Teaching International Relations

ELGAR GUIDES TO TEACHING

The Elgar Guides to Teaching series provides a variety of resources for instructors looking for new ways to engage students. Each volume provides a unique set of materials and insights that will help both new and seasoned teachers expand their toolbox in order to teach more effectively. Titles include selections of methods, exercises, games and teaching philosophies suitable for the particular subject featured. Each volume is authored or edited by a seasoned professor. Edited volumes comprise contributions from both established instructors and newer faculty who offer fresh takes on their fields of study.

Titles in the series include:

Teaching Cultural Economics
Edited by Trine Bille, Anna Mignosa and Ruth Towse

Teaching Nonprofit Management
Edited by Karabi C. Bezboruah and Heather Carpenter

Teaching the Essentials of Law and Economics
Antony W. Dnes

Teaching Strategic Management
A Hands-on Guide to Teaching Success
Sabine Baumann

Teaching Urban and Regional Planning
Innovative Pedagogies in Practice
Edited by Andrea I. Frank and Artur da Rosa Pires

Teaching Entrepreneurship, Volume Two
A Practice-Based Approach
Edited by Heidi M. Neck, Candida G. Brush and Patricia G. Greene

Teaching Environmental Impact Assessment
Angus Morrison-Saunders and Jenny Pope

Teaching Research Methods in Political Science
Edited by Jeffrey L. Bernstein

Teaching International Relations
Edited by James M. Scott, Ralph G. Carter, Brandy Jolliff Scott and Jeffrey S. Lantis

Teaching International Relations

Edited by

James M. Scott

Herman Brown Chair and Professor of Political Science, Texas Christian University, USA

Ralph G. Carter

Piper Professor of Political Science, Texas Christian University, USA

Brandy Jolliff Scott

Lecturer, Department of Political Science, Texas Christian University, USA

Jeffrey S. Lantis

Professor of Political Science, College of Wooster, USA

ELGAR GUIDES TO TEACHING

Cheltenham, UK • Northampton, MA, USA

© James M. Scott, Ralph G. Carter, Brandy Jolliff Scott and Jeffrey S. Lantis 2021

All rights reserved. No part of this publication may be reproduced, stored in a retrieval system or transmitted in any form or by any means, electronic, mechanical or photocopying, recording, or otherwise without the prior permission of the publisher.

Published by
Edward Elgar Publishing Limited
The Lypiatts
15 Lansdown Road
Cheltenham
Glos GL50 2JA
UK

Edward Elgar Publishing, Inc.
William Pratt House
9 Dewey Court
Northampton
Massachusetts 01060
USA

Paperback edition 2022

A catalogue record for this book
is available from the British Library

Library of Congress Control Number: 2021939137

This book is available electronically in the Elgaronline
Political Science and Public Policy subject collection
http://dx.doi.org/10.4337/9781839107658

ISBN 978 1 83910 764 1 (cased)
ISBN 978 1 83910 765 8 (eBook)
ISBN 978 1 80392 605 6 (paperback)

Printed and bound by CPI Group (UK) Ltd, Croydon, CR0 4YY

Contents

List of figures and tables	vii
List of contributors	viii

1   Introduction to *Teaching International Relations*   1
James M. Scott, Ralph G. Carter, Brandy Jolliff Scott and Jeffrey S. Lantis

PART I   CONTEMPORARY TRENDS IN COURSE STRUCTURES AND GOALS

2   Essentials for Introduction to International Relations   11
Paul F. Diehl and Mark A. Boyer

3   Teaching with purpose: commitment and innovation in IR pedagogy   27
Jeffrey S. Lantis

4   Teaching IR in the Global South: views from Brazil and South Africa   38
Jacqueline de Matos Ala, Cristina Yumie Aoki Inoue and Marcelo Valença

5   Toward an intersectional pedagogy in IR: how to take feminist interventions seriously   52
Dovilė Budrytė

PART II   INNOVATIONS IN THE CLASSROOM: TECHNIQUES AND APPROACHES

6   Teaching with case studies   66
Ralph G. Carter

7   Experiential learning through faculty-led study abroad programs   77
Amy Below, Amanda Nydegger and Mary Jane Parmentier

8   Using Statecraft in the classroom   90
Eric Cox

9	Teaching political violence with games and simulations *Amanda Rosen and Victor Asal*	105
10	Teaching with the IR theory toolkit *Eric K. Leonard*	117
11	Teaching IR with literature and film *Gigi Gokcek and Patrick James*	129
12	Engaging in inquiry: problem-based and research-focused teaching and learning *James M. Scott*	145
13	Engaging with diversity through technology *Yasemin Akbaba and Filiz Başkan*	160
14	Becoming an effective online teacher: five considerations for better teaching and learning in IR courses *Brandy Jolliff Scott*	176
15	Collaborative learning in the IR classroom *Heather A. Smith*	189

PART III   ASSESSMENT AND EFFECTIVENESS

16	Assessment and effectiveness of active teaching and learning in IR *Matthew Krain and Kent J. Kille*	201
17	The vital role of assessment in active teaching and learning *Kerstin Hamann*	214

References	224
Index	257

Figures and tables

Figures

12.1	Approaches to undergraduate research	149
12.2	The "Assertive Multilateralism" peace operations puzzle	155
16.1	Two concept maps from a research methods and design course	210
16.2	Cartooning an article's research design	211

Tables

2.1	Comparison of topical emphasis in introductory IR textbooks	17
2.2	Three most important things for students to learn cited in ISA workshop surveys	20
2.3	Topical coverage cited in ISA workshop surveys (N = 62 participants)	22
2.4	Theory coverage cited in ISA workshop surveys (N = 62 participants)	23
9.1	Exercises discussed and related concepts and theories	108
13.1	Course assignment performance comparison	167

Contributors

Yasemin Akbaba	Gettysburg College, USA
Victor Asal	SUNY–Albany, USA
Filiz Başkan	Izmir University of Economics, Turkey
Amy Below	California State University, East Bay, USA
Mark A. Boyer	University of Connecticut, USA
Dovilė Budrytė	Georgia Gwinnett College, USA
Ralph G. Carter	Texas Christian University, USA
Eric Cox	Texas Christian University, USA
Jacqueline de Matos Ala	University of the Witwatersrand, South Africa
Paul F. Diehl	University of Texas-Dallas, USA
Gigi Gokcek	Dominican University of California, USA
Kerstin Hamann	University of Central Florida, USA
Patrick James	University of Southern California, USA
Brandy Jolliff Scott	Texas Christian University, USA
Kent J. Kille	College of Wooster, USA
Matthew Krain	College of Wooster, USA
Jeffrey S. Lantis	College of Wooster, USA
Eric K. Leonard	Shenandoah University, USA
Amanda Nydegger	Arizona State University, USA
Mary Jane Parmentier	Arizona State University, USA
Amanda Rosen	Naval War College, USA
James M. Scott	Texas Christian University, USA
Heather A. Smith	University of Northern British Columbia, Canada
Marcelo Valença	Brazilian Naval War College, Brazil
Cristina Yumie Aoki Inoue	Radboud University, the Netherlands

1. Introduction to *Teaching International Relations*

James M. Scott, Ralph G. Carter, Brandy Jolliff Scott and Jeffrey S. Lantis

INTRODUCTION

We are delighted to introduce this new volume on *Teaching International Relations*. Instructors and students alike face a complicated and increasingly interconnected world in which security, prosperity, identity, and quality of life all have international and transnational components that are growing in relevance. Engaging with our students to encourage them to understand what happens in world politics and how and why it happens is thus both important and challenging.

Our approach to this challenge rests on a philosophy of student engagement and active learning focused on efforts to facilitate subject mastery and the development of critical/analytical thinking and writing skills. As professors and mentors, we believe that the foundations of excellence in education include a participatory environment where students are engaged in and are owners of their learning and instruction occurs in an active, applied fashion. These elements help to build the substantive expertise necessary for mastery of a discipline and they encourage critical inquiry and facilitate discovery, as students are engaged in asking questions and seeking answers. We believe, and extensive research indicates, that when students are the owners of learning, they learn more and develop faster. So, teaching international relations (IR) – or any subject – in ways that emphasize student participation, discovery, critical/analytical thinking, and intellectual independence promises substantial benefits.

In this volume, we have assembled contributions from outstanding and experienced professors and mentors in IR who consider course structure and goals; classroom approaches, techniques, and activities to foster engaged learning; and assessment of teaching effectiveness and learning outcomes. Together, we share the commitment to helping students make sense of world politics, and to do so with a learner-centered, engaged approach that contributes to both substantive mastery and a range of critical/analytical thinking, writing, and communication skills.

This introductory chapter describes the transformational era in which we are living and highlights the value of innovation in teaching and learning for a new generation of students. We identify and discuss contemporary trends and innovative approaches for the active IR classroom and the need for broad and inclusive approaches that expand perspectives. We also provide an overview of the rest of our volume that highlights the purposes, approaches, and techniques addressed in the chapters that follow.

A CRITICAL TIME FOR TEACHING IR

The world has experienced dramatic changes during just the past 20 years, or the lifetime of many of today's college students. The post-Cold War optimism of the early 1990s – based on expectations of an era of democratic peace – was soon dashed. Terrorist attacks on Western targets resulted in a Global War on Terror and seemingly never-ending conflicts in the Middle East, Africa, and Asia. A second shock was the sharp rise in intrastate wars and genocidal violence. Refugees and asylum seekers scrambled to reach safer areas by any means necessary. A third shock came in 2020 with the devastating global pandemic and its costly effects on the lives and wellbeing of people and societies around the world. These and other pressures on Western countries gave rise to an increasing number of populist or nativist political parties and backlashes against democracy in many places. Concurrently, a wide range of environmental challenges arose, with societies struggling with global climate change, rising seas, increasing desertification, and resulting wildfires, all of which created additional migration and refugee flows. New pandemic diseases spread quickly, often going global before national health organizations could adequately respond. Globalization, previously touted as the remedy for many ills, has clearly benefited some societies. However, unanticipated costs in terms of human rights, workers' rights, environmental indifference, and increased economic competition have created pressures to wall societies off from such negative consequences. In the midst of all these changes, the international system saw the renewal of Great Power competition between the United States, China, and Russia.

These transformations produce new challenges for the study of IR. For example, concepts of national security must move beyond interstate wars, safety from violent harm, or protection of narrowly-defined national interests to include a greater emphasis on economic security and the need for sustainable economic development and an acceptable quality of life. Other human security interests also have greater salience, including protection from dangers like disease, environmental harm, and systematic violations of human rights. Scholars from the Global South increasingly question the assumption that North American and European perspectives on IR and IR theory are universally valid. For them, regional or local issues – and values – demand and deserve more attention (Acharya 2014). Finally, new technologies like drones and cyber weapons pose new challenges, not to mention government struggles to manage public expectations in a world that is increasingly connected by smartphones and social media.

Traditional Westphalian notions of state sovereignty have shuddered in the face of these pressures. Governments have struggled to manage challenges from both outside and within. New norms, such as the idea that if a government would not protect its own people then foreign interventions would be legitimate, represent dramatic shifts (not to mention contested concepts). These and other developments have challenged the future of the Liberal International Order, assumptions like the inviolability of military alliance obligations, and the need for regional or global cooperation. In the face of these profound changes and challenges, effective teaching in IR in the twenty-first century must go well beyond the focus of what was taught to prior generations of undergraduate and graduate students.

RENEWING OUR COMMITMENT TO ACTIVE TEACHING AND LEARNING

Given these dramatic transformations, this seems a propitious time for reflection, reinvention, and recommitment to learner-centered approaches and interactive methods of teaching and learning. Indeed, our discipline has always been shaped by efforts to make sense of and analyze major developments. This has driven both the process and product of our work in the IR classroom. Committed teacher–scholars identify learning objectives and select methods for teaching that reflect a sense of purpose (Kolb; Hutchings, Huber, and Ciccone). This helps students formulate conceptual linkages between theory and real-world examples, both past and present (Shulman; Cusimano), as well as increase retention of knowledge (Jensen; Brock and Cameron).

Why Active Teaching and Learning? Why Now?

Beyond its implicit appeal to instructors and students, there are good reasons for teacher–scholars to engage with active teaching and learning in IR. First and foremost, participatory approaches to teaching and learning can help us study the complex changes in global politics discussed above. Revisiting our approach to teaching IR should begin with reevaluation of learning objectives for our courses in the twenty-first century. For example, how do we help students learn about trends like globalization and fragmentation, as well as challenges in new realms like global health policies and cybersecurity? How should we present information about civil wars, under-studied regions of the world, and diverse cultures and societies?

Changes in global politics in the twenty-first century have fueled innovations in our teaching and learning approaches – from greater attention to post-colonial discourses and social constructivism in the contemporary IR classroom to the study of cybersecurity, transgender rights, and wartime sexual violence. In short, committed teacher–scholars are seizing learning opportunities and identifying new puzzles and new "ways of knowing" about IR in a dynamic period.

Second, advancements in our understanding of the science of learning represent a second inspiration for teacher–scholars to reevaluate our instructional methods. Neuroscience research has underscored the educational value of student engagement. For example, advances in neuroimaging have helped to illuminate the pathways of the brain that are stimulated by specific teaching and learning techniques. Studies show that "multi-modal" or multi-sensory learning can help promote education and retention of knowledge (Mueller and Oppenheimer). Neuroscience tells us that a mixture of exercises in the classroom like speaking, interacting, movement, writing, and listening can help activate memory pathways and allow new information to be physically linked in the body's neural, cognitive, and emotional, and motor pathways (Ward). Results of student ownership and learner-centered pedagogy can be promoting higher order thinking and deep learning (Dubinsky et al.; Blakemore and Frith; Glisczinski).

A third reason to revisit our modes of instruction, which we discuss further below, is diversification of our pedagogical understandings and the expansion of global perspectives on teaching and learning. As our authors discuss throughout this volume, IR is truly becoming more global and open to perspectives from around the world. Voices from the Global South are increasingly contributing to the scholarship on teaching and learning, for example, dramatically expanding the potential for pedagogical innovations. Instructors and students alike are learning more about the power of diverse cultural perspectives and understandings to enrich our worldviews.

Trends in Active Teaching and Learning

The expansion of the scholarship on teaching and learning (SOTL) in IR over the past two decades has helped promote engagement and activism in the classroom. It has also had a compound effect on the exchange of ideas and the encouragement of teaching and learning through professional development opportunities. For example, one finds a richer SOTL in publications in leading journals on teaching such as *International Studies Perspectives* and the *Journal of Political Science Education.* And today there are also more teacher-training opportunities in IR than ever before, including the International Studies Association's (ISA) Innovative Pedagogy Conference series and the American Political Science Association's (APSA) Teaching and Learning Conferences. Collectively, these initiatives and other initiatives have helped promote the further development and exchange of ideas.

Instructors in IR are embracing a much wider set of opportunities for student engagement today. For example, they are building on and expanding simulations and games as platforms for innovations in teaching and learning (Brynen and Milante; Glasgow; Usherwood; Dahlgren, Fewnwick, and Hopwood). These can help students deepen conceptual understandings of a particular phenomenon, institutions, or socio-political processes by using student interaction to bring abstract concepts to life (Meibauer and Nøhr; DiCicco; Matzner and Herrenbrück; Evans, Tse, and Baker). Problem-based or case-based learning exercises represent a second popular trend in the modern IR classroom (Savery; Majeski and Stover). These approaches often place real-world problems at the center of the learning process and are designed to foster an atmosphere of student-centered engagement with the issues, while also promoting critical thinking and group problem-solving, or teamwork (Kille, Krain, and Lantis; Krain).

Other trends in active teaching and learning focus on the use of popular culture touchstones, or what Kille, Krain, and Lantis (2019) call "alternative texts," such as films or popular literature to teach important concepts (Glover and Tagliarina; Van Belle; Stump; Sachleben). Among these, film and video are some of the most widely used alternative texts for teaching IR (Lobasz and Valeriano; Lantis; Gregg 1998, 1999; Gibney; Giglio; Cooley and Pennock). In addition, teaching IR today naturally extends beyond the traditional classroom. Not only are conscientious instructors bringing the world "in" to their classes, some are taking students "out" for direct engagement and experiential learning. While off-campus and study abroad semester programs represent the classical approach to this type of immersion and engagement (Lantis and DuPlaga), many instructors also help connect students directly to their wider communities through service-learning (Kille, Krain, and Lantis; Robinson; McIlrath and MacLabhrainn; Krain and Nurse).

INCLUSIVENESS, BROADER PERSPECTIVES, AND GLOBALIZING CONTENT

A contemporary examination of teaching must also consider how to broaden IR teaching away from exclusively Western and Global North lenses and towards more inclusive and diverse perspectives and practices. Calls for diversity and inclusiveness in IR are not new. They can be traced in part to the development of Feminist IR theory as a critical perspective on Realism and other traditional schools of IR thought, as well as challenges from voices in the Global South (Acharya 2014).

Currently, both ISA and the APSA are beginning to address issues of diversity and inclusion more actively as part of their agendas. For example, in 2017, the APSA included the promotion of diversity and inclusion in its 2017–2019 strategic plan and subsequently published its *2018 Diversity and Inclusion Report*. At ISA, the program for the 2020 Annual Meeting, "Multiple Identities and Scholarship in a Global IR: One Profession, Many Voices" invited participants to acknowledge and reflect upon the state of the discipline as a product of patriarchal, Western identities and promote discourse and action to diversify the field. The call for papers focused on the need to make space for gender, racial, ethnic, Global South, LGBTQIA+ (lesbian, gay, bisexual, transgender, queer, and intersex), and marginalized group access to the organization and the field. ISA also actively promoted panels on issues surrounding the problems of "Structuring Inclusion/Challenging Oppression" as a part of this program. Nevertheless, significant progress remains if we are to more accurately construct undergraduate and graduate IR courses that truly recognize issues and perspectives from women, minorities, and the Global South that have so often been ignored by mainstream scholarship and pedagogy.

Decolonization and Inclusion of Diverse Perspectives

The goals of recognizing and incorporating diversity and inclusion into our teaching are both simple and complicated. At its most basic level, inclusivity refers to the act of making space for more individuals and ideas from a wide array of backgrounds, and in a safe, equitable, and respectful manner. Conversations about inclusion and diversity have increasingly focused on the need to "decolonize" the academe, or to "recognize that knowledge is inevitably marked by power relations," (Gopal) and to "scrutinize the colonial and racist foundations and practices of the field of international relations" (Koomen). However, as Koomen and others have noted, students of IR remain primarily exposed only to the traditional, outdated version of IR limited to the -isms and primarily influenced by white, male voices.

While some are invariably threatened by calls for decolonizing IR, it is important to note that efforts to decolonize do not mean erasure of these traditional, elite voices. Rather, the need for decolonization and inclusion reflects the increased awareness that if we do not incorporate the voices and experiences of non-white, non-Western, and non-heterosexual male voices alongside the Anglo-European male experience, we are inevitably limiting our knowledge in both theoretical and empirical terms. If the aim of both research and teaching is to increase knowledge, then we do a disservice if we fail to strive for inclusion, diversity, intersectionality – what is effectively decolonization – in our teaching practices. Rather than increase knowledge, we limit it.

Methods and Approaches for Decolonizing IR Teaching

Fortunately, there is a growing scholarship and conversation devoted to decolonizing the teaching of IR, both for the sake of broadening perspectives and content and because of the need to accurately reflect the experiences and identities of the students we teach. Restructuring syllabi to include more non-white scholarship and to be more critical of our dependence upon the "-isms" is one place to start, as is thinking critically about the content of the textbooks we assign and opting for choices that include diverse perspectives alongside the foundational texts so many rely upon (see Atchison; Baylis, Smith, and Owens; Olivo).

Beyond restructuring course content, purposefully incorporating more readings from women and POC (people of color) scholars in the subject matter we teach can help to broadly diversify the field of IR. The "gender gap" in IR scholarship has been well-documented (Maliniak, Powers, and Walter; Mitchell, Lange, and Brus). To overcome this gap, not only must we do a better job of citing diverse scholars in our research, we must also normalize the work of women and minorities in the material we teach. If overcoming the gender/race/ethnic/Global South gap in IR means we must amplify these works in bibliographies, how much more progress can we make if we also include these voices in the foundational educational experiences of future IR scholars, too?

Of course, finding additional strategies to decolonize teaching in thoughtful and pedagogically-informed ways is also important. Engaging students in dynamic classroom practices taught by well-informed teacher–scholars can help enhance student engagement with diverse material and topics to which they were previously not exposed. Some of these approaches include active learning strategies, the assignment of both fiction and non-fiction literature – including novels and biographies – and the use of film and other media (Rasmussen). The use of social media as a vehicle to connect students in the Global North with peers in Global South countries, promoting exchanges of ideas and firsthand interactions that many students would otherwise remain unexposed to is another option (Shaw 2016). "Empathic scaffolding," where students are exposed to diverse perspectives through "content and pedagogy to strategically expand students' zones of comfort from very personal experiences with the material to broader groups of people and course concepts" (Bauer and Clancy, 73), may prove especially useful.

Among such approaches, making individual students responsible for tracing one country, idea, perspective, or issue throughout the course and enabling students to develop more intimate connections with a new and different subject allows for greater depth of experience and understanding, which may create long-lasting, empathic effects. Finally, we also note that the burgeoning scholarship on teaching IR from diverse and inclusive perspectives includes a lively online presence of active teacher–scholars regularly experimenting with and sharing ideas that promote active student learning from different and diverse perspectives. Blogs like *Active Learning in Political Science* and *The Tatooed Professor*, by historian Kevin Gannon, provide resources for simulations and related exercises that challenge student thinking in new and diverse ways.

In sum, the need to teach IR from and make space within the field of IR for diverse and inclusive voices and perspectives is increasingly pressing. Crossing boundaries and crossing cultures have always been important dimensions of IR training, but there is a greater urgency for attention to these perspectives in twenty-first-century discourses. Today, there are more contributions to dialogues about active pedagogy underway in the profession – and much greater respect for and recognition of the value of these contributions to our discipline. In many ways, this book celebrates this diversity and seeks to further fuel the dialogue in the SOTL on future pathways. If knowledge is the key to combating discrimination, then diversifying and decolonizing our teaching is a task of utmost importance.

A PREVIEW OF WHAT FOLLOWS

Our volume is organized into three sections: Contemporary Trends in Course Structures and Goals; Innovations in the Classroom: Techniques and Approaches; and Assessment and Effectiveness. The contents are designed to capture important trends in pedagogy and contribute a continuing dialogues on pedagogy in the field.

The remainder of the volume proceeds as follows. In **Part I: Contemporary Trends in Course Structures and Goals**, our contributors focus on course structure and goals. It includes chapters that provide broad overviews of theories of learning and pedagogy and identifies prominent themes to be explored in the IR classroom. In Chapter 2, Paul F. Diehl and Mark A. Boyer address the essentials of introductory IR courses, while Jeffrey S. Lantis discusses learning goals, engagement, and outcomes in Chapter 3. In Chapters 4 and 5, Jacqueline de Matos Ala, Cristina Yumie Aoki Inoue, and Marcelo Valença focus on teaching IR in the Global South, while Dovilė Budrytė focuses on on feminist approaches and intersectionality.

Part II: Innovations in the Classroom: Techniques and Approaches contains ten chapters that feature contributions on active and engaged approaches, techniques, and activities, grounded in the scholarship of teaching and learning. Ralph G. Carter discusses teaching with case studies in Chapter 6. Amy Below, Mandy Nydegger, and Mary Jane Permentier consider the nature and opportunities of faculty-led study abroad in Chapter 7. The next two chapters feature a discussion of teaching with *Statecraft*, an online simulation, by Eric Cox (Chapter 8), and the use of simulations and games more broadly by Amanda Rosen and Victor Asal (Chapter 9). Eric Leonard takes on the use of IR theory in Chapter 10, while Gigi Gokcek and Patrick James discuss the use of literature and film to teach IR in Chapter 11. James M. Scott then takes up problem-based and research-focused approaches to teaching (Chapter 12), while Yasemin Akbaba and Filiz Başkan devote their attention to using technology to teach cross-cultural diversity in Chapter 13. Continuing the technology topic, Brandy Jolliff Scott explores teaching IR online in Chapter 14. Heather A. Smith concludes this part with her chapter on collaborative learning (Chapter 15).

In **Part III: Assessment and Effectiveness**, we bring our volume to a close and focus on approaches to assessing teaching effectiveness and learning outcomes. Matthew Krain and Kent J. Kille discuss assessment and effectiveness of Learning in IR Courses in Chapter 16. Kerstin Hamann then addresses the role of asessment in active teaching and learning in Chapter 17.

We hope you find the contents of our volume helpful.

PART I

CONTEMPORARY TRENDS IN COURSE STRUCTURES AND GOALS

2. Essentials for Introduction to International Relations

Paul F. Diehl and Mark A. Boyer

Although it might go by different names beginning with "Introduction to" (followed by "International Relations," "World Politics," "Global Studies," "International Studies" to name a few), the first course in international affairs is a staple for undergraduate curricula in colleges and universities around the world. That course has changed substantially over time as the world has evolved from one of 50 or so countries after the Second World War to almost 200 today. International organizations, non-governmental organizations (NGOs), and even individuals play a greater role in international affairs than ever before. Although some global problems, such as war, have long-standing pedigrees, others, such as climate change, are of more recent vintage. Still others, such as human rights, have existed for centuries but have only been recognized and made acutely salient in the twentieth century. This greater diversity and complexity poses challenges for teachers who are constrained by university structures and practices (such as semesters or core curriculum configurations) that have not necessarily changed in over a century.

Instructors always face the dilemma of having more content than could be covered in a single course, and indeed including too much content might undermine student learning when they are overwhelmed with information. What are the essential elements of an introductory course in international relations (we use that nomenclature to represent the variety noted above and IR for short)? This chapter focuses primarily on the content of such courses, understanding that it is but one aspect, and many other chapters in this handbook elucidate a range of other dimensions for many courses in IR. Recognizing that answers to this question can vary across instructors, we nonetheless consider key answers to that question by reference to common practices of IR teachers, evidenced by common textbooks used in these courses as well as the responses to informal surveys of instructors attending International Studies Association (ISA) meetings. We begin, however, with two interrelated influences on content that set some of the parameters or affect content choices in the Intro IR courses: context and learning goals.

CONTEXTUAL FACTORS

In determining the essential ingredients of an introductory IR course, one cannot and should not conclude that one size fits all. No one teaches this course in isolation from the configuration of students in the course, its place in the department/program curriculum, and the political and cultural setting of the state and region where the institution is located. In this section, we cover some of those contextual factors and how they broadly influence the content of IR courses.

The basic course in IR occurs in the context of a broader curriculum in political science, global studies, and IR offerings more generally. This has several effects. In some colleges and universities, Intro to IR is a single, one semester course that is a gateway to the rest of the curriculum in that academia area. The result is that some topics will be covered only superficially (e.g., foreign policy decision-making) or deferred to later in the curriculum (e.g., a semester-long treatment of international political economy or conflict and war). In contrast, some institutions envision the Intro IR course as a series of two to four courses that allow in-depth examination of multiple topics (see Vlcek and Bower); such flexibility permits examination of different theories (e.g., post-colonial theory) and subject matter (e.g., global health) that might otherwise be ignored. Of course, multiple introductory courses also allow greater in-depth treatment of topics that are regarded as core elements in any configuration.

In many countries, Intro IR instructors have the academic freedom or at least significant discretion to design this course in the manner that they see fit. We know that faculty have divergent views on epistemology, methodology, and a series of other concerns, and this would suggest substantial differences in how Intro IR courses look according to the instructor; as we demonstrate below, however, this is less the case than one might expect. Nevertheless, the content of Intro IR courses is not always left to the whims of the individual instructor; course design could be the result of coordination with other faculty members teaching other sections of the course or even teaching the course according to a required syllabus decided by others. These are not necessarily undesirable situations, as there is some value in faculty discussing pedagogical issues perhaps to the same extent that they tend to discuss research agendas. There is also a positive outcome to greater consistency across the teaching of this course as students in different sections might then have similar knowledge and skills finishing that course, and instructors of upper-division courses can assume a common base among students as they enter those advanced courses. Although there is perhaps less consensus on what should be included in the Intro IR course than gateway courses in physics or chemistry for example, there is likely to be more commonality when content choices are not purely individual.

A third contextual factor that affects content concerns is the student population in the course and this will be driven in large part by how the Intro IR course is embedded within the university curriculum. If the course is for IR or political science majors only, the content might be driven more by an eye for providing the groundwork for future coursework, especially if the course serves as a prerequisite for advanced study. Less concern for student motivation might also lead instructors to include topics or material that is not as elementary or designed to meet some of the goals elucidated in the next section. As the audience includes students who are taking the course only to fulfill a core curriculum, general education, or similar university distribution requirement, the course might require adjustment to enhance student motivation. Moreover, in this context, the course might be the only exposure that those students have to IR. Still other students might choose the class as part of a requirement for a degree minor or just as an elective. For many instructors, the reality is that there will be each type of students – majors, minors, those meeting a requirement, those taking it as an elective – in a typical classroom. This can require a delicate balancing act in meeting the different goals below, and some consideration should be given to meeting all these needs rather than deciding to teach to only one group.

Fourth, and certainly neither last nor least important, is the influence that stems from where in a geographic sense the course is taught. Although the type of institution (e.g., elite, public, private) is certainly important, the country or region where the course is taught can have a significant effect on course content (see the essays in Frueh and Diehl). Courses taught in Africa will have topics and readings (e.g., colonialism) that might not be found in similar courses taught in Europe and vice-versa. This is not to say that a Western-centric orientation isn't persistent across the globe (Knight), but there will be substantial differences based on geography. We discuss more about this issue and the associated debates toward the end of this chapter.

STUDENT LEARNING GOALS

The fundamental starting point for any course should be goals, and these goals should focus on student learning. This is consistent with the so-called "backward design" model for course development (Wiggins and McTighe); rather than beginning with activities and assessments, course design and content are driven first by what the instructor wants the students to learn. Specific learning goals are dependent on both context and faculty perspective, especially with respect to the student population in the course (see also below the workshop results on desired outcomes in Table 2.2). In the analysis below, we discuss general goals in terms of different student groups, but there are several caveats. First, the goals are not mutually exclusive with respect to different groups; there are essential skills and knowledge that apply to all. Second, and somewhat related, basic knowledge can be, and in some cases should be, a goal, but hardly the only goal. The aspiration level extends beyond that to what is usually referred to as critical thinking. Students won't generally retain factual knowledge (e.g., how many members are on the United Nations Security Council – UNSC?) and "factual" knowledge can change over time (e.g., the kinds of actions authorized by the UNSC). As a result, "knowledge" becomes dated. Some other kinds of knowledge (e.g., the UNSC is dominated by major power interests) is more enduring and broadly applicable to understanding a range of UN actions. Third, even as some goals might be student group specific or emphasized more than others, many instructors will teach classes in which students from all types of student audiences are enrolled. This is certainly the case when Intro IR is part of a core or general education curriculum.

For students whose only course in IR will be this one, goals relating to citizenship education will be primary. Whatever their major, students will enter a society in which they will, to varying degrees, make political decisions that require some sophistication about global affairs and one's place in the world. This is especially important in an increasingly globalized and interdependent world where events and actions in one part of the world affect lives elsewhere whether the subjects are trade, pandemics, or war. Of some concern, one recent study jointly published by National Geographic, Gallup and the Council on Foreign Relations (*U.S. Adults' Knowledge of the World*) shows limited knowledge of global affairs among American adults, even if they exhibit a desire to learn more. Accordingly, this knowledge gap should be addressed in Intro IR courses.

For students who will major in IR, political science, or related disciplines, the Intro IR course is foundational and should be designed to lay the groundwork for future study. The scaffolding of skills and knowledge might not be as clear and linear as is the case for successive courses in mathematics, but nevertheless Intro IR should be the gateway to further coursework in the curriculum. The type and scope of those advanced courses will vary by degree and institution, but as our analysis below reveals there will be commonalities. In other cases, institutional variation will necessitate some additions or modifications to what are considered essential skills. For example, if a curriculum for majors already requires an undergraduate course in methodology or research design, Intro IR instructors might not build those elements into the course, whereas the absence of such courses might require instructors to introduce such matters so that students can read and understand some research findings as part of the course.

Returning to the goal of knowledge gains, many of us will also consider the degree to which we are developing basic social science analytical skills. Specifically, if we can't expect high levels of factual knowledge retention (assuming we wanted that in the first place), we can help students begin to develop the skills to analyze world events in part to cultivate their roles as citizens mentioned above. To put it simply, perhaps if our Intro IR students can read world news in the *New York Times* or critically assess an internet source on world affairs a year after finishing the course and be able to analyze the factors underlying a story, then maybe that is real goal achievement. Whether we call this "critical thinking," "analysis," or something else, such skills will serve the student well after graduation (Haber) and we believe that the Intro IR class is uniquely suited for that foundational work.

Thus far, we have discussed Intro IR students as either majors or non-majors with associated learning goals, but this should not imply that individual classifications are not malleable. Indeed, introductory courses in a discipline influence the choice of major (Chambliss and Takacs). Students with good experiences might choose to major in international studies (in whatever the appropriate department at the institution); this can reinforce their original choice, lead them to choose a new major after being undecided or undeclared, or induce them to switch majors away from something else. Of course, bad experiences can have the opposite effects.

Along these lines, relevance to student lives is often cited in terms of courses they enjoy and that impact their careers. For this group of students who might be less initially engaged, the challenge of emphasizing relevance as opposed to abstract concepts is acute. By definition, introductory courses are designed for audiences in which there is limited background knowledge or understanding; the purpose of those courses is to provide that initial knowledge. Yet, Intro IR might still require some basic background in order to make sense of the material, and there can be large variation among students entering the class. Instructors might face the task of providing that necessary background information at the outset of the course content. Indeed, that is one of the concerns that some textbooks and instructors address by including a section of the course on key historical events. Finally, although students might have limited knowledge about IR when entering this course, it doesn't mean that they lack political opinions about the subject or believe that they know about it already. Intro IR will no doubt challenge some of those tightly held beliefs and there may be resistance to new ideas. Some instructors attempt to navigate these waters by having associated readings that present two sides of a debate over contemporary issues. Such a strategy has the virtue of allowing students to be exposed to different perspectives, but it runs the risk of reinforcing the misperception that different views are merely opinions that have equal value and therefore can be dismissed.

INSIGHTS FROM TEXTBOOKS

An important element in Intro IR courses are the readings that are assigned to students and the centerpiece of those is typically a textbook around which other readings and assignments are constructed. There is a recursive relationship between an instructor's preferences and the content of textbooks. Instructors choose textbooks that most closely resemble the subjects and approaches of their personal predilections; the same instructors will also structure their courses according to and include other topical matter that is contained in the textbook chosen. This recursive relationship is further reinforced in that textbook authors and their publishers do extensive work to provide a book that meets the needs and wants of the instructor and his or her students.

Looking at the content of textbooks therefore reflects, to a significant degree, how Intro IR courses are taught. The goal is to determine what topics or subjects are common across them, suggesting then what could be considered as essential or core elements of the introductory course. One caveat is in order for any inferences about commonalities across textbooks. The books reflect the orientations and judgments of their authors, but they also reflect marketing concerns of the publishers as mentioned just above. Accordingly, the latter discourage approaches and content that are deviant from the norm and might not have a large enough market; thus, there is a homogenizing effect from this pressure and textbooks are not as different as one might expect from the diversity of research and orientations among IR scholars.

To find out what textbooks can tell us about the core elements of the Intro IR course, we examined nine prominent books, ones that are widely adopted and, in several cases, have gone through multiple editions over an extended period of years. For each of these works, we examined detailed tables of contents, their subject matter, and the amount of space devoted to that subject matter. Based on that, we identified a series of topics or subjects common to the books. In Table 2.1, we list those topics/subjects by row and indicate whether they are contained in the textbooks examined, each with its own column. In fact, most or all are covered in some way in all the books, but we only considered a topic to be a key part of a textbook (marked with an "X" in the column) if there was at least a half of a chapter devoted specifically to it. In some cases, certain topics (e.g., historical background) appear in pieces throughout multiple chapters and we acknowledge that our survey might miss such an emphasis. Nevertheless, the results in Table 2.1 reveal many common elements among the textbooks.

Most textbooks begin with two key elements that are designed to lay the analytical groundwork for students to understand the substantive elements that follow. Textbook authors assume that students have limited knowledge

Essentials for Introduction to International Relations

Table 2.1   Comparison of topical emphasis in introductory IR textbooks

Book	1	2	3	4	5	6	7	8	9
Topic/subject									
History/background	X	X	X	X			X	X	X
Theory	X	X	X	X	X	X	X	X	X
Levels of analysis	X		X						
Actors	X					X	X		X
Power	X					X	X	X	
Foreign policy decision-making	X	X	X	X		X	a		X
War/conflict	X	X	X	X		X	X	X	X
International political economy	X	X	X	X	X	X	X	X	X
Human rights	X	X	X	X		X	X		X
Global South/development	X	X		X			X	X	X
Environment/global commons	X	X		X	X	X	X	X	X
International law	X	X	X		X	X	X	X	X
International organizations/NGOs	X	X	X	X	X	X	X		X
Migration/refugees			X	X					
Health			X	X			b		
Security/terrorism	X	X		X	X		X	X	X
Globalization/transnationalism	X	X		X		X	X	X	
Nationalism/state	X		X						X
Integration/regionalism	X	X		X					
Ethics									
Gender/race							c		

Editors' Note: [a] Foreign policy decision-making is one of six theoretical perspectives (across two chapters) included and applied in this text, and thus does not reach the half-chapter threshold.
[b] Global health is included in this text as part of a chapter on managing the global commons, and thus does not reach the half-chapter threshold.
[c] Feminist theory is one of six theoretical perspectives (across two chapters) included and applied in this text and thus does not reach the half-chapter threshold.

Key: Columns by textbook in Table 2.1: 1. Boyer et al.; 2. Goldstein and Pevehouse; 3. Mingst et al.; 4. Lamy et al.; 5. Shiraev and Zubok; 6. Blanton and Kegley; 7. Scott et al. 2022; 8. Shimko; 9. D'Anieri.

of key historical events and changes in international affairs. Thus, usually an early chapter is designed to fill that gap and make sense of the historical references that follow in later chapters. Similarly, all textbooks devote a chapter or more to IR theory. Most students are unaccustomed to thinking in terms of analytical frameworks, and indeed might have fundamental misunderstandings of what social scientific theory is; commonly, they might confuse theory with opinion or tools that policymakers "use" rather than something that scholars employ (there are some approaches to redress this – see Frueh and Youde). The full range of IR theories in the discipline are not covered in these books; most often, realism, liberalism, and constructivism are privileged, with some reference to feminism or Marxism made in certain works.

Some themes common to textbooks in the 1950s–1970s have fallen by the wayside at least in terms of having their own chapters. Rather, they are still critical to IR, but are now integrated into chapters about specific process or phenomena; these include levels of analysis, actors, and power. Nevertheless, foreign policy decision-making (how policy is made) retains its place in two-thirds of the textbooks examined.

Substantively, war and international political economy (IPE) are near universal parts of Intro IR textbooks. The former reflects the traditional focus of international relations studies, although a concern with civil war because of its relative importance and frequency has joined interstate war and associated issues (e.g., deterrence) as a topic of coverage. Terrorism and general security issues are sometimes included in chapters on war, but they also receive separate treatments as well; in all, seven of the nine books give significant attention to these subjects. Political economy – typically including trade, finance, foreign aid, and related topics – has a shorter pedigree in the study of IR (often dated as beginning in the late 1970s), but it is a major subfield of international relations. Accordingly, it receives extensive treatment in all texts. Globalization/transnationalism is related to IPE in many ways, but raises other concerns that span borders (e.g., transnational social movements) and accordingly often receives separate or semi-separate treatment from textbook authors.

International organizations (IOs) and international law are increasingly the source of social science research, and they also receive prominent attention in Intro IR courses. With respect to the former, the UN receives the most attention, although other IOs (e.g., International Monetary Fund) and NGOs (e.g., Amnesty International or Greenpeace) are covered in the context of specific issues, such as finance, human rights or the environment. Similarly, international law can be embedded in certain concerns (e.g., humanitarian intervention or war crimes) as well as a stand-alone subject. Integration and regionalism receive less attention. Foci such as the European Union are not ignored, but do not necessarily get their own chapters. It might be that regional issues are covered elsewhere in an international studies curriculum, perhaps under the comparative politics rubric.

Also an influence on textbook content, there is a lag between the time that new issues arise on the international scene and when they are reflected in the content of textbooks. Textbooks are typically published a year or so after the author has finished writing, and they stay in print for several years thereafter.

Accordingly, the politics of immigration and health (e.g., COVID-19) are not deeply considered in IR textbooks at this time, although they might receive some indirect attention (e.g., hunger) and will likely be featured more in future editions or in rapidly produced supplements by authors and publishers.

Some IR research areas – specifically ethics, gender, and race – fall short of our cutoff of at least half of a chapter devoted to them to qualify as core elements of a textbook.[1] Gender-related material is sometimes found in discussions of feminist theory, and ethical discussions can be contained in international law and subject matters. Nevertheless, these subjects do not receive the concentrated attention that other matters do.

INSIGHTS FROM ISA WORKSHOPS

In trying to tease out the modal components of teaching IR in varied places, we also draw on experiences of classroom teachers gained at interactive workshops around this topic. That meant structuring our workshop as we would an active-learning classroom space by providing ample time for the participants to be involved directly in the discussion and in understanding how others in the room approached the field. To date, this workshop has been held seven different times, four of those sessions as part of the ISA Innovative Pedagogy Conference (IPC) – in 2018 (two sessions at ISA-Midwest, St. Louis) and 2019 (two sessions at ISA-West, Pasadena, CA) – and the remaining three at other ISA events in Accra, Ghana (2019), Belgrade, Serbia (2019) and Singapore (2019).

Each workshop section and its results are discussed below and are in order of the questions and foci posed for participants:

- Student Learning Goals – what are top three things you want your students to learn?
- Topical Coverage – using a brief survey of topical coverage to understand the breadth of coverage in the participants' classrooms;
- Theory Coverage – using as brief survey again to understand which theoretical approaches are taught.[2]

As is evident below, there was a remarkable degree of agreement across participants about the foundational components of the Intro IR course. Nevertheless, there were also points of variance among participants and also some across the different geographic venues. We summarize the results of the workshops in the tables and discussion below.[3]

Table 2.2 lays out the different responses from the participants when they were asked to list the three most important things that they want their students to learn. The responses show wide variation, but also a fair degree

20 *Teaching international relations*

Table 2.2   Three most important things for students to learn cited in ISA workshop surveys

Learning category	Responses
Academic skills	Analytical skills
	Writing skills
	Career/profession building skills
	Working with others
Applications	Collective action problems and solutions
	Global literacy/awareness
	Links to real world decision-making
	Local or regional issues
	Theory and practice interface
Alternative perspectives	Non-traditional issues
	Differences in ways of life
	Non-Western worldviews
	North vs. South perspectives
Critical analysis	Critical theory
	Critical thinking
	Debate positions on issues
	Gaps in IR theory
	Levels of analysis
	Evaluating sources of information
Cross-discipline	Differences with comparative politics
	Current events
	International v. domestic politics
	Global economics
	Historical North–South power dynamic
Intra-discipline	Actors
	Myth-busting
	Interconnection with IR with all other things
	Concepts and frameworks (e.g., sovereignty)
	Theory basics
Miscellaneous	Empathy
	Interconnectivity
	Evidence
	Empowerment
	Explanation
	Affect
	Curiosity

of commonality. Some of the responses also reflect some overlap with the topical coverage responses discussed below. As for commonalities, perhaps the most striking one across the workshops was a desire to introduce students to non-Western (or non-traditional) perspectives on IR. These responses might indicate some sampling bias, as IR scholars are perhaps more apt to focus broadly on geographic, conceptual (e.g., use of the "worldview" and "perspectives" term in responses), and normative terms than the average social science instructor might. A second commonality was evident in collective action concerns. Quite logically, as IR focuses on decision-making and action in an anarchic system, the struggle to develop collective action is indeed central to many areas of IR study.

The third area of consensus focuses attention on critical thinking and analytical skills. This is hardly surprising, especially in an academic era in which pedagogy emphasizes the value of cultivating evaluation capabilities, as they build citizenship skills and provide methods that are broadly applicable in a range of career sectors in the world post-graduation.

Moving to the substance of the Intro IR course, as taught by our participants, the survey results about topical coverage are displayed in Table 2.3. Consistent with the topical coverage in textbooks above, participant responses also showed significant agreement. Topics such as "war/conflict", and "theoretical approaches" were consensus core topics, as well as "actors" and "power" even as the latter two do not have specific chapters devoted to them in textbooks. "human rights," "environment," "international development" and "IPE" were also frequently listed, even if slightly less so than the first grouping. Much less focus is given to both "foreign policy decision-making" and "IR history," which might be surprising given some common assumptions about what might be necessary to cover in the IR basic course and what textbooks emphasize.

Results did not differ substantially in comparing participants attending US conferences and those in other areas of the world. Indeed, there were greater differences between participants across US regional meetings than relative to those from Europe, Asia, and Africa, although the numbers analyzed were relatively small in those latter sessions.

A few outliers are worth some attention. "Norms" and "international law" were mentioned by multiple respondents at one workshop in contrast to the respondents elsewhere. It is possible that these are covered in the context of other topics from the upper half, such human rights, actors (IOs), or perhaps even when discussing the differences between realism and liberalism. Second, "international cooperation" also received mention at the same workshop, but again cooperation might be embedded in other places mentioned above. Perhaps the most notable, though hardly surprising, finding were the responses on "colonialism" at the workshop in Ghana. Again, these considerations might also be embedded in sections focusing on IPE, international development, human rights, the environment, or others. Nevertheless, they might also reflect region-specific concerns or topics addressed relevant to the audience in question, something we discuss below.

22 Teaching international relations

Table 2.3   Topical coverage cited in ISA workshop surveys (N = 62 participants)

Topical coverage	% Cited (N)
IR history or background	51.6 (32)
Theoretical approaches	85.5 (53)
Power	64.5 (40)
Foreign policy decision-making	45.2 (28)
Actors	82.3 (51)
War/conflict	82.3 (51)
International political economy	66.1 (41)
International development	71.0 (44)
Human rights	72.6 (45)
Environment	74.2 (46)
International cooperation	8.1 (5)
Norms/international law	8.1 (5)
Other (7 other topics)	24.2 (15)

IR Theory was an important focus of textbooks and in participant responses in Table 2.3. Table 2.4 lays out the responses of workshop participants concerning the specific theories they cover in their courses. The first pattern that jumps out is that the so-called "Big Three" – realism, liberalism and constructivism – appear to have become the canonical core of IR theory with feminist theory and Marxism (in varied forms) following close behind. Critical theory and post-modernism also show up prominently and might be more so if they were parsed out from variants of other perspectives (e.g., feminist theory). Again, there was little difference across US regions or international

Essentials for Introduction to International Relations 23

Table 2.4   *Theory coverage cited in ISA workshop surveys (N = 62 participants)*

Theory coverage	% Cited (N)
Realism	83.9 (52)
Liberalism	88.7 (55)
Constructivism	79.0 (49)
Feminist theory	61.3 (38)
Critical theory	38.7 (24)
Post-modernism	29.0 (18)
Marxism	62.9 (39)
English school	14.5 (9)
Post-colonialism	16.1 (10)
Other (11 other theories)	19.4 (12)

settings. Indeed, that included some participants at different venues identifying post-colonial theory as important to their teaching of Intro IR.

REGIONAL VARIATIONS

In general, there is a Western-centric bias in IR instruction (Knight), given that many instructors were trained in Global North universities and most of the textbooks and instructional materials are published in English and written by Western authors. Although there is considerable consensus about the content of Intro IR from textbooks and ISA conference participants, there are variations that stem from the historical and cultural contexts in which those courses are offered (Frueh and Diehl).

There has been a movement toward what has been dubbed "Global IR" (Acharya 2014), that calls for research in IR to consider non-Western subjects and ideas actively and intensively, including those from the Global South. Applied to teaching (Acharya 2020), this means, among other elements, going beyond post-Westphalian history to include: the contributions of other civilizations (see also Powel); exploring local actors and their resistance to and modification of global norms and institutions; problematizing the alleged universal applicability of certain fundamental IR concepts, such as nation-state, territorial sovereignty, balance of power, and free markets; and recognizing multiple conceptions and processes of ideas such as human rights and just war. Some of this is already reflected in the ways that Intro IR is taught in different parts of the world, but the call for Global IR also aims to broaden what is taught in the West as a means of expanding the space for discussion on new topics and ideas. It also aims to challenge the canon wherever possible both substantively and theoretically.

Even putting the Global IR movement aside for the moment, Intro IR differs by institutional context, defined in large part by the university or college in which the course is taught and the student audiences it serves. The relevance of IR for the student audience also prompts variations in content. This might take the form of a companion introductory course that relates the home country to international affairs as is true of at least one Chinese university (Liu). Instructors might also seek resonance in the examples or cases employed such as covering actions of the African Union instead of the European Union for students in South Africa (de Matos-Ala). It also might mean the development of curriculum materials with a specific regional focus when and where possible. Similarly, active-learning exercises might be used to teach core topics, but the applications might emphasize or avoid politically sensitive concerns; for example, model UN simulations in the Middle East (Kalpakian) might shy away from the Palestinian issue when some students would be placed in the role of an Israeli delegate. As a result, even with the high degree of commonality noted above, there will inevitably been unique variation on-site to accommodate instructor preference, student demand, regional circumstance or even socio-political sensitivities.

CONCLUSIONS

For two long-time instructors of IR who have witnessed many changes, expansions, and extensions of our field over the past four decades, the degree to which we uncovered common threads in the teaching of Intro IR was rather surprising, but also quite important from several vantage points. First, the common threads across learning outcomes, topics, and theory show that there appears to be a significant level of cumulation in IR learning. For social scientists, cumulation of knowledge is a foundational goal and in that way our field does seem to be building on itself. It is also encouraging to find that the teaching of IR also seems to reflect cumulation in coverage and approach. Still, the study and teaching of IR have many continuing elements, including the need for understanding through theoretical frameworks and the enduring place of realism and liberalism as the approaches that have informed generations of scholars and students. Similarly, concerns with war and peace continue as focal points for the way that IR is taught. It is also heartening that an appreciation of history and the development of key critical and analytical skills remain as student learning goals for instructors around the world.

Second, although the essentials of Intro IR have retained common elements over time and across different geographic regions, that course, and the IR field more broadly, have been flexible and adaptable. For those IR scholar–teachers more critical of social science epistemology and traditional theoretical approaches, they can take heart in the knowledge that many of the edges where IR research and instruction have grown are ones that have pushed outward to create intellectual spaces that allow for creative, non-mainstream discussions of alternative interpretations of the phenomena that we study. This is reflected in several ways from our analysis of textbook coverage and the workshop discussions. One is the emergence of different analytical frameworks – most notably constructivism and feminism – that challenge the ways we ask students to comprehend the world. Somewhat related are the efforts not only to incorporate non-Western perspectives in concepts and subject matter, but to make the understanding of such ideas a specific learning goal, even among students in Global North institutions. Core subjects have also evolved to give prominent treatment to political economy a few decades ago and more recently to human rights and the environment. We would be remiss to ignore the emergence of post-colonial perspectives and discussions of race and ethnicity in IR, the latter of which has been persistent in IR scholarship, but historically not addressed (see Henderson; Zvobgo and Loken). Both threads have highlighted the lasting impact of colonialism and the persistence of structural factors within IR teaching and practice. Recent events around the world have emphasized this point and have highlighted the ways student interest has driven part of the expanded agenda. We expect that the expansion of the agenda for what constitutes IR to continue and that will further push for expansion and revision in the classroom.

The reality also means that the IR classroom becomes a living laboratory for analysis of the world as we try out new perspectives while still preserving the valuable foundational work of our own teachers. In this highly globalized, highly changeable global socio-political environment, providing our students with the ability to analyze in a nimble fashion what they are seeing, reading, and receiving through news platforms, social media, and other sources is an invaluable tool for citizenship. That also argues for the on-going need for revision, expansion, and reevaluation as we move forward. The status quo of content or pedagogy won't help the next generations to cope with the world around them.

NOTES

1. In fairness, there are instances in which one-third of a chapter is devoted to such concerns.
2. The reader should note that each survey is a simple list of possible responses including an open-ended response area where participants can include any other responses not listed.
3. Note that we do not have aggregated summary data for the Belgrade and Singapore workshops, as each group of participants numbered only about five and thus it was difficult to generalize from such a small N. That said, neither of those workshops showed as much variance from the four in the United States than was the case for the Accra group. In addition, we do not assert that these data have been generated from a random or representative sample of teachers of IR, but they do provide an impressionistic picture of what is the perceived state of the art in Intro IR.

3. Teaching with purpose: commitment and innovation in IR pedagogy[1]

Jeffrey S. Lantis

The modern discipline of Political Science was developed in the late nineteenth century to help individuals gain a better understanding of social and political dynamics that shape the world. From the beginning, political scientists acknowledged deep roots in Philosophy and the Humanities, as well as the natural sciences. Critically, the emergence of the discipline was also inspired by a commitment to teaching and learning. Innovation and engagement with students remain at the heart of our work today, as we seek to make sense of both prevailing patterns and dramatic changes in the world around us.

This chapter discusses our historical commitment to pedagogy in the discipline, including its inspirations in the Aristotelian philosophy of formal education and examples of achievements through more than a century of work in Political Science. This chapter also addresses the ebb and flow of the professional community's relationship with pedagogy over time and the role of key voices and developments in spurring innovation. Next, the chapter discusses insights on "teaching with purpose" developed over my 25 years of teaching and learning. It concludes with a call for continued engagement in effective pedagogy and surveys emerging trends that could help to define the next century of teaching and learning in international relations (IR).

A BRIEF HISTORY OF "PEDAGOGICAL THINKING"

Our techniques for meaningful student engagement in the discovery of knowledge have evolved over centuries, from Aristotle and Socrates to the works of John Dewey (1938), Benjamin Bloom (1956), Paulo Freire (1970/2000), Cynthia Enloe (2014), and Darby, Flower, and Lang (2019). Committed instructors select goals and methods for teaching that reflect a sense of purpose, and they draw their students into an exploration of knowledge (Kille, Krain, and Lantis; Hutchings, Huber, and Ciccone). Engaged teacher–scholars are also creative and willing to experiment. Today's IR professors are equally as likely to facilitate role-playing simulations of crisis policy-making, to teach power politics by using examples of a zombie apocalypse, or to lead discussions on constructivist interpretations of the latest popular series on Netflix as they are to offer traditional lectures on Realism.

The resonance of these examples for many readers is itself testimony to how far we have come in the discipline. Yet, we also know that we cannot rest on our laurels. Commitments to pedagogy in the discipline today have not always been so strong, and teacher–scholars face a constant challenge to remain engaged and relevant in increasingly diverse educational and global contexts. Advocates for purposeful pedagogy play a key role in this process. Indeed, a closer look at the history of the Political Science engagement with pedagogy suggests a sometimes fraught relationship between teaching and research, debates about how best to share the scholarship of teaching and learning, and potential disconnects between classroom instruction and analysis of real-world developments. Recognizing and embracing these dynamic tensions can serve to inspire and energize teacher–scholars on their own "pedagogical journeys" (Frueh).

Engagement with pedagogy has always required a conscious process, driven by committed professionals who stimulate pedagogical discussions and share their ideas widely. For example, the American Political Science Association (APSA) was founded in 1903 and began publication of its flagship journal *American Political Science Review* in 1906. After a decade of publishing articles solely on research, members of the APSA established a committee in 1911, "to consider the methods of teaching and studying governments now pursued in American schools, colleges and universities, and to suggest means of enlarging and improving such instruction" (Haines, 251). This was the beginning of a series of studies aimed at enhancement of teaching, even as research programs for the discipline were beginning to take shape.

So long as persistent voices have promoted the value of engagement with pedagogy, they have remained an important part of our professional discourse. In an article published in 1933, for example, political scientist A. Gordon Dewey, raised a call to arms for instruction. Dewey described "growing dissatisfaction" in the discipline "with the purely descriptive approach in teaching political science … which fails to answer the intelligent student's recurrent question: 'Why am I studying this stuff?'" His prescription was greater student engagement and efforts to find real-world connections between theory and research (quoted in Craig, 27). In 1941, APSA President Frederic Ogg called for even "more contemplation of the characteristics and methods of the great teachers of our subject," and he suggested that members of the discipline should be "assembling, digesting, and preparing for publication the data that might conceivably be gathered (chiefly from past students) throwing light on the approaches, methods, techniques, innovations, success and failures of a representative group" (511) of teachers. In the 1950s, Benjamin Bloom developed a taxonomy of educational goals that helped provide a vocabulary for levels of instruction in the classrooms that followed a progression from lower to higher orders of complexity, and from a static possession of knowledge to more creative forms of thinking in categories of synthesis and evaluation (Mulcare and Schwedel). Teacher–scholars have employed this common vocabulary in course and curricular design ever since.

However, attention to pedagogy in Political Science appeared to ebb in the post-Second World War period. Cold War priorities, coupled with the behavioral revolution and the rise of quantitative methods for research in Political Science, served to marginalize some pedagogical pursuits. As the discipline became more "professionalized" (Desch), one observed a centralization of foundation support for major graduate programs and an overarching disciplinary focus on research and publication. The evidence of a shift in emphasis was also manifest in the empirical record of publications. Craig found that the number of published works related to pedagogy and instruction was lower during this period, despite the establishment of a new journal, *Teaching Political Science* (published from 1973 to 1989). To some degree, attention to teaching as a craft seemed to fade from professional discourse and professional graduate training.

The End of the Cold War and the Resurgence of Pedagogy

Thankfully, we have witnessed the resurgence of attention to pedagogy in IR in recent decades. Professors began to consider new topics and means of instruction in the post-Cold War era. Gone were some traditional conventions that dominated the curriculum, such as studies of the arms race or Soviet history or behavioralist-driven research. In their place, instructors saw opportunities for newfound attention to instruction on topics like human security, environmental politics, human rights, and civil and ethnic conflicts. Many institutions of higher learning have also faced new attention and pressure from state legislatures to conduct assessments of learning and to confirm the value of public education at taxpayer expense. In addition, positivist and behavioral revolutions in Political Science have come under scrutiny from scholars who questioned standards for the cumulation of knowledge (Hamati-Ataya). This has prompted the proliferation of theoretical development and paradigmatic alternatives to positivism and realism. Charitable foundations and even the federal government have also provided valuable support for teacher training and internationalized education. The Pew Charitable Trust Foundation program at Harvard University helped draft a new generation of teacher–scholars to use the case study method, for example, and the American Council on Education and the U.S. State Department promoted global learning programs in the post-Cold War era (Shaklee and Bailey; Hudzik).

Globalization and democratization have also profoundly influenced our disciplinary approaches to teaching and research. Transitions to democracy helped to breathe new life into the philosophy of education and enlightenment for its own sake. Indeed, John Dewey and others describe pedagogy as central to democracy itself. Democracy depends upon the communication process and the dynamics of how others live as collectives, with the future contingent on the involvement and interaction of everyone in the community (1997[1938]). Dewey returned to the critical nature of education to build these habits and norms of democratic life. He actively challenged the traditional education system that relied on transmitting a "fixed body" of knowledge to the students and instead championed an alternative approach that would not only improve learning but also have positive impacts on society and democracy. Instead of presupposing the static and external objective of knowledge, Dewey argued for the "intimate and necessary relation between the processes of actual experience and education" (20). Student experiences themselves become a resource for constructing knowledge and a critical part of the curriculum, a starting place and a continual touchstone from which students can draw and to which they can relate, developing their understanding of new concepts.

These patterns of engagement were also evidenced in peer-reviewed publications in the 1990s and 2000s. In a study of publications on the scholarship of teaching and learning (SOTL), Kehl reported that 495 articles on the subject appeared between 1990 and 2001. The number of these publications increased significantly between 1998 and 2001. Similarly, Ishiyama (2013) found 176 articles on active learning that were published in three key journals on pedagogy from 2005 to 2011.[2] At the same time, there has been a growth in peer-reviewed journal articles on teaching and learning and patterns of publications and content. Using data drawn from the International Political Education Database (IPED), Craig found 1600 articles on teaching and learning in politics published between 2005 and 2012.[3]

Finally, the discipline experienced a tremendous resurgence of interest in pedagogy in the face of unexpected challenges during the COVID-19 pandemic. Thousands of teacher–scholars had to quickly pivot in their traditional or preferred means of instruction to new, hybridized forms of teaching and learning. They joined many colleagues who already had established online instructional training to explore creative approaches to student engagement in a complex era. As the pandemic wore on, instructors came to recognize that these were not short-term transitions in our instruction that were to be quickly forgotten; rather, our profession appeared to be undergoing a long-term transformation in teaching modes, technologies, and assessment. Ideas that had been circulating in the profession for years—such as teaching online, hybrid and "flipped" classroom formats, using Zoom and Microsoft Teams for meetings with students, and bringing in guest speakers virtually from around the world—suddenly became a reality for the vast majority of the profession. These dramatic changes have provided fertile ground for critical thinking and asssement of means of instruction, as well as serious opportunities for professional growth. The scholarship on teaching and learning was poised for advancement in the aftermath of the COVID-19 crisis.

Powerful Voices

Despite the progress that has been made, we must also remember that this is not self-perpetuating. The discipline will remain committed to these types of pursuits only so long as important voices and members of the profession demand introspection, assessment, and refreshment of our methods and practices. It is critical that we acknowledge that some of these perspectives are emerging from the global South. Paulo Freire, a Brazilian educator, advocated for a form of critical pedagogy drawing from his personal experiences and vocational work in adult literacy education. Freire criticized instructional methods that he said resembled a "banking system," where knowledge was deposited into the heads of students, stored there and later withdrawn by the instructor's assignments. Instead, he argued, education should focus on posing problems in relations with the world. The goal was not to solve the problem, he argued, but rather to engage in a "critical analysis of the problematic reality" (Freire, 168). Freire called for both the imagination of civic education as a way to overcome domination and oppression—the opportunity to know more about oneself, the structural forces shaping our lives, and how to imagine and create a new life (Giroux 2010, 716). Pedagogy in this sense is a political practice. We need to recognize our space and open our worldview and create an equal and democratic space—a space capable of promoting social reform and justice (Longview Foundation).

Voices from the South have continued to inspire reflective thinking about global engagement. In Amitav Acharya's presidential address to the International Studies Association (ISA) in 2014, for example, he argued that it was important for teacher–scholars in our discipline to critically reflect on the question of whether our discipline truly represents the global society that we live in today. His new non-Western or "post-Western" paradigm called for us to endorse "an aspiration for greater inclusiveness and diversity in our discipline" (Acharya 2014, 649). Ultimately, Acharya called for empowerment and education to promote a new universality in IR education (649).

Alternative voices are also challenging the traditional Western canon in teaching IR. If we are truly committed to educating global citizens, teacher–scholars should heed these perspectives and revisit the hallmarks of our teaching and research. This represents more than simply embracing diversity; it involves uplifting disparate voices and promoting critical conversations about identity, class privilege, power, and place. Culturally responsive pedagogy includes the embrace of diversity of perspectives, acknowledgment of potential bias or Western-centric worldviews and theoretical constructs, and embracing narratives of traditionally marginalized groups (Deardorff). This is about communicative consciousness and awareness, recognition and critical engagement. This is about challenging "received wisdom" and empowering students and faculty (Bhambra et al.).

TEACHING WITH PURPOSE

There is no doubt that teacher–scholars who are committed to collaboration can help enliven the educational environment and achieve learning objectives. Best practices in our discipline include the importance of designing exercises that have clear educational objectives, exploring examples and alternative ways of engaging students, detailing clear procedures, and implementing assessment protocols (Kille, Krain, and Lantis). Examples of popular and successful active teaching and learning approaches include problem-based learning in international studies, structured debates, or the use of popular cultural touchstones, like the TV series *Game of Thrones*, to engage students with critical themes. In this section, I discuss several important dimensions of an approach to "teaching with purpose" that reflects both on development of the discipline and best practices in pedagogy.

Looking Backwards to Move Forward

Instructors in IR should constantly consider educational outcomes of classes as they relate to pedagogy, innovation, and course design. The importance of educational objectives has been discussed in the SOTL literature in the past, particularly in relation to assessment. But over the past two decades, the innovation of "backward design" in Science, Technology, Engineering, and Mathematics (STEM) fields and other disciplines has reinvigorated a goals-based approach. Designing classes first around the key or essential questions of a course, then focusing on the learning goals and outcomes, and only then on assignments, readings, and exams has provided helpful logic (Davidovitch; Kuh et al. 2010). This also fosters consideration of connections between content and pedagogy, as well as promotes innovation. Backward design fits well with broader curricular design considerations (considering major program goals, for example) and provides core logic for development of online, hybrid, or remote classes. Indeed, many of us learned more about this during the COVID-19 pandemic in 2020–2021.

Backward design helps instructors focus on educational objectives and consider creative means to get there. Bloom's taxonomy of learning goals and assessment mechanisms provides a good starting point for this approach (Mulcare and Shwedel). Once our goals are established, we can foster learning-centered and student-centered approaches in the classroom to help achieve them. These can also foster powerful and engaging dialogues between students and instructors (and fuel vibrant exchanges among instructors in the wider profession). The logic of backward design is also critical for innovation, and we have seen more attention to the approach by instructors who are committed to active learning and to re-thinking the traditional curriculum, such as challenges to teaching the traditional Western canon by "de-colonizing" the IR curriculum. This allows us to move beyond trying to simply transfer knowledge, in the spirit of Freire's critique and towards student engagement and ownership.

Embracing Dynamic Tensions

We are fortunate to teach and research in a field that is rife with dynamic tensions of its own. Political Science and International Studies are never boring. To the contrary, there are tensions between contending theoretical perspectives, for example, that we articulate with our students as we analyze issues from different perspectives. There are inherent tensions in different subject areas, such as the study of international political economy, peace and conflict, or identity. They are manifest in methodological treatments of subjects. And, dynamic tensions are the core of an educational focus on critical thinking and analytical reflections on major themes. We teach by tapping into these strains, while at the same time mentoring student applications of critical thinking.

The contemporary literature on pedagogy in IR is rife with examples of applications designed to promote this type of engagement. For example, instructors can deviate from the "traditional" approach to study of major theories or themes by employing alternative texts or source material (Glover and Tagliarana). Possibilities abound—from the use of graphic novels and comics to generate discussions about power and responsibility (Dougherty; Juneau and Sucharov; Worcester) to the use of films or filmed events to generate discussion (Haney; Corrigan; Franklin). Such material frequently draws on controversial subjects or popular culture to connect students to subjects in the classroom (Stump; Sachleben; Van Belle). Current events also provide a ready supply of "alternative texts" in the form of news articles or editorials or subjects to analyze using tools developed in the classroom. Additional possibilities include the use of novels (Lang and Lang; Morgan; Vachris and Bohanon; Dreyer), memoirs (Deibel), music (Soper; Levy and Byrd; Hawn), video games (Hayden), dance (Rösch), and art-making (Alexander).

If we are to remain conscientious teacher–scholars, it is important for us to embrace the tensions of a globalized world. These themes come through in many different ways, including reckoning with inherent Western or Northern biases in our means and subjects of instruction. In this context, one should never be completely satisfied with one's professional expertise or understanding of common themes. It can be valuable for us to repeatedly second-guess and practice mindfulness when it comes to the topics that we teach, as well as the way that we teach them. With acceptance comes the opportunity for creative reflection.

Innovation: Thinking Big and Small

Committed teacher–scholars are constantly thinking about how best to communicate valuable information, engage students, and enliven the classroom. Indeed, some of the most important innovations in the classroom require continual trial and error. Innovation often demands a level of *dis*comfort that can be professionally exhilarating. I believe that one should always consider one's class syllabi and course designs as "works in progress." Teaching innovations should be part of our efforts to push the envelope, raise important questions, and get uncomfortable. If, for example, we instructors find that we tend to "default" to teaching with lectures regularly, then I believe it is incumbent upon us as innovators to add new exercises in classes, to design discussion groups or listserv conversations, or "minute papers" that all facilitate more creative and critical engagement. If we change our natural defaults, we stand poised to gain a great deal from the political process.

Innovation also requires us to seize "teaching moments" whenever possible and to tap directly into students' lived experiences. Dewey argued that "problems are the stimulus to thinking," and through a problem-based learning frame students may become more invested in the learning process and more connected to their learning and lived communities (Dewey, 79). Students must come from a starting place or a foundation that they can continue to relate lessons back to or be used to force critical thinking and cognitive dissonance. Traditional forms of education focused on memorization do not necessarily provide opportunities for reflection and analysis for students to learn from these experiences. Without this reflection, individuals tend to move on, both consciously and unconsciously and continue with everyday activities and leave issues unexamined (Hildreth, 924). In this sense, difficulties or challenges become critical junctures for the learning process, affording opportunities to question and challenge habits, routines, and ways of thinking.

Student interest and support in their knowledge development and application to critical questions represents an important professional commitment. On a good day, some of our students may learn a great deal from excellent lectures; others will draw inspiration from the great readings that we select so carefully; and a few of our students may even go on to become PhDs themselves and professors at colleges and universities. But studies show that what most students will remember are those occasions when they were *engaged*: when there was a discussion that they had to take part in, when they watched a powerful film together or read a good book, or when they gave a presentation (Dewey; MacLabhrainn; Robinson). These arguments also served as the inspiration for a problem-based curriculum structure. "Problems are the stimulus to thinking," Dewey argued (79), and the problem-solving process promotes greater learning and connection to community.

Innovation has become even more critically important for teaching in the COVID-19 era. A global pandemic has forced instructors in IR to learn quickly about different philosophies of teaching, develop creative approaches to online learning, and to find ways to connect and engage with students from a distance. A subject like a global pandemic creates opportunities for teaching and learning in every discipline in higher education, and politics seems central to this. To suggest that developments in 2020–2021 will be transformational to our pedagogy and the way that our institutions work is an understatement. But the degree to which these changes will resonate and "stick" in higher education are yet to be determined.

RENEWING OUR COMMITMENT TO ACTIVE TEACHING AND LEARNING IN IR

Given dramatic transformations in global politics over the past two decades, this is a propitious time for reflection, reinvention, and recommitment to interactive methods of teaching and learning. Our discipline has always been shaped by efforts to make sense of and analyze changes in IR. This has shaped both the process and product of our work in the IR classroom. Committed instructors select goals and methods for teaching that reflect a sense of purpose, and they draw their students into an exploration of knowledge (Kille, Krain, and Lantis; Hutchings et al.).

Pedagogy and purpose have a synergistic relationship. Revisiting our approach to teaching IR should begin with reevaluation of our learning objectives for our courses in the twenty-first century. How do we help students learn about trends like globalization, fragmentation, international cooperation, conflict, and challenges in new realms like global health policies and cybersecurity? How should we present information about civil wars, under-studied regions of the world, and diverse cultures and societies? Successful active teaching and learning certainly should begin with consideration of educational objectives—'what' we seek to teach to our students (Kolb), allow students to make conceptual linkages between theory and real-world examples (Shulman 1997), and increase retention of knowledge (Jensen; Brock and Cameron). This includes identification and exploration of new means of instruction—seizing a teaching moment or harnessing new technologies for broader objectives.

There is a great deal of room for optimism about pedagogy in IR today, and I believe that our discipline has "caught up" to the idea that teaching and learning are important. For example, both the ISA and the APSA are sponsoring initiatives designed to promote active teaching and learning. In 2017, the ISA Governing Council launched a three-year pilot program in 2017 to support innovative teaching and learning initiatives. The ISA now sponsors a series of Innovative Pedagogy Conferences (ISA–IPC) linked to regional ISA section conference meetings. These conferences include a variety of workshop sessions and graduate student teacher training workshops on topics ranging from decolonizing the teaching of IR and faculty-led study abroad programs to simulations and games for teaching political violence. Similarly, the APSA sponsors bi-annual Teaching and Learning Conferences, designed to offer participants the opportunity to engage in days of critical discussions about teaching innovations and assessment. All of these initiatives also went online during the COVID-19 pandemic, expanding our audiences and enriching our dialogues about pedagogy.

These conferences have been very successful over the last 20 years. Participants have appreciated the variety of offerings, the level of engagement expected in each workshop, and learning from some of the best-known names in the field. Participants also agreed that the graduate student teacher training session was an outstanding component of the experience. In summary, the general consensus among all participants with whom I spoke was that this was successful, and many people asked when and where the next conference on pedagogy might be held.

Finally, one of the most promising avenues for advancement of the scholarship on teaching and learning in international studies for the twenty-first century has been to make our enterprise truly international. That is, work should intentionally seek out and promote a more global viewpoint while encouraging cross-national engagement and understanding of active teaching and learning across different areas. This advancement is not only promising, it is necessary in order to counter a Western/Northern-centric bias in the literature, and to help move this part of the field toward a truly Global IR (Acharya 2014). The international studies discipline will benefit from examination of different teaching contexts across the globe (e.g. Ferreira; Tan; John), consideration of the impact of students transitioning from one teaching context to another (Hammersley-Fletcher and Hanley), and teaching dimensions of cross-cultural competence (Raymond et al.). To date, efforts to evaluate the utility of exercises that cut across different national and cultural contexts have been limited (Inoue and Krain; Shaw 2016), even though many of the IR courses analyze similar phenomena.

Exploring cross-cultural active teaching and learning dimensions will also promote understanding of how different student learning styles, expectations, perceptions of the learning experience, and levels of comfort with interactive learning may be recognized. This could help open pathways in the SOTL for approaching cultural context with intentionality and awareness, along with promoting cross-cultural sensitivity and diverse viewpoints (Krain et al.). Teacher–scholars from different backgrounds could better engage with central questions such as what teaching approaches have been employed, why these approaches are being used, how well these are working, and what advantages and challenges does this evaluation reveal for the various uses of active teaching methods in different situations.

In conclusion, this chapter has summarized insights from decades of teaching—and a survey of decades of the scholarship on teaching and learning. It promotes the commitment to teaching with purpose and details some of the qualities that can make for effective pedagogy, including engagement, innovation, and discomfort. It also underscores the idea that teacher–scholars must remain vocal, persistent champions of advancing our craft.

NOTES

1. I express my thanks to the thousands of students and colleagues who have helped motivate and inspire my teaching. I'd like to extend special gratitude to Kent Kille and Matthew Krain for their collaborative spirit and ideas that helped inform this chapter.
2. These were the *Journal of Political Science Education, PS: Political Science & Politics*, and *International Studies Perspectives*.
3. IPED data draws on a significantly wider range of journals than other literature surveys, and Craig, too, identifies a significant increase in the Political Science SOTL around the year 2000.

4. Teaching IR in the Global South: views from Brazil and South Africa

Jacqueline de Matos Ala, Cristina Yumie Aoki Inoue and Marcelo Valença

INTRODUCTION

The concept of Global South reflects a political construct that comprises a myriad of socio-cultural, political, and economic realities. It is both a geographic location and a metaphysical space. As such many scholars located in the geographic North are associated with the Global South due to their origins, backgrounds, or research agendas.

These unclear borders make it difficult to generalize about what the Global South represents for the scholarship of teaching and learning in international relations (IR). First and foremost, any attempt at reducing IR pedagogy in the Global South to a single reality or experience may reinforce an Orientalist approach to the discipline. Many criticisms of the Global South by Western theories are due to the generalized belief that these theories are universally applicable, irrespective of the local context, culture, and society. Nevertheless, as academics of the Global South, it is inevitable that we assume positions that express our particular loci of enunciation, even if they represent our own experiences.

Thus, in this chapter, we discuss some of the challenges we face as academics teaching IR in the Global South. We present our reflections not only from our experiences teaching at our institutions but also as participants in national- and international-level discussions about what constitutes IR as a discipline and an academic field of inquiry and teaching. The field is filled with both an established and a critical scholarship on the process of knowledge-making and a diversity of perspectives, ontologies, and epistemologies as to what constitutes the "international" in IR. Still, little has been said about teaching and learning IR in the Global South. It is relevant, therefore, to tackle this silence. How we teach is a central aspect of the process of reproducing, perpetuating, and creating new IR narratives by bringing other voices into the debate (Wemheuer-Vogelaar et al.). With the proliferation of IR-related departments and majors around the world, the discussion on teaching in/from the Global South is a large, overdue task to which we can just add a small piece.

Teaching IR in Brazil and South Africa is challenging enough given the lack of resources, internal inequalities, and institutional constraints. Arguably, a more fundamental problem is the fact that current curricula and textbooks reflect neither a global (Acharya 2014) nor a pluriversal IR (Blaney & Tickner 2017a). IR as a discipline, and its theories, in particular, have been grounded in knowledge derived from Western philosophy and historical events. If this is a problem in the Global North classrooms, it is magnified when what is taught does not relate to students' realities in the Global South. The first years of higher education are highly influential in students' development within a discipline as well as in their worldview after university (Powel, 9), so presenting a body of knowledge compatible with students' experiences is not only recommended: it is imperative.

In order to develop strategies to overcome the lack of plurality in IR, we make a claim for a "global pluriversal IR" perspective in the classroom that recognizes regional and local contributions from History and Social Sciences to IR as well as contributions from other knowledge systems, worldviews, and other epistemologies and ontologies. To illustrate the challenges and possibilities entailed in this claim we present two cases: Brazil and South Africa. The former gives a general picture of IR teaching in a country as large and diverse as the United States and discusses some challenges we face, bringing a few examples of where we can start to build a more plural IR classroom. The latter brings a concrete example of IR theory teaching and how it can actually be made in a way that resonates with the local realities. We initially focus on IR curricula, as theories are an essential part of the construction of a field's identity. However, a global pluriversal IR perspective should not be restricted to theory teaching. In our view, any IR area can benefit.

Our chapter unfolds as follows. Following this introduction, we introduce in the second section the so-called Global IR debate, which critically engages IR knowledge-building processes. We point out IR foundational bases as structured on Western knowledge (Acharya 2014; Tickner 2003b) and how these bases have been recently challenged by a growing scholarship that tries to redefine and reimage ways for a more plural IR field (Blaney & Tickner 2017a, 2017b; Acharya 2014). The third section conceptually delineates the challenges and possibilities we face as scholars teaching in the Global South. We then present the cases of Brazil and South Africa to illustrate how these challenges and possibilities play out in our countries and some of the strategies we developed in order to engage with these issues. We conclude our chapter with a few remarks about how a global pluriversal IR perspective in the classroom can also be important in other contexts even in the Global North.

DELINEATING OUR MAIN CHALLENGES AND POSSIBILITIES

Many – if not most students – usually study IR theories by referring to the Great Debates of the twentieth century. These debates relate, in different ways, to historical events that affected the world in the last century, but mainly Europe and the United States. The narrative proposed by the Great Debates since 1919 goes hand in hand with the interaction between the great Western powers, the changes they face, and the strategies developed to achieve their goals.

The dominance of academia from the United States has been so substantial that Stanley Hoffman characterized IR as an American Social Science. This statement is not limited to the field of theory but also to others. Sub-areas like foreign policy analysis, international security, and political economy are equally dominated by the American academy and its understanding of what science is and how knowledge is constituted.

Despite its predominance in the twentieth century, this epistemic hegemony has been challenged in the last two decades. There is a growing body of scholarship criticizing how IR theory is anchored on Western knowledge and reflects a Western-centered disciplinary interest (Acharya, 2014; Tickner 2017a, 2017b; Barasuol & da Silva; Hovey; Blaney; Liu). Even critical IR theories that supposedly address such biases – including Critical Theory, Feminism, Post-Structuralism, and Marxism – are structured on Western knowledge. These theories hide their own contradictions under a rhetoric of neutrality, misleading to the universal applicability of their premises (Odoom & Andrews). In order to overcome such limitations, there has been a concomitant growth in scholarship defining and re-imagining the ground rules for creating knowledge plural IR theories (Blaney & Tickner 2017a, 2017b; Acharya 2014).

It is important to note that our understanding of knowledge plurality is more than just bringing ideas, values, or concepts originating in the Global South into the existing Western theoretical canon. It also involves including the ontologies and epistemologies from the Global South because they represent potentially different ways of knowing and understanding IR. Thus, pluriversal IR theory-building embraces multiple and divergent realities in which all forms of knowing and understanding are equally present (Blaney & Tickner 2017a). Moreover, "responding effectively and respectfully to the pluriverse presumes that we learn to bend in the face of and to walk with others in the cosmos, thinking and being beyond the familiar" (Blaney & Tickner 2017a, 310).

Despite the significance of this scholarship, little consideration has been given to the need for establishing knowledge-plural IR theory curricula, nor has there been much reflection on the institutional implications as well as the pedagogical choices and outcomes accompanying such initiatives. It is this intellectual gap that our chapter seeks to make some contribution towards filling. Thus, we argue that if our students are to study IR from Global South's locus of enunciation, then our curricula must not only critically engage with Western narratives on history and theory, but also inclusive of the histories and the knowledges – i.e., incorporating their unique ontologies and epistemologies – that elucidate the IR of the Global South.

IR THEORY CURRICULA AND KNOWLEDGE PLURALITY

The literature on knowledge plurality within IR theory curricula is of varying usefulness to the research we seek to undertake. Tickner (2003a) has undertaken research into whether endogenous Latin American IR theories were included in the curricula taught to Latin American IR students. Her findings revealed that Western-based IR theory comprised most of the curriculum. Critical IR theories were also largely absent. Contradictorily, she noted that Latin American scholars were incorporating endogenous Latin American knowledges in their research. They had also developed hybrid theories by merging select aspects from a range of theories to either explain or analyze their findings, as nothing suitable existed in the current cannon. Despite these innovations, almost none of these models had found their way into Latin American IR theory curricula.

More than a decade later Barasuol and da Silva redid Tickner's 2003 study. Their aim was to see if the growing demand for theoretical plurality in IR scholarship had led to more research either producing or utilizing Latin American knowledges as well as whether more endogenous based scholarly knowledge had permeated into the curricula. They concluded that Latin American scholars are more inclined to apply Western IR concepts to their field of research to formulate analytical frameworks. However, little development of theories derived from local knowledge had occurred in the interim between the two studies.

In terms of curricula, the range of theories taught to students had expanded to include critical Western IR theory but Latin American theories were still absent. Both Tickner's and Barusol and da Silva's empirical studies suggest that despite the existence of theories derived from Latin American endogenous knowledges, these were still not being selected as IR theory curricula content. Whether this situation is similar to other regions or countries located in the Global South cannot be ascertained, as to the best of our knowledge there is currently no published research that expressly addresses this issue. Besides pointing out the problems that exposure to a limited range of Western-based theoretical perspectives poses for students' academic capacity (which has numerous implications for the range of post-graduate research they would be capable of undertaking) and their ability to understand and solve problems related to their context, no recommendations are made for expediting knowledge plurality in curricula, especially knowledge originating and developed in the Global South.

Blaney's (2002) and Hovey's (2004) analysis of IR curricula at US higher education institutions showed that content focused exclusively on the IR of the West was counterproductive to developing awareness of IR beyond US borders. As a consequence, IR graduates remained largely ignorant in their knowledge of the rest of the world. Liu (2016) investigated IR theory teaching from a Taiwanese context. Similarly to Blaney and Hovey, Liu advocates for curricula content that is inclusive of diverse cultural contexts given the strong representation of foreign students in Taiwanese IR courses. Western-based IR theories have limited explanatory and analytical capacity for the study of Taiwanese IR. They further tended to produce reductionist solutions to problems. Hence the need to either modify the ways in which we get students to apply these theories or to develop more suitable alternatives. Significantly Krishna (2001) actually draws attention to how pedagogical practices can be used to either reinforce or subvert the dominant status quo held by Western-centric knowledges and theory. He advocates that as teachers we should be mindful of how theoretical discourses in IR eradicate motivation to study issues such as race and genocide, as well as the theft of territory and culture, choosing to focus instead on combating terrorism, illegal migration, securing state sovereignty, and the competitive nature of state interaction. Consequently, in teaching IR theory we must disrupt this dominant discourse by including its contrapuntal narrative.

In summary, current research primarily focuses on how limited knowledge diversity in IR theory curricula is and how it stunts students' capacity to develop a rich conceptualization of the study and practice of IR. Moreover, most argue that students only exposed to Western IR contexts fail to acquire both the knowledge and related dispositions they require to function in a multicultural, globalized world. Additionally, these studies also focus on the important role of curriculum content in shaping the development of student dispositions that determine their ability to be a productive member in a globalized world. However, these studies often only consider one or two elements about the curricula or knowledge choices and do not consider larger curricula contexts (this is probably due to most IR academics lacking the pedagogic knowledge to engage in such debates). Those that do interrogate the issue of the inclusion of knowledge from the Global South in curricula exclusively examine a single country or region.

GLOBAL PLURIVERSAL IR IN THE GLOBAL SOUTH CLASSROOM?

The above Global IR debate denounces the Western centrism of knowledge and the epistemic violence it provokes when silencing other voices and cultures. It highlights the need for changes to create a more inclusive field, to make visible what has been kept invisible. However, this debate is still incipient in the IR scholarship of teaching and learning.

We propose a "global pluriversal IR" perspective to the classroom to recognize the need to go beyond Western centrism, as there is a myriad of ways of undertaking this exercise (Acharya 2014; Blaney & Tickner 2017a, 2017b; Escobar; Sousa Santos 2007, 2015). Acharya and Buzan (2010, 19) argued that the problem is not that non-Western theories do not exist but that they need wider circulation. For Buzan (2016, 156), IR goes beyond world politics and how political science sees it, "IR is multidisciplinary, comprising, and interweaving, the macro ends of most of the social sciences as well as world history". Behera makes a call for reinventing IR by ensuring that "the singularities and universal claims of key concepts of IR must yield to diverse notions and understandings, informed by varied geo-cultural epistemologies derived across the globe" (2016, 154). Consequently, for us, a global pluriversal IR should go beyond multidisciplinarity, in that it reflects the plurality of worldviews, ontologies, and knowledge systems that exist. This would require a double effort of looking both within and beyond IR into other disciplines, other knowledge systems, and worldviews to decenter and pluralize IR.

The rationale for our approach is evident in the recently published *International Relations from the Global South. Worlds of Difference* (Tickner & Smith), For Smith and Tickner (8), there is a need to recognize the role that the Global South has played in shaping world politics, which means recognizing Global South scholarly work, and paying attention to distinct starting points for talking about the world. Most of the book's authors concur that there is a "disconnect" between IR theories, concepts, categories, and themes and their "lived realities" when teaching IR in a Global South, non-West locale (2020, 1 and 2). This is identified consistently throughout the book as a problem that requires immediate engagement. Thus, we need to realize that what we teach is as important as how we teach it. Powel (2019, 9) argues that teaching goes beyond building particular skills, in that it plays a constitutive role in students' understandings of a discipline. Querejazu (2016) states that how students are introduced to IR theory particularly in terms of ontological scope and epistemological range influences not only how they come to perceive and engage with the discipline but also the type of research they will produce. Consequently, it is essential to expose our students to a wider range of ontological and epistemological perspectives together with the different theories they embody as possible. This is not merely a matter of "re-centering" how we teach IR, by trying to delineate schools based on national perspectives of IR, or by focusing only on local realities, but making our theory curricula inclusive of a plurality of theories, concepts, and narratives, based on different ontologies and epistemologies. The act of decentering IR involves challenging the existence of the center that creates, defines, and polices what is deemed to be legitimate knowledge, through questioning the politics, concepts, and practices that enable such centering of IR (Nayak and Selbin, 4; Smith and Tickner, 8). In sum, our initial call is for a global and pluriversal IR theory curricula, de-centering conventional narratives and making many worlds visible. This is an important first step, as theoretical education/instruction is a fundamental element in building a field's identity. Ideally, we should move beyond IR theory curricula into other courses to create a global pluriversal IR classroom.

TEACHING IR IN SOUTH AFRICA AND BRAZIL: DISSENT VOICES?

By and large, this is the ethos that fundamentally informs our approach to IR theory curriculum design. It is not only a matter of "one world many theories" (Walt) but "many worlds, many theories" (RBPI). Moreover, we contend that global pluriversal IR theory curricula are inherently predisposed to student-centric pedagogical approaches and facilitate a participatory approach to help students become more familiar with global IR. As many chapters in this book call for teaching innovations and approaches that are student-centered, we argue that creating learning environments that are collaborative and focused on dialogues between instructors and students means that we must pay attention to context. A learning paradigm should be accompanied by changes in curricula. Freire's pedagogy of the oppressed departs from the students' contexts to build knowledge in a mutual learning process. Thus, how we teach and what we teach go hand in hand. In our diverse contexts, it is a contradiction to focus only on histories, theories, and concepts from distant realities.

In practical terms as instructors, teaching in and from the Global South, we face a double challenge of changing what we teach and how we teach. In the former, we are conscious of the challenges of adding multiple voices to our curricula. In the latter, we are aware of the transformations in higher education, from an instructional paradigm to a learning one (Kille et al; Valença, 30–31) and the impacts of critical pedagogy approaches (Freire). Considering our political and social contexts, these challenges need to be addressed to provide relevant knowledge to students.

Brazil

Concerning the Brazilian case, we would like to highlight two aspects of this debate. First, Brazil's locus of enunciation is not a clear one. Despite the recent construction of its foreign policy based on the leadership of the Global South, Brazilian society still has difficulties in defining its global insertion. As with South Africa, Brazilian society is multicultural. Several social, religious, and ethnic groups coexist, promoting their values and identities in a relatively stable environment. Adding such diversity to the regional peculiarities results in an eclectic and hard-to-define collective identity. However, differently from South Africa, the relatively recent colonial past is not contested, which leads to a mainstream reading of IR theory, aligned with the European and American elite worldview. Thus, it is difficult to speak of a collective Brazilian identity to embrace either the Global South or the West as a reference, but the latter seems to predominate, especially among political elites and the wealthier classes.

The political rhetoric of belonging to the West ends up permeating society as a whole, although dissenting voices are more and more frequent. Still, this image of a Western identity is strong and must take some time to be deconstructed, impacting society in different ways, mainly in how education – especially higher education – should be offered, accessed, and understood.

By and large, higher education in Brazil has traditionally been exclusive to elites. When accepted, poor classes and minorities were mostly limited to lower status majors. Traditional courses, such as Law, Medicine, and Engineering, are almost exclusively filled with students from the elite segments, as well as majors of greater appeal, such as IR. Courses' structure and curricula are aligned with the idea of international and knowledge construction by this elite. Even with the popularization of access to higher education through affirmative action policies, this reality remains, largely due to the institutional constraints and federal regulations themselves. This broad context influences what IR undergraduate programs look like in Brazil.

Second, the reflection on teaching and learning of IR in Brazil is relatively recent. Despite institutional incentives – such as the creation of working groups and sections on teaching and learning in the two most important professional associations of the field – and the publication of special editions focusing on teaching IR, the research on the scholarship of teaching and learning is still incipient and lacks empirical data beyond the experience of the authors.

The emerging active learning literature mostly describes activities conducted in classes, such as games, simulations, the use of alternative texts, and seminars, without structuring proposals or establishing pedagogical goals (Valença and Tostes). This emerging literature, however, does not reflect much on questions related to curriculum building. A few empirical studies like

Barausol and da Silva's do indicate the lack of plurality, or how far IR undergraduate curricula is from being more plural. Thus, considering the lack of systematic studies, it is difficult to identify what theories, themes, and subjects have been taught, or what should or should not constitute the core of the field in the country.

In that sense, it is useful to point out that all IR undergraduate programs in Brazil have to follow the 2017 National Curriculum Guidelines (NCG – Diretrizes Curriculares Nacionais in Portuguese) for IR undergraduate courses. The NCG is the result of a debate involving civil society, universities, and lobbying groups and presents the basic requirements for all IR curricula in Brazil. The document mentions (Art. 2, Para. 1, XI) that IR curricula should integrate environmental education, human rights, race, African and indigenous histories, and cultures, and also that each program should consider its regional context and specificities. However, little is mentioned in terms of promoting diversity or the need to rethink what an IR major should look like. It is emphasized that all undergraduate programs must include security, strategic studies, and defense, but there is a silence on human security, technological changes, sustainability, diversity, and racism, as well as on the planetary challenges that are to come (of which the current COVID-19 pandemic is just an illustration).

A closer look at IR theory handbooks published in Brazil replicates the scenario described elsewhere by the literature (Hagman and Biersteker; Wemheuer-Vogelaar et al.). The orthodox narrative about the Great Debates and major traditions still prevails. One study that analyzed a set of undergraduate IR theory syllabi from four major Brazilian universities concluded that they replicate traditional approaches to the discipline as a way to provide epistemological authority and the autonomy of IR as a coherent body of knowledge (Pini). But, what about local/regional theories, histories, perspectives, and narratives that speak of the global/international? Are they invisible? Or are they hidden somewhere else?

In Latin America, one may find significant contributions from Social Sciences and History that speak of IR, but these are not recognized as IR. These contributions range from different ontologies and epistemologies, including the several strands of dependency theory, regionalism, and decolonial perspectives. For example, Deciancio, echoing Acharya's call, proposes a regional research agenda for global IR. She argues that regions are central for understanding the global IR agenda, which highlights the importance of conceptualizing forms and functions of non-European regionalisms as well as being more aware of local demands.

More specifically, Deciancio (2016, 107) argues that regions and regionalism have been central to Latin American IR, where "regionness" developed before nations (2016, 108), and where there is a rich tradition of describing and conceptualizing alternative forms and functions of regionalism and regionalization processes. Such an agenda is connected to the various strands of dependency thinking, and the ideas of development and autonomy, which are important lenses through which Latin American scholars have approached the international. In this light, regionalism can be seen as a more distinct process than the European-led approach to regionalism (2016, 107). In another vein, Latin American scholars (Inoue and Moreira; Inoue; Inoue et al.) have called attention to how indigenous knowledge systems and voices can contribute to the study of global environmental politics. However, we should note that concepts like "living-well" and reciprocity or the awareness about the destruction of the Amazon forest named as the "Falling Sky" (Kopenawa and Albert) not only speak of different society–nature relations, but also of relations among ourselves, and the societies in which we live. In sum, there are theories, concepts, and theoretical notions that could become part of the IR theory curricula. It is more a matter of recognition than to prove the existence.

In the Brazilian higher education system, IR is an independent – and quite popular – major, and schools design their curricula in a multidisciplinary fashion. Theoretical approaches to IR are underestimated, as "they would not provide employable skills". In that sense, IR theory tends not to feature prominently in curricula and is not usually taught in stand-alone courses. However, many of the theoretical approaches mentioned above are included in other courses such as international political economy, Latin American studies, or global environmental politics. These are built as stand-alone courses but do cover concepts and theories that could potentially be IR theory curricula.

For instance, at the University of Brasília, regionalism and decolonial perspectives are taught in a Latin American IR course. Dependency theories, on the other hand, are part of the International Political Economy course. Students get to know the importance of indigenous voices when enrolled in a Global Environmental Politics course. In this sense, one first step to pluralize the IR theory curricula involves the recognition of these local/regional perspectives as contributions to the field.

Currently, students are still inclined to understand the Great Debates and the theories of IR in a linear fashion, one theory leading to another. The Debates are inserted in a historical narrative built on a Western-focused approach. Major events, such as the World Wars, the Cold War, or the 1970s' Oil Crisis seem to impact more significantly than local/regional events. Thus, and as an attempt to build a global IR mentality, it is important to highlight the diversity of approaches and theoretical concepts occurring concomitantly. Our experience at the Rio de Janeiro State University and the Brazilian Naval War College showed that teaching IR theory by exploring multiple approaches to key concepts does break this linear perception. By realizing that multiple theories can coexist and do not have the monopoly over a given concept, students are able to understand how plural is the field and how their realities are

48   *Teaching international relations*

shaped not only by world events but by regional events, much like Deciancio suggested.

Due to the constraints posed by the NCG, teaching IR in Brazil is strongly limited by institutional restraints, unlike South Africa. By recognizing local/regional contributions to the field, in terms of both theoretical and agenda-setting, it would be possible to take these discussions to universities committees, national associations, and the federal government guidelines.

South Africa

In South Africa, there is already a growing body of literature that calls for changes in curricula, to decolonize it or to make it include a diversity of knowledges (Luckett; Matos Ala 2017) to better dialogue with students' realities. Nevertheless, this is usually confined to studies examining higher education pedagogy in general and is not discipline-specific. This section will examine my attempt to create a global knowledge plural IR theory curriculum in IR at the University of the Witwatersrand, South Africa, which is the only independent IR department in the country.

Even before the rise of the "Rhodes Must Fall" and the "Fees Must Fall" student movements at various South African universities in 2015 and 2016, one of whose principal demands was "decolonized" or "de-Westernized" curricula, we have been engaged in trying to de-Westernize the part of the undergraduate theory curriculum that we have been responsible for teaching since 2012.[1] However, the strong demands by both our university as well as broader social movements have encouraged us to be bolder in designing curricula that present a broader range of knowledges from the Global South. As our students are located in Africa, we especially wanted a course that strongly incorporated African knowledges relevant to the study of IR. We should also note from our experience that creating knowledge plural theory curricula is not merely a case of adding extra readings pertaining to the application of IR theories in the Global South. It involves a radical re-conceptualization of the types of knowledge that can be included when one steps out of the strictures imposed by traditional thinking on what an IR theory course should look like.

We teach a final year undergraduate course entitled "Thinking, Theorizing, and Researching International Relations". A central focus of the course is critically examining the power dynamics within IR theory that determines the dominant narratives regarding the discipline's ontology and epistemology. It explicitly engages with how the theoretical narrative of the discipline has been predicated on Western philosophies and concepts that reflect various Western academic interests and ideologies.

In terms of the development of academic skills we felt that it was imperative that the course develop students' ability to critically engage with knowledge.

Teaching IR in the Global South: views from Brazil and South Africa 49

Thus, the course was structured to develop students' critical analytical and evaluative skills so that they will eventually develop the skill to use theory discerningly and where necessary in innovative ways. An important skills component was to encourage students to create or tailor the application of a theory to suit an African context, which develops the ability to create and synthesize. Developing students' skills to critically analyze the efficacy of Western IR theory for African contexts also enables them to critically engage with the debate on what the decolonization of knowledge should entail.

The course is divided into two sections. The first is focused at a meta-theoretical level and examines how Western derived knowledge is used to conceive of or conceptualize the Global South resulting in it being designated the role of the "other" in IR. The aim of this section is to get students to ask questions not presently found in any mainstream theory textbook – namely why and how IR theories are founded on Western-based knowledges and the implication of this for understanding and studying IR in the Global South. A fundamental component of both sections is contextualizing the study and theorizing IR within a Global South context. Thus, examining the IR of colonization is vital for understanding why there are no African theories of IR. The first section therefore engages with the colonization of knowledge as an integral part of the colonization process of Africa by the West. African philosophies already enter IR at a disadvantage, with Africans having already been declared by both Kant and Hegel as being devoid of the capacity for complex, abstract, intellectual thought. Indeed, one of the expounded benefits of colonization by Western powers was bestowing modernity which encompassed more complex ways of reasoning on colonies and which is perpetuated by dominant Western ontological and epistemological standards into the postcolonial period. The course, using the works of Franz Fanon, examines not only the consequences of the continued colonization of knowledge but how the decolonization of knowledge is a crucial but often overlooked part of decolonization. As this has not occurred in IR, we have a discipline that has produced theories that misfit, misinterpret, or misunderstand the IR of the Global South.

The second section of the course looks at African philosophies that have explanatory potential in the realm of IR, particularly, in terms of their usefulness in explaining and understanding African IR. The main African philosophy we examine is Ubuntu. The course makes an important distinction between the practice of ubuntu and the philosophy of Ubuntu. "ubuntu" has been practiced by a wide range of ethnic groups in Southern and East Africa dating from pre-colonial times to the present. The concept is encapsulated in the Nguni expression "Umuntu ugumuntu ngabantu", translated as a person is a person through other persons (Metz & Gaie). In other words, a person's survival, or well-being is causally dependent on their interaction with others. One strives to become fully human by entering more and more deeply into community with others. Thus, in a metaphysical sense you do not exist outside your community. In fact, ubuntu is not something that an infant or young child could possess, it develops as your interactions with and obligations to your community deepen as you progress into and through adulthood. Although the ultimate aim of ubuntu is personal fulfillment, this must be obtained by community immersion and engagement. It cannot be attained by selfish actions that benefit an individual either primarily or exclusively at the expensive of your community. The practice depicts the centering of African society within what Patrick Chabal terms a political economy of obligation (Praeg, 45) It is from the practice of ubuntu that a philosophy of Ubuntu has been derived. This has seen the practice of ubuntu being abstracted and de-contextualized from the communal environment of the ethnic group, so that it could be applied to African liberation movements and finally the diverse ethnic populations of African states and beyond African borders. In contrast to Western prioritizing of individual identity Ubuntu centers on communal identity. Thus, it represents the antithesis of humanist philosophies like neoliberalism.

The course further critically evaluates the explanatory capacity of Ubuntu versus Western normative theories of IR. Ubuntu can elucidate many intra-African IR practices, giving explanations for individual or collective state behavior. As case studies we consider South Africa's practice of "quiet diplomacy" towards Zimbabwe during the Mbeki presidency as well as the African Union's refusal to enforce an International Criminal Court warrant of arrest for former Sudanese President Bashir. From the perspective of Ubuntu these cases reveal collective attempts of African leaders to alter the negative behavior of a member of the group through dialogue and negotiation with them. Ubuntu in these instances would see reconciliation and rehabilitation as more important than punishing the wrongdoer.

Finally, the course discusses the benefits of global knowledge plurality in equipping scholars to more fully study and understand IR. The course helps students question the utility of Western IR theories beyond their social and historical context. It also allows them to conceive of a world where knowledges from the Global South, although ontologically and epistemologically different from those of the West, are seen as equally intellectually valid ways of understanding IR. From our point of view, this is the ultimate way to decolonize knowledge within the field of IR theory.

FINAL CONSIDERATIONS

In this chapter, we discussed some of the challenges we face as academics teaching IR in the Global South, more specifically in Brazil and South Africa. We shared experiences and strategies based on our experiences both as instructors and as participants in national- and international-level discussions about what constitutes IR as a discipline and an academic field of inquiry and teaching.

We advocate for a global and pluriversal IR in the classroom. This could initially start in IR theory curricula and move beyond. A global IR de-centers conventional narratives and makes visible the logic of "many worlds, many theories" that goes beyond multidisciplinarity, and entails the recognition of the plurality of worldviews, ontologies, and knowledge systems worldwide. Moreover, we argued that "what" we teach goes hand in hand with "how" we teach. This pedagogical approach is context-based and student-centered. As many chapters in this book share assumptions about creating learning environments that are collaborative and focused on dialogues between instructors and students, we think that more plural IR context-based curricula can enhance learning in both the Global South and North.

NOTE

1. Rhodes Must Fall and Fees Must Fall were student driven movements that have distinct as well as overlapping demands. The focus of Rhodes Must Fall was the decolonization of tertiary institutions. Hence their demand for the removal of Western iconography from campuses together with the contesting the pre-eminence given to Western knowledge in course curricula. The core demand of Fees Must Fall was securing free education for all students from low-/middle-income households. However, this movement also supported the decolonization of curricula knowledge.

5. Toward an intersectional pedagogy in IR: how to take feminist interventions seriously

Dovilė Budrytė

In her recent contribution to H-Diplomacy Teaching Roundtable on Teaching Gender in International Relations (IR), Laura Sjoberg, one of the leading feminists in IR, wrote:

> Many colleagues omit explicit mentions of gender in their politics and IR syllabi, either because they truly believe gender is irrelevant to their substantive interests or because they have difficulty sorting through the relevant work to select the most appropriate readings for their syllabi. Even syllabi which do address gender often treat the subject quite marginally. (H-Diplo ROUNDTABLE XXI-39)

She went on to suggest that such attitudes affect the ways in which the students view gender in IR—as a marginal, unimportant topic, somehow less important than the "traditional" foci of IR. However, there are many reasons why teaching gender and other identities should become central in IR classes. These reasons include a rich and growing feminist literature in IR which has demonstrated the many ways in which women and gender play an essential role in world politics in areas such as women and war or women and international development. In addition, there is a solid feminist pedagogy that can be applied in IR classes. This pedagogy encourages reflection, student engagement, and the importance of connecting theory and individual human experiences—all of which are excellent active learning strategies conducive to effective teaching and learning. As Kathryn M. Fisher, one of the contributors to this roundtable, points out, teaching gender in IR suggests paying attention to issues such as situatedness, "self-reflective engagement," as well as the importance of connecting IR literature with individual human experiences—which helps to improve teaching and learning (H-Diplo ROUNDTABLE XXI-39).

Drawing on the insights from this roundtable and the rich feminist literature in IR as well as feminist pedagogy, this chapter focuses on the ways in which teaching gender can overlap with other important identities, including national belonging, ethnicity, race, and socioeconomic class. Theoretically, it is rooted in the literature on intersectionality, which here refers to teaching strategies that address complex variables such as global developments, linguistic differences, ethnicity, gender and national identity and their combination in an effort to determine an individual's role in a global context. I am also interested in practical questions related to course design and specific assignments: How should IR courses that draw on feminist perspectives and take intersectionality seriously be structured? How can gender be applied to concepts that are taught in a traditional IR classroom? How can specific assignments be structured with intersectionality in mind? Following this line of questioning, this chapter is divided into four sections. The first section surveys the ways in which various feminist interventions have attempted to transform the field of IR. This section also mentions the contributions of postcolonial gender studies, which stem from the feminist literature and which suggest integrating intersectional perspectives, studying gender together with other identities, including race, ethnic identity, and socioeconomic class. The second section outlines an intersectional pedagogy in IR, which would allow us to take the contributions of feminist interventions seriously. The third and the fourth sections focus on the application of intersectionality and other feminist perspectives in teaching, addressing the ways in which insights from an intersectional pedagogy could transform the teaching of topics such as state and security and thus enrich or even transform traditional IR courses.

TRANSFORMING THE FIELD: FEMINIST INTERVENTIONS IN IR

Early feminist interventions, focusing on gender as the main category of analysis and highlighting the centrality of social relations in global politics, criticized the IR discipline as "based on a masculine worldview" (Tickner, 1993, 429) and offered alternative understandings of essential IR concepts, such as power and security. Instead of linking power to security-seeking behavior by autonomous states in an anarchic international system, feminist scholars offered the definition of power as "a relationship of mutual enablement," suggesting that scholars should focus on concepts such as coalition-building, communities, and persuasion. They argued that security should be focused on individuals and should include the notion of structural violence, development, and the environment (Tickner, 1993, 434). Feminist perspectives challenged the image of states as security providers in the international system, arguing that structural inequalities, the main sources of insecurity in global politics, have been "built into the historical legacy of the modern state and the international system of which it is a part" (Tickner, 1993, 625). This examination of the foundational concepts in the discipline, including power and security, suggested a different research and teaching agenda, focusing on a broader concept of security and the examination of the lives of powerless and marginalized individuals (mostly women). Feminist scholars and teachers have been interested not only in criticizing injustices and inequalities, but also in promoting social change. Anne Sisson Runyan and V. Spike Peterson, leading feminist scholars, have identified a strong "political commitment to thoroughgoing social justice" as one of the key elements of feminist lenses of looking at world politics. This commitment often translates into action research, which attempts to erase the borders between the "knower" and "the object of knowledge" and embraces a normative commitment to improving the lives of people in a community which is studied (Runyan and Peterson). Often a feminist scholar is not only an observer, but also an activist as well. According to Susanne Zwingel, this connection between activism and knowledge creation helps feminist IR scholars to challenge "the idea of objective knowledge" and make their research agenda visible and politically salient (H-Diplo ROUNDTABLE XXI-39).

Attentiveness to boundaries and relationships has inspired feminist scholars in IR to engage the concept of intersectionality, which focuses on the interplay of complex variables such as linguistic differences, ethnicity, gender or national identity in an effort to determine an individual's role and responsibility in a regional and global context. Feminist investigations of inequalities that affect women's lives revealed other systems of oppression linked to economic divisions, racial inequalities and discursive practices studied by (neo) Marxist, postcolonial, and poststructuralist schools of thought (Runyan and Peterson). In particular, the studies of women and gender in the Global South demonstrated the need to study intersecting systems of oppression. Postcolonial feminists who are skeptical of the notion of a "global sisterhood," which is embraced by some feminists, have argued for a deeper and more radical acknowledgment of feminist struggles and women's issues in specific historical and geographical contexts. They have argued that there has been a "discernable First World feminist voice" in IR which does not sufficiently recognize the intersectionality of race, class, and gender as well as related erasures (Chowdhry and Nair, 14). The goal of postcolonial feminist perspectives in IR has been to reveal the silences and omissions regarding race and representation, linking these identities to the study of gender (Whitworth, 395).

TAKING FEMINIST INTERVENTIONS SERIOUSLY: AN INTERSECTIONAL PEDAGOGY IN IR?

Since the 1980s, various feminist interventions have significantly affected the discipline of IR, and currently they are considered an important part of the field. But how can these interventions be taken seriously in teaching IR? Contributing to the H-Diplo Teaching Roundtable on Teaching Gender in IR, Sjoberg has identified several highly problematic patterns of teaching gender in IR classrooms. One pattern is to devote one class period or one week for teaching gender. This usually happens during the time when a professor does not treat gender as a very important part of IR and plans to cancel class anyway. Students are asked to do their own investigations into this topic. Another pattern is to promote essentialist work on gender, portraying women as peaceful and eternal victims in violent conflicts. The third pattern has been to discuss only the status of women in IR, linking gender to women only (and not to men). Opposing these patterns, the contributors to the roundtable suggested that gender should be "mainstreamed" when teaching IR to investigate the ways in which the state system has been constructed and maintained by various actors, including women, and that gender essentialism (associating certain traits with a certain category) should be avoided (H-Diplo ROUNDTABLE XXI-39). Jessica Auchter suggested that instead of portraying women as peaceful and victimized, those teaching gender in IR should try to capture the variety and complexity of people's experiences, centering the discussion on the problem of masculinity and femininity (H-Diplo ROUNDTABLE XXI-39).

Following this line of argumentation, this section outlines an intersectional pedagogy in IR. Drawing on the broad and rich literature on intersectionality, such an approach would not only attempt to avoid gender essentialism, but also takes the insights of postcolonial gender perspectives seriously, paying attention to different contexts and the impact of other factors, such as race, socioeconomic class, and national belonging on individual lives. Applying intersectionality to the study and teaching of IR should capture the "rising importance of ordinary individuals in the practice of international politics today" because traditional IR theories and approaches have still not addressed the issues faced by individuals, their subjectivities and their lives sufficiently (Riegg, 1). Making this step will empower us to gain a deeper understanding of traditional IR issues, such as terrorism, popular unrest, or the promotion of democracy. Thus, when teaching about democratic transitions, for example, or about the resistance to the presidential election results in Belarus in summer 2020, it may be useful to include perspectives from the streets (the voices of demonstrators), which can be easily obtained from online sources. In addition, developing an intersectional pedagogy in IR means "an increased requirement to take the cultural dimension of international politics into consideration" (Riegg, 4), paying attention to various expressions of identity and their impact on policies and international interactions. In the case of Belarus in summer 2020, it may be useful to analyze the gendered dimensions of this popular unrest, which included women's marches and female opposition leadership.

Leslie McCall's description of intersectional methodology provides ideas about how to take the cultural dimension of international politics seriously. She described three major approaches in intersectional methodology (McCall, 50). Consistent with the insights of poststructuralist theories, the first approach, or "anticategorical complexity," deconstructs analytical categories by arguing that fixed categories (including gender) simplify complex social realities and (re)produce inequalities. Those embracing this approach argue for the deconstruction of "master" categories that are used to impose a "homogenizing" order on messy realities. The project of deconstructing categories marking the boundaries of social groups was linked to the possibility of social change (McCall, 53). By questioning categorization and separation, this approach helps to avoid gender essentialism, which may lead to erroneous assumptions that associate women with peace and beliefs that women are more peaceful than men. In the IR classroom, when discussing issues such as terrorism or war, it may be useful to include case studies of women warriors or women terrorists (e.g., Sjoberg and Gentry) to demonstrate various roles that women can play in war. The second approach, or "intracategorical complexity," also questions boundary-making. Those embracing this approach tend to "focus on particular social groups at neglected points of intersection" (McCall, 51) to reveal the complexity of belonging and to question group boundaries. To apply the insights from this approach in the IR classroom, it may be useful to include the study of struggles for recognition and often survival by marginalized groups. Such case studies help to enrich discussions about human security and who is entitled to it. Finally, the third approach, or "intercategorical complexity," focuses on various relationships of inequality among groups and aims at mapping out the configurations of inequality and their causes. Applying this approach in the IR classroom would help to identify different patterns of racial, gender and class inequality across different regions when discussing international development.

Drawing on rich intersectionality studies, Amy Cabrera Rasmussen (2014) proposed an intersectional pedagogy for political science that can be adapted to a variety of courses, both introductory and upper level. Such pedagogy consists of four dimensions. The first dimension is the commitment to multiple identities. Policy studies could definitely benefit from taking various identities, not just race and gender, but also disability and religion, into account. Students could use their own experiences and positionality to better understand the topics covered in such classes (Rasmussen, 106). The second dimension focuses on power ("foregrounding of power and processes," Rasmussen, 102), how power operates and affects different aspects of political life. The study of power is essential for the study of marginalization and applying intersectionality lenses would help students to understand the "complexity of inequalities and privileges" (Rasmussen, 107) in a given country. The third dimension is the transformation of courses through inclusion. Adopting an intersectional pedagogy may imply that, instead of covering traditional political science subject areas, the focus could shift to themes, processes, and policies. The experiences of minorities and marginalized groups would become the essential parts of such courses. Finally, the fourth dimension is a "normative commitment to equality" (Rasmussen, 102). Many political science courses have a normative component already, such as a better civic consciousness. An intersectional pedagogy implies a commitment to a better understanding of inequalities, which implies that topics such as violence against women, including women of color, would become relevant to the study of politics (Rasmussen, 109).

Rasmussen's pedagogical model could be adapted to teaching IR. Different dimensions of this model could be enriched with feminist insights and feminist critiques of IR, thus making sure that these interventions are taken seriously. The first dimension, or commitment to multiple identities, implies the inclusion of postcolonial feminist insights about the importance of race and related representations. Other identities, such as religion and nation, also impact the lives of "real people" in significant ways and must be included in analyses of international politics. Attention to complexity and multiple intersecting identities should help to avoid simplistic essentialist categories, such as "women" or "nation states," and inspire an exploration of the multiple meanings associated with these categories. In practice, it may be useful to ask students to be careful when using "we" (usually to refer to the United States or US foreign policy) and ask them to identify specific actors. Furthermore, pursuing intersectional pedagogy means being aware of simplified depictions of various actors in global politics, and acknowledging complexity of human beings. Mary Ann Tétreault and Ronnie D. Lipschutz's textbook *Global Politics as if People Mattered* is an example of such an approach. Applying an intersectional pedagogy also implies reflection on the situatedness of the teacher and students as well as the use of personal experiences to explain international politics. In the classroom, such reflections may involve the acknowledgment of multiple privileges of living in the Global North and hypotheses about the ways our sociopolitical situation affects the ways in which we participate in IR.

The second dimension, or the workings of power, offers many opportunities for integrating the insights of feminist IR. This concept is essential even for those who embrace more traditional perspectives in IR; thus, this area offers room for engagement between feminist IR and traditional IR (Whitworth, 397). For feminists, explaining power means focusing on "real people" (including women and other marginalized groups in IR) and understanding the ways in which gender works. Thus, social relations become an important part of IR. An intersectional approach to the study of IR implies that various configurations of power and various politically relevant identities, not just gender, should be explored. For example, as demonstrated by Nira Yuval-Davis, "nationed gender" (the workings of gender in national contexts) and "gendered nation" (the ways in which gender affects the construction of nations) play a major role in international politics (Yuval-Davis, 21). A proper understanding of either one of these concepts is impossible without looking at the ways in which they intersect. In the classroom, this means the inclusion of feminist insights about the private and the public, and the ways in which this division has influenced the rise of gendered states and gendered citizenship as well as the inclusion of women in the military (focusing on the concept of gendered militaries).

Similarly, the third dimension, or the transformation of IR courses through inclusion, could integrate one of the most important insights of feminist IR—that marginalized actors matter in IR in various ways, and paying attention to their activities is essential for understanding the international system. Case studies of marginal actors and their perspectives on security could definitely enrich IR courses. The principles of "curious feminism" articulated by Cynthia Enloe inspire us to explore processes of trivialization (e.g., associated with prostitution) and silences (e.g., silences surrounding sexuality in many cultural contexts) (Enloe 2014, 74–75). These strategies can help to reveal intersecting structures of oppression that have produced such outcomes. Furthermore, transforming courses through inclusion can make a study of "traditional" topics, such as international crises, more interesting—if the focus is shifted to the "weak" and "silent" actors and if we pay attention to the ways in which they perceive and construct these events. (For an example of how to "decolonize" the study of an international crisis, see Laffey and Weldes.)

Finally, the fourth dimension of intersectional pedagogy includes a "normative commitment to equality" (Rasmussen, 102). Various feminist approaches to IR suggest different ways to address inequality and hierarchies in IR, and regard "gender emancipation" (Sjoberg and Tickner, 5) as a goal. Liberal feminists do not advocate the full deconstruction of existing political orders, and argue for the inclusion of women in positions of power. Constructivist feminists argue that it is important to change the norms related to femininity and masculinity. Critical feminists focus on various manifestations of gendered power and argue for a change in the "gendered balance of global politics" (Sjoberg and Tickner, 6). Poststructural feminists focus on discourses, and the ways in which the inequalities associated with femininity and masculinity are constructed through various discourses. Similarly to the anticategorical and intracategorical approaches in intersectionality studies, postmodern feminists question "the naturalness of the categories of 'woman' and 'gender'" (Sjoberg and Tickner, 6), and look for different ways to get rid of gender hierarchies. Postcolonial feminists interrogate the hierarchies imposed by imperialism and try to address "gender subordination in particular cultural and sociopolitical contexts" (Sjoberg and Tickner, 6).

A "normative commitment to equality" in an IR classroom could include exposure to these feminist approaches and reflection on their proposed strategies to achieve emancipation as they apply to other categories, including race and national belonging. Furthermore, a "normative commitment to equality" could transform classroom dynamics and perhaps even lead to teaching "with students," not teaching the students. Teaching with students implies that learning would be based on interconnectedness, reciprocity and cooperation in the classroom. The students would become part of a responsible relationship based on dialogue, the goal of which is to understand the complexities of global realities and the sources of inequalities. In practice, "normative commitment to equality" and "teaching with students" may involve letting students construct their own assignments and their own knowledge. Natalya T. Riegg has described how her students wrote scenarios for simulations about international conflicts. Students chose the topics for simulations by following the international news. They were allowed to decide on the timetable, divide up tasks and set the deadlines for completion. Such strategies helped to "acknowledge the individuality of every student in class," (Riegg, 10), and they were consistent with "the principles of egalitarianism, inclusiveness, and cooperation" (Riegg, 10).

APPLYING INTERSECTIONAL PEDAGOGY: TEACHING ABOUT IDENTITIES IN IR

Applying the principles of intersectional pedagogy in an IR classroom implies analyses of various inequalities, which means that students' lived experiences may become relevant to the class material and the whole discipline (Rasmussen, 112). Sharing experiences means that it is essential to think about ways to create a safe learning environment and a sense of community in which students would feel comfortable discussing their experiences and even revealing aspects of their identities. Rasmussen suggests using a questionnaire during the first class that would ask the students to share their "first memories of aspects of difference" (Rasmussen, 111), their own political experiences and concerns about discussing difficult and challenging topics in a classroom. One way to signal to students that the class will engage difference in global settings is to ask the students to reflect on the demographic breakdown of the campus, city, state, nation, and its political institutions (Rasmussen, 111), perhaps expanding it to the region or even the whole world. Barbara Tedrow recommends a teaching strategy called "sense of place mapmaking that can decolonize teaching" (Tedrow, 75) to help create a relaxed atmosphere in the classroom during the first meeting, which is conducive to the discussion of various identities and inequalities. Tested with students in South Africa, Tedrow's strategy invites students to remember a favorite place, explore its elements, draw a map of this place and explain the emotional connection to this place, reflecting on their relevant experiences (Tedrow, 77).

The principles of intersectional pedagogy (e.g., a commitment to the exploration of multiple identities) can help breathe new life into the main concepts used in IR, such as states and sovereignty. Even the early writings of feminist scholars revealed the gendered aspects of state and citizenship, demonstrating that throughout the centuries political communities became associated with male bodies, and women had a difficult time becoming full citizens of the states (Pettman, 3). Incorporating feminist perspectives into teaching about the main concepts (e.g., state system and sovereignty) can help to trace the development of patriarchal states, the constitution of separate "public" and "private" spheres and the exclusion of women and other groups, such as foreigners, from the public sphere. As noted by feminist scholars, the Athenian polis is associated with the emergence of male citizenship, and the association of the public space with masculinity (Pettman, 6). Similarly, the concept of sovereignty can be linked to the discussion of identities by pointing out that states demand loyalty from their citizens, thus homogenizing political identities and disguising differences within the states to create differences between the states. States are charged with the task of defending borders and keeping "the right people in and the wrong people out" (Pettman, 4). Ideologies, such as nationalism and militarism, are used to achieve these tasks. Through colonization, European state-making processes, including the strengthening of the public/private divide, were introduced to other parts of the world (Pettman, 6).

The discussion of the dynamics of exclusion and the use of force by states, including the exclusion of some groups from citizenship and other areas of the public sphere, can prompt discussions about current political developments (such as systemic racism or the privileges enjoyed by some groups, either domestically or internationally). These discussions can be extremely polarizing and difficult, but unfortunately they may be unavoidable if intersectional pedagogy is used. Bryan L. Dawson suggests a useful teaching strategy on how to discuss sensitive topics such privilege and diversity. He argues that it is important:

> to relate this information [about white privilege, the privilege of being heterosexual, living in a rich "developed" country or another type of privileged identity] in a manner that does not blame individuals for their privilege or assign fault for societal privileges but rather to question the validity of privilege and its origin. (Dawson, 69)

He suggests using handedness as a way to help the students "to articulate the feelings of what it is like to be different from their peers" (Dawson, 69). It may be useful to ask left-handed students (usually, there are one or two in class) to identify themselves and respond to the stereotypes identified by right-handed students about left-handedness. This exercise leads to a discussion about the ways in which left-handed individuals are faced with challenges in life (such as experiences opening the doors, notebooks made for right-handed students, and so on). It helps to illustrate several important points, such as the fact that privileged individuals are usually unaware of their privileges. Upon learning about their privileges, they are likely to "question the unfair system and seek answers" (Dawson, 71). Similar exercises can be useful when discussing privilege associated with inequalities in international development and similar topics.

A commitment to the exploration of multiple identities and related questions, such as privilege, can help instructors to enrich their teaching of international organizations in their IR courses. In particular, the European Union (EU) has viewed itself as a leader in developing programs and policies to combat discrimination and achieve equal treatment. During the last several decades, policies designed to address inequality in the EU have been expanded to include different dimensions, including religion, sexual orientation, disability, and so on (Verloo, 212). Although there have been attempts to apply the principles of intersectionality to various anti-discrimination forms, there are calls to apply these principles even more widely, to migration policies, discrimination laws and laws regulating the EU labor market (ENAR). Non-governmental organizations pushing for more intersectionality argue that operationalizing intersectionality in policymaking can help to reduce "the severity of multiple discrimination" and develop more effective equality policies, even though it has been quite challenging to do it (ENAR). Some EU member states, such as Sweden and the UK (Scotland in the UK) have attempted to base some of their anti-racist policies on the principles of intersectionality (ENAR). Given the rising interest in battling racism in the United States in 2020, the exploration of various attempts to apply intersectionality by international organizations and EU member states can lead to interesting insights on whether such policies can be replicated domestically.

APPLYING INTERSECTIONAL PEDAGOGY: STUDYING SECURITY "AS IF PEOPLE MATTERED"

A "normative commitment to equality" in intersectional and feminist approaches suggests radically different perspectives on security than embraced by traditional IR. Although there is no unified feminist perspective on security, war and peace are conceptualized as gendered processes (Pettman, 87), and different types of violence, including structural violence are seen as sources of insecurity. Structural violence refers to a situation when security means not only protection from physical violence but also "addressing underlying political structures that give rise to it" (Basu, 105). "Security as emancipation" is a leading feminist perspective on security. Drawing on Ken Booth's concept of "security as emancipation" (in which he argued that individuals, not states, should be the ultimate referents of security), feminist authors have argued that "security does not lie in victory or defeat but in the transformation of the oppressive social relations underlying structural violence" (Basu, 105). Patriarchy is considered to be an example of such oppressive social relations. An intersectional approach to security would necessitate taking multiple identities into account. Individuals with multiple identities would be the ultimate referents of security. Here, the search for security would imply attempts to get rid of oppressive hierarchies and transform society to overcome the structures of domination.

In addition to outlining the theoretical dimensions of the concept of "security as emancipation" in the IR classroom, it may be very useful to enrich the discussion with examples of real lives, perhaps using anthropological and biographical studies. Students could perform independent research to locate such life stories and could be asked to relate them to theoretical insights. In my class, I ask the students to read about Tatu, a member of the Waluguru tribe in central Tanzania (as recounted by Boos and Boos, 73–74). Her life story provides an illustration of the disastrous effects of multiple oppressions, including patriarchy. Married at 13 to an abusive husband 20 years her senior who already had two other wives and 13 children, Tatu had to feed herself and her children by working in a small garden (that wasn't her own). If seasonal rains were insufficient, Tatu went hungry and had to beg for food. With no formal education and no job skills, Tatu could not be employed outside the home. One time, Tatu's husband went drinking and gambling and amassed a large debt. To cover the debt, he let three other men gang rape Tatu. One of the men also took Tatu's hut and garden (to cover the debt). Tatu went to live with another wife, and together they were able to produce a good crop; however, Tatu's husband took away their money and beat them. Non-compliance was not a real option for the women because "legally" he could divorce them and expel them from his property. Not having a title to property, the women remained at his mercy. When the abusive husband died, his creditors took away whatever little property the women had. The suffering depicted in this story is quite common in Tanzania and other countries where women and other minorities cannot claim rights to land due to customary law and other patriarchal traditions. The legacies of colonialism (when new hierarchies were implemented and dubious claims to land were made by national and community leaders) complicate the picture even more.

Focusing on personal stories like Tatu's is at the heart of feminist approaches to war, another concept essential in traditional IR. One of the major contributions of feminist IR has been to demonstrate that "modern constructions of the citizen and the soldier universalize (some) men's experiences and exclude women, especially from the prerogative state and war" (Pettman, 95). Feminists have investigated the ways in which war and violence are normalized through nationalism and militarism, and have explored the construction of militarism (e.g., Peterson; Via). They have strongly resisted placing women "ontologically outside war" (Sylvester 2013, 41), insisting that it is necessary to pay attention to women warriors and women terrorists (Sjoberg and Gentry). As suggested by Christine Sylvester (2011), one way to study war is to steer away from "national interest politics of war" and start focusing on individuals who have bodies and experience war first-hand in various roles—not only combatants, but also grave diggers, casualties, enemies, and so on. The "experiencing war" approach developed by Sylvester suggests that the study of multiple experiences and identities is essential for understanding war because "difference exaggerated, invented, or politicized in the extreme can explode into large-scale armed conflict between groups that find others so 'other' that they must be killed" (Sylvester 2011, 1). Her approach encourages us to explore the ways in which people in various locations "touch war and are touched by it in physical, emotional and intellectual ways" (Sylvester 2011, 3). Integrating this approach into the IR classroom opens the door to a variety of perspectives, including art, anthropology and history, which is likely to enrich the study of war.

Feminist revisions of the study of security (with a focus on individual experiences) suggest that the concept of security should be necessarily broad and include various types of violence and oppression. As argued by J. Ann Tickner, "any feminist definition of security must... include the elimination of all types of violence, including violence produced by gender relations of discrimination and subordination" (Tickner 1993, 58). Feminist authors generally have welcomed the theoretical moves to broaden the concept of security to include issues such as migration and environmental degradation, but warned about the dangers related to excessive securitization of issues such as food, water, energy, or health security by linking them to war and "continual justifications for violence" (Runyan and Peterson). Including the study of issues such as migration into the study of security in IR classrooms can definitely lead to lively class discussions and help to integrate students' personal experiences (especially if the student population includes immigrants). Exploring this issue using intersectional pedagogy means analyzing multiple identities and overlapping structures of oppression, especially in the case of refugees and undocumented migrants. Ellen G. Rafshoon recommends using experiential learning techniques, such as role play, to study migration because such pedagogical approaches "are considered the most effective in cultivating empathy for those who are considered strangers" (Rafshoon, 83). When studying migration, Rafshoon's students read a novel depicting a life of an immigrant and written by an immigrant. They engage in playing the roles outlined in that novel. In my International Studies classes, I used Mohsin Hamid's (2008) novel *The Reluctant Fundamentalist* to explore issues related to identity and belonging felt by a Pakistani in New York after 9/11. Although there was some resistance among students to the study of fiction in a social science class, I found that the use of novels can definitely help to discuss complex topics such as the multiple identities and oppressive structures that are essential parts of intersectional pedagogies.

CONCLUSION

Reflecting on international studies education at the beginning of the twenty-first century, Jeffrey Lantis, Lynn Kuzma, and John Boehrer (2000a) argued that in the post-Cold war era it was essential to switch from a "lecture-oriented paradigm" to a holistic, student-centered approach that was conducive to learning. This transformation includes focusing on transnational challenges, such as the competition for scarce resources and economic and social justice. Twenty years later, in the age of the Me-Too and Black Lives Matter transnational movements, these principles remain important. It remains essential to establish egalitarian dialogic relations in classes where students are engaged in learning and construct their own knowledge. Transnational issues such as economic and social justice necessitate an investigation of various systems of inequality. The intersectional pedagogy for teaching IR presented in this chapter does both. On the one hand, it mandates the inclusion of various voices, including the voices of students, in the learning process. On the other hand, it is committed to exploring and even potentially challenging various inequalities in global politics. Furthermore, as argued in this chapter, with its commitment to multiple identities and equality, it is well equipped to take feminist interventions in IR seriously.

One of the major contributions of feminist IR has been to take the lives of women and other marginalized groups into account, arguing that they are essential for the (re)construction of power relations in the current international system. Furthermore, feminist IR has offered revisions of major IR concepts, such as state sovereignty and security. With its focus on inclusiveness and its attention to multiple identities, intersectional pedagogy necessitates that these insights are integrated into the teaching of IR. During times of crisis, such as the COVID-19 pandemic, when human security effectively becomes national security, taking human experiences and multiple oppressions into account can definitely enrich the study of IR and make it more relatable to the students.

PART II

INNOVATIONS IN THE CLASSROOM: TECHNIQUES AND APPROACHES

6. Teaching with case studies
Ralph G. Carter

INTRODUCTION

This chapter illustrates four key steps in employing case-based teaching in the international relations (IR) classroom. Those steps include (1) finding the right cases, (2) the preparation needed before the classroom session, (3) the class session itself, and (4) what to do after the class session. But before we get to those steps, we must acknowledge that there's nothing new about using case studies in a classroom. Law, medical, and business schools have relied upon case-based teaching for decades (Redlich; Reed; Barrows; McNair). The appeal of case-based teaching is easy to understand. Most people love stories, because they engage us and help us to both remember and understand things. Immersing students in a narrative, a story, about something that actually happened, is a way to draw them into the study of that academic subject or discipline (Golich, 12). Stories make the material more intuitive by making our subjects seem real. Thus, they help students relate to issues and events on a more personal level. In short, case studies promote learning as they foster *intellectual engagement* with the material under study (Holsti, "Case Teaching", 7–13). Case studies have another advantage in that they can overcome a shortcoming typically found in textbooks. Most textbooks are forced to rely on generic descriptions of recurring phenomena, but examining actual historical cases reveals the unique nature of those events. Even for patterned behaviors – often found in organizational politics, for example – as the individuals and the roles they play change, as times and contexts change, behaviors change from the generic pattern. Case studies help reveal these idiosyncrasies. They help students understand how the involved participants perceived events and identify possible explanations for those perceptions and the resulting actions (Boehrer and Linsky, 41). Simply put, case studies make subjects – and lessons – come alive.

For example, a case study of the Syrian civil war could illustrate much about contemporary IR. It could shed light on issues like great power politics, war crimes, refugee-related human rights issues, roles of non-state actors, autocratic regime behavior, the difficulties coordinating allied military action, religious motivations of political actions, the challenges of diplomacy, and much more. Examining the rise and demise of the Joint Comprehensive Plan of Action (also known as the Iran Nuclear Deal) could not only make the analogy of the "stag hunt" come alive, it also could illustrate the challenges of multilateral diplomacy, resolving nuclear non-proliferation issues, dealing with so-called "rogue" regimes, and so on. Moreover, both these cases could be examined through the lenses of IR theories like realism, liberalism, constructivism, feminism, and Marxist-based critical theories.

Beyond increasing subject knowledge, good case-based teaching promotes skill building on the part of the students. To master their assigned role in case-based teaching, students must listen carefully, think critically, and reason inductively. They must also communicate effectively, as they listen to others and then share their viewpoints on the events of the case, either orally or in written formats. These are lifelong learning skills, the type "needed to identify and apply relevant knowledge in specific situations; and coping with the problem-oriented, interdisciplinary nature of the real world of practice involving synthesis, judgment, and application" (Lynn, 38). The key benefit of this approach is the promotion of active, as opposed to passive, learning (Golich, 13).

Active learning has another advantage. In passive modes of learning, students tend to better understand, remember, and retain information that seems to reinforce their preexisting biases and values more than information which challenges their own views. If our goal is for students to think critically, including about their preexisting biases and values, the give-and-take environment of case-based learning, where they may be called upon to promote a position contrary to their preexisting ideas, can be a valuable approach (Budesheim and Lundquist).

In addition to the benefits of intellectual engagement, case studies help our students in another sense. Many students have never traveled to other countries or experienced another culture or societal context. They've never done a study abroad tour. Some have never taken a world history course or a regional or world geography course. If they have never had the chance to experience or study such things, even demonstrably "smart" students can be surprisingly ignorant of the world that exists beyond the borders of their own country (Warf). We've all probably been amazed at times at the things even our best students don't seem to know. The use of case studies in IR courses can help reduce this parochialism.

Finally, there is another benefit to using case studies. As instructors, we see cases through the lens of our own experience and education. We cannot see cases in the same way as our students who are confronting that knowledge for the first time. They will often see the cases quite differently, based on the background of their age and unique experiences. Consequently, we may learn from our students, as they glean different meanings or messages from these cases than we do.

Yet despite the many benefits of the use of case studies in class, there are obvious costs as well. Preparation for case-based teaching is different and often more time-consuming – and perhaps more challenging – than preparing a more traditional lecture or seminar. As Golich et al. (3) note:

> A case teacher resembles an orchestra conductor. Much as a conductor creates music by coordinating individual performances, providing key signals, and knowing what the outcome should sound like, a case teacher generates learning by eliciting individual observations and analyses, asking key questions, and knowing what learning outcomes s/he wants students to achieve.

To do so, the first challenge is finding the cases to use. Not all cases work well. Second, the instructor has to know the chosen cases very well. A superficial understanding of a case will not suffice. Engaged students will ask questions that we do not anticipate. Thorough knowledge of the case events and the individual players involved can help us navigate our way through such questions. Third, we have to be willing to give up some of our control of the classroom environment. Case-based teaching empowers the students to be active learners, and that means classroom dynamics are often unpredictable. Some of us may be uncomfortable with a loss of classroom control and the possibility of unpredictable classroom outcomes.

Finally, we have to know how to teach in a case-based format. So, how is this done? Let's turn to that now.

STEP 1: FINDING THE RIGHT CASES

As previously noted, the first task in case-based teaching is to identify the type of cases you want to use. Not all cases are the same. If our goal is active learning, the emphasis should be on teaching cases, not research cases. Teaching cases tell the story of what happened. *They do not analyze the case for the student.* If the "why" questions have already been answered in a research case, further examination of the case is normally less likely. For example, hypothesis-testing case studies – like those of the 1914 outbreak of the First World War or the 2003 US decision to invade Iraq – provide the reader with theoretical expectations by which to understand the key case events. The opportunity for students to explore how they would have reacted in those situations, other possible alternative explanations, or how alternative decision outcomes could have been achieved is reduced. Learning still occurs in research cases, but that learning is via a more passive, rather than more active, learning method. Teaching cases promote active learning by leaving it up to the students to determine why events transpired as they did, what factors were most important to understanding the case and its outcomes, and what broader lessons can be learned. In research cases which already provide the analysis of the case, the intellectual engagement and interactive teaching aspects of the case are minimized, if not totally lost (Golich).

Teaching cases tend to fall into one of two major types. *Retrospective cases* are the more common type. These cases previously occurred, and the resolution of the case is known. So for students, the initial task is to determine why the case arose in the first place. In other words, why did policymakers think this situation needed to be addressed at this time, if at all. From that point, the emphasis for students is to determine which people were involved in making the ultimate decision, why those individuals were involved rather than other possible decisionmakers, and how the relevant decisionmakers perceived both the issues in the case and how they would be impacted by its resolution. This impact could be personal or professional regarding themselves, or the impact could affect the entities they care about – their political party, agency or organization in government, the regime at large, the society/nation/state at large, or possibly even the human race. As Allison (168) initially described this: What are the personal stakes for each of the individuals involved and, based on those stakes, what stands on the issue do they take? Once those stakes and stands are understood, the students seek to explain why the resultant output occurred; which individuals seemed to have the most influence and what arguments or perspectives persuaded the decision-making group. Once the case has been decided, a final step is to ask the "so what?" question. What difference does this output make? How is it significant in any broader sense? What are the broader consequences of this decision when it comes to long-term outcomes? What does this case help us to understand?

The other major types of cases are those that force students to make the decisions themselves. These *decision-forcing cases* have no resolution provided. Instead, they describe a situation and put the students in the role of policymakers. As such, the cases could be completely hypothetical or they could be based on actual cases. However, one has to be careful with the use of well-known real cases, as some of the students might know how the case was actually resolved, thus potentially short-circuiting the goal of the exercise (Golich; Christensen et al.). In such cases, one could mask a real-life case by putting the situation and the relevant factors into hypothetical terms with new names of players, entities, and so on. Then, once the students have finished the case with their resolution, the instructor could reveal what the real case was and how the class resolution compared to the real one. Then the interesting part begins; if different decisions occurred in the class discussion than did in real life, how and, more importantly, why? Did the policymakers overlook something that the students chose to consider? Were the policymakers blinded by their assumptions, biases, or shared values? Or did the lack of governmental experience on the part of the students lead them to an output that might not be "realistic" in the applied setting of real-world politics?

Once the type of cases to be used has been determined, one has to go find them! Relevant cases can be based on current events, where a series of articles in newspapers or other periodicals may provide sufficient information for the case study to proceed. For example, one could pick a recent but retrospective case, such as a particular European state's response to the refugee crisis arising from the Syrian or Libyan civil wars or virtually any state's response to the 2020 COVID-19 outbreak. A decision-forcing case might involve what to do about ongoing Russian pressures on Ukraine or Belarus, Myanmar's continued repression of the Rohingya, or how to deal with North Korea's nuclear weapons and missile programs.

Beyond these cases found by the instructor, there are websites with case studies to be used. Hundreds if not thousands of cases are available online. Many of these are free to use, but some require purchase. Some of the websites include:

- Columbia University's International Affairs Online: http://www.ciaonet .org/catalog?utf8=%E2%9C%93&search_field=all_fields&q=case+studies (accessed July 1, 2020)
- Georgetown University's Institute for the Study of Diplomacy: https://isd .georgetown.edu/case-studies/ (accessed July 1, 2020)
- Harvard University's Kennedy School of Government's Case Program: www.ksgcase.harvard.edu/ (accessed July 1, 2020)
- Princeton University's Institute for Successful Societies at the School of Public and International Affairs: https://successfulsocieties.princeton.edu/ about/faqs (accessed July 1, 2020)
- The University of Washington's Hallway program at the Evans School of Public Affairs: https://www.hallway.org/browse (accessed July 1, 2020).

There are also books of case studies or books heavily featuring case studies. A number of them focus on the United States, its foreign policymaking system and actors, and issues. These include those by Carter, Devereaux et al., Houghton, Rose, Snow (*Regional Cases*), and Strong. Others present cases involving a range of international actors – states, international governmental organizations, and international nongovernmental organizations. These include de Swielande et al., Hastedt et al., Mingst and Mori, Mislan and Streich, and Smith et al. Others provide a focus on transnational actors and issues. See, for example, Ramsey and Kiltz, Rhodes, Snow (*Cases in International Relations*), and Styles. Some volumes focus on selected issues in IR, such as diplomacy (Hutchings and Suri, Kiehl), global health (Glassman and Temin, Matlin and

Kickbusch, Rosskam and Kickbusch), or international ethics (Amstutz). As one can see, these selections of cases can fit in a wide variety of IR courses.

STEP 2: PREPARATION BEFORE CLASS

The next step on our part is to choose what general classroom approach we prefer. One approach that may be familiar was developed by the partnership of Harvard's Kennedy School of Government with the Pew Charitable Trusts. That approach stressed providing no cueing questions to the class in advance about the particular case at hand and letting the students work through the case with the instructor only asking questions. A slightly modified version of that approach is for the instructor to provide some cueing questions to the class in advance but, again, to let the students determine why and how things happened. A very different way to handle a case study is to assign the students roles to play from the case. They assume the roles of key policymakers in a simulation format, basing their roles off the case study material. Another method is to assign the case and have students engage in a debate or even game show format, with teams answering questions from the instructor. We are only limited by our imaginations as to how we approach the examination of particular cases. Regardless of the approach, we must be clear about what we want students to learn from this exercise. What's the educational payoff?

Once the cases and approaches have been chosen, we must get to work to carefully prepare ourselves for the case study. This is unlike preparing a lecture or a seminar discussion. We need to know as much about the case as possible. In retrospective cases, we need to be able to answer questions like:

- Why did the case arise? Why at this time?
- What issues were involved? How important were they?
- How did the events play out?
- Within the circle of decisionmakers, who did what?
- Why did the decisionmakers or participants speak and act as they did? What were their stakes and stands?
- What led to the output being chosen?
- Were there clear winners/losers in the case, or was the output some form of compromise solution?
- Was there slippage between the output being chosen and its implementation?
- Could the output be considered successful in the short term?
- What were the longer-term consequences of this case and its resolution?
- What does the case demonstrate or what can be learned from it?

In decision-forcing cases, a somewhat different set of questions can be asked, to paraphrase Golich et al. (1):

- What information here is important and what is peripheral?
- What's the real problem, its context and parameters?
- What are likely possible solutions?
- How can such solutions be implemented, and might problems arise in that process?

As Lynn points out, instructors must also take into consideration class size and the physical layout of the classroom. Employing a case-study approach in a seminar setting with a class of a dozen or so students is vastly different than trying to do the same with 30 or 60 or more students. Small classes can usually engage organically as a group in a case-study approach. Larger classes may require other accommodations. For example, classes of 30 or more students may seem too large for the normal give-and-take we desire from the students. A way to rectify that is to divide large classes into smaller groups. Such groups may be charged with working through the details of the case on their own with the instructor watching the interactions and evaluating student participation in some manner. After a suitable amount of time – perhaps 15 or 20 minutes – the class could reconvene as a whole to discuss the case and to see if different groups understood and dissected the case in similar or different ways. Another approach for dealing with the large class issue is again to divide the class into smaller groups but to assign certain questions to each group to answer – such as why did the case arise, what were the important issues, who played key roles in the case, what made the key players so influential, why was the 'winning' solution chosen, what are the consequences of the case, etc. Then after a suitable amount of time, the class can reconvene to work through the case together. Either of these tactics can work quite well with larger classes. However, without breaking into smaller groups in some fashion, the passivity often found in larger group dynamics can often work to derail the discussion of a case that seemed promising. Free riders may abound, and only a few interested or serious students may willingly participate in the discussion (Holsti, "Reflections on").

The physical layout of the class matters as well. Regardless of the class size, case-study dynamics improve if the students can see each other. Is the number of students small enough to fit around a table? If so, does your classroom have one, and if not, can another room with one be found? If not, can chairs or desks be moved so students can more easily interact with each other? Are whiteboards available with markers that work? Do you have chalk if using chalkboards? Are flipcharts available if needed, and are the markers for them sufficiently dark to be easily read? If students rely on laptops, tablets, or classroom computers, can they be connected to classroom projectors if desired? For extremely large classes, are microphones necessary and available for all to hear student comments? Do they work?

A final task before the classroom session is to prepare the students for their role in this active learning exercise. The key is to find a way to get students to buy into an active learning approach in advance and to be ready to participate on the day the case study is discussed. There are probably as many ways to accomplish this task as there are instructors. We each find what works for us in our particular situation. When teaching an honors section of a course or teaching at a small, liberal arts-oriented college, getting such student involvement may not be that difficult, as it may be the norm. It may be what the students already expect. On the other hand, at universities with larger class sizes or in courses that count as a general education or core curriculum requirement, the task may be more difficult. Some ways to ensure that they do the preparatory work are:

- If the entire course is going to be case-based, address this on the first day of class. Make sure they know this course will be different from others they take. If only occasional class sessions involve cases, talk to the class at least several days before the case study is scheduled. Make it absolutely clear that students need to carefully read the case and understand it well. Be candid about the fact that not reading the case is unacceptable, and reading it only superficially is only marginally better. Without their compliance in this regard, employing a case-study approach will almost certainly cause both you and the students great stress and the probabilities of classroom failure rise dramatically.
- Consider giving them prompts in the form of questions to consider when reading the case, letting them know that these will be important in the discussion of the case.
- Commit a class session, either in full or in part, to conduct a "training session" where you walk them through the steps they can expect when working through a case study.
- Let them know in advance that passivity and disengagement are unacceptable. If desired, tell them their active involvement and participation in the group or class effort will be evaluated by you. If you choose this option, share a template or rubric of how you will evaluate their participation.
- When all else fails, go with the "nuclear option" by telling them that, yes, this information – about both the case events and what we conclude about the case – will be on the next exam. Then make sure to include such questions in that exam!

74 *Teaching international relations*

STEP 3: THE CLASS SESSION

Now the "rubber hits the road" and we all hope for traction. We need to be sure to follow the structure of the session that we earlier alerted the students to so they know what their roles are. As noted earlier, larger classes may need to be divided into groups and time provided for the groups to do their work. Once the discussion of the case begins, we need to follow through with the structured format the students have been led to expect. To quote Golich et al. (46), the typical stages of case-study analysis are:

- What is the situation?
- What are the possibilities for action?
- What are the consequences of each?
- What action, then, should be taken?
- What general principles and concepts seem to follow from this analysis?

For many of us, our key role will be asking the right questions. Our goals may be to "obtain information; clarify a point; confirm a point; draw attention to related points; foster debate; resolve a debate; change the direction of the discussion; suggest a hypothesis; stimulate abstract thought; and, begin a summation" (Golich et al., 46–47). To get the class started, we can begin with easy questions about the case events or the issues involved and move on from there. To get at the more analytic aspects, we need to ask 'how' and 'why' questions. To get more evaluative, we can ask what else might have been done or do others agree. To finish, we need to ask questions about what can be learned from the case of what the possible consequences of the case could be (Golich et al., 47).

We all hope for a positive and energetic classroom experience. Yet despite all our efforts, sometimes the experience falls short of our goals. There are many things that may go wrong during the case discussion. Works by Andersen and Schiano, Golich et al., Lantis et al. 2000b, Lynn, and others try to help us with some of the more typical dilemmas. Distilling their suggestions, here is what to do if confronting:

- The silent class: Don't answer the questions for them. Wait them out, be patient, make it clear that they must respond to such prompts. If necessary, rephrase the question another way, but don't let them escape their responsibility to participate.
- The silent student: Some students just will not want to participate. If this becomes a pattern, you may have to call upon them. If they don't respond, find other ways to rephrase the question. If they still refuse to respond, move on, but later privately let them know that their unwillingness to participate hurts both the group effort and potentially their understanding of

the case. If necessary – and if you have previously made this clear – remind them that lack of participation will impact their grade.

- The student whose responses are not germane or are uninformed: Stop them when the situation becomes apparent and ask them or others how those responses relate to the case. Redirect the class attention back where it needs to be.
- The student who wants to dominate discussion: These are very common. These students may be impassioned about the case issues, ideologues who believe they are right, those who just want to score points with the instructor or demonstrate their mastery of the case, and so on. When it becomes a problem, ask for others to respond or if everyone agrees. If necessary, speak to that student outside class, noting that you value that person's contributions but that you also have a duty to involve the others as well. Students generally respond well to this approach when it is couched in ways that recognize that person's investment in the material or makes that student a tacit partner in the classroom learning activity.
- The disruptive or rude student: When this first occurs, make the point that such comments or behavior are inappropriate. Be respectful but firm. If that doesn't work, ask the others in class what would make a person say that or act that way. It is hard to handle such students without embarrassing them at least to some degree, but that may be necessary to allow the case-study approach to proceed as hoped. Of course, the worst-case scenario would be the student who is unwilling to change the unacceptable behavior or language. The 'nuclear option' in such a case may be to ask them to leave the classroom or, if necessary, to drop them from the course and contact the relevant campus administrators or services.

STEP 4: AFTER THE CLASS SESSION

We always want to know the extent to which our students are learning, but when we go to this much effort and preparation, we'd really like to know that the students benefited from the case-study approach. There are several ways to go in this regard.

If time permits at the end of the class session, anonymous surveys could be distributed asking open-ended questions about what was learned in the exercise, or this could be done as an overnight exercise. Another straightforward method is to rely on some form of brief reflection assignment, perhaps a one-page paper with lessons learned from the case study. These could be a component of the student's course grade or could represent some form of "bonus points" at the end of the term. Another method is to have a longer paper assignment, in which similar – or different – cases are compared in terms of the educational value they had in the eyes of the students. Still another method is to require the students produce a case analysis of their own, using the approaches and rubrics employed in class. Such more extensive assignments can demonstrate the degree to which the students have embraced and understood the case-study method and thus should be at least an indirect indicator of students' abilities to learn from this approach. Finally, there is the option of asking questions on subsequent exams about either the events of and the actors in the cases themselves or the lessons and interpretations the class discussion drew from those case studies.

Another somewhat different approach would be to evaluate whether the case-study approach is a better learning tool than other approaches used in class. One way to do this would involve the same course being taught in case-study and non-case-study formats by the same instructor, with the learning outcomes at the end of the course compared. A less precise way would be for comparisons of learning outcomes in the same course taught by different instructors with some employing case-study approaches while others do not. Of course, the variation in instructor effectiveness would be a potentially confounding factor.

In summary, many instructors in varying fields have found the use of case-study approaches to be worth the time and effort required. They can enhance active learning and skill building on the part of the students, but they require different types of preparation, and sometimes more effort in preparation, on the part of the instructors.

7. Experiential learning through faculty-led study abroad programs

Amy Below, Amanda Nydegger and Mary Jane Parmentier

One key to teaching international relations (IR) effectively is to transform students' perspectives to reach beyond their own national contexts and to see global dynamics through multiple and expansive lenses. Students of IR will fail to comprehend varying national interests and priorities if they view behavior solely through their own domestic lens. Many techniques exist to teach IR in a way that broadens students' perspectives and engenders critical thinking, and a rich array is offered throughout the chapters of this volume. This chapter focuses on faculty-led, short-term study abroad (SA) programs, and argues that if these programs are carefully designed and implemented, this transformation to a broader world view can happen in a relatively short period of time. On the other hand, students can return without reaching the learning objectives we may have set for them. Thus, just as in the classroom, active and innovative learning pedagogy needs to be carefully and thoughtfully designed.

While SA professionals may encourage students to spend a semester or year abroad to maximize cultural and linguistic immersion, a well-designed, short-term faculty-led program can accomplish the sort of transformative experience that opens students' minds to other cultural and national contexts. Short-term SA programs typically span one week to one month, and faculty-led refers to programs designed, implemented, and actively taught abroad by faculty members from the home institution.

The innovative design and careful implementation of short-term programs by faculty is essential for successfully attaining learning outcomes, both for subject matter and cross-cultural awareness (Giedt et al.; Hulstrand; Strange and Gibson; Mule et al.; B. Anderson et al.). SA programs can have many foci for subject matter, and teaching IR abroad could include topics from foreign policy to comparative politics, economic issues, and history. The scholarship on short-term SA examines transformations in cultural sensitivity and awareness, and there is research that supports these programs' potential in achieving these outcomes, depending on how they are designed (Tarrant; Rexeisen; Gaia; Bai et al.; Strange and Gibson; Edmunds and Shore). B. Anderson et al. found that service-learning SA programs can broaden students' views. However this is not automatic, and without careful programming, students can cling to their assumptions. Other research has shown that short-term faculty-led programs need to be well designed, with clear objectives and expected outcomes (Parmentier and Moore; Mule et al.).

Service learning and student research abroad have been emphasized as innovative elements of SA that can enhance active learning (Strange and Gibson; Shostya and Morreale; B. Anderson et al.), leading to broader effects on students' understanding of themselves and their host country. Both service projects and field research tend to engage students in local communities, working alongside host-country citizens in both formal and informal ways. Shostya and Morreale emphasize the importance of local partner institutions in allowing students access to local resources. Strange and Gibson found that the more experiential learning elements such as service learning and research that are incorporated, the more transformative learning took place. The goal of this chapter is to provide a guide to developing and running high-quality and impactful short-term faculty-led SA programs. It provides guidance for first-time SA and experienced faculty alike.

DREAM SEQUENCE

This chapter is modeled after a workshop we led at the 2018 and 2019 International Studies Association (ISA) Innovative Pedagogy Conferences. We began the workshop with an individual brainstorming activity we entitled the "Dream Sequence." We now invite you to participate. First, grab a notebook or piece of paper, or open a new document on your computer. In one to two minutes, brainstorm what your ideal SA program would look like if you could craft it to your every desire. Erase concerns about funding, potential administrative hurdles, and political limitations. Consider where you would go, for how long, who you would take, what students would study, and any ideal activities or people to meet. Ready? Brainstorm!

Now that you have imagined your ideal program, including ideas about locations, course content, and ideal activities, we hope the following pages will help you determine which aspects may be feasible, which might need adjustment, and which will require detailed attention. We also hope to highlight issues you may not have considered or realized might be your responsibility. We propose a series of questions to ask yourself and/or others in your field or on your campus to help best design and implement your "close-to" dream program.

Though not perfect due to overlap and other complex realities, the chapter begins with a discussion on program design, focusing first on important logistical considerations and then shifting focus to curricular and faculty considerations. It ends with suggestions for thinking about your program holistically, including pre-departure and re-entry programming. As you contemplate program design, you may find it more useful to consider your curriculum first and then adapt the logistics accordingly, and that works well, too. In either case, it is important to recognize that logistics and curriculum are interconnected and that changes to one will inevitably impact the other. Program design can begin from either perspective; regardless of your approach, the questions and discussion below will be useful.

PROGRAM DESIGN

Because creating and leading a SA program requires serious work, you want to ensure that you have the bandwidth to commit to this project and see it through to completion. Before you dive in, evaluate your resources at a macro level. You need to know how much assistance you might expect to receive during this process, but, even more important, you need to understand the culture of education abroad at your institution. Howard and Keller write that the "development process should only commence after student interest has been confirmed and departmental and institutional support obtained." Otherwise, "designing and implementing a study tour can be at best challenging and at worst fruitless" (136). You can gauge institutional support by asking the following questions:

- Does your institution already offer SA programming?
- As a whole, does your institution support the creation of SA opportunities?
- Does your particular unit support the creation of SA opportunities?
- What, if any, barriers have you encountered that would prevent you from developing a SA program?

According to Howard and Keller, "if there is institutional or departmental resistance to education abroad, an inaugural study tour may also be viewed as an opportunity to showcase how positive and valuable students find this learning experience" (136). Identifying possible barriers early and working to overcome them may allow you to facilitate a SA program that paves the way for others at your institution to do the same.

As you look around, start to assess the resources on your campus. What, if any, offices focus on international education? Is there an education abroad office that can support your endeavor to create and deliver a SA experience for your students? If yes, what services does this office offer, and what will you be responsible for doing on your own?

If you do not have an education abroad office on your campus, you will need to dig a little deeper. Are there any champions of international initiatives on campus—anyone to whom you can look for mentorship and advice on building a program? Finding mentors and champions of SA, on your campus or even at other institutions through your network of contacts, can make your job easier. They can share tips and lessons learned and, when you encounter barriers, they can help brainstorm solutions or alternatives. According to a study by Madden et al., "most respondents noted that informal mentorship was their most useful resource because it produced program-specific information" (194–195). Even if you do not know of others on your campus who have developed SA programs, quite a bit of scholarship from the field exists regarding program development (Howard and Keller; Marine; Womble et al.; Eckert et al.; Hulstrand). It may require a more piecemeal approach, but developing a SA program, even without a dedicated office, is possible.

The next step is to evaluate your particular situation. Given your teaching load and the level of institutional support you expect to receive, is developing and leading a SA program a project to which you can commit? When would your program take place, and how would it fit into your teaching load? Would you be compensated for your time, and what does compensation look like at your institution? Will developing a SA program impact your promotion and tenure file, and, if so, how? What are your responsibilities on-site? Veteran SA leaders will tell you that much time and energy are required to create a strong program. Madden et al. found that although faculty leaders expected developing a program to take time, they still underestimated the requisite "time commitments" and "range of unanticipated activities" in which they were required to engage (189). Taking time at the onset to evaluate your context and determine if this is the right time for you to develop a SA program can save you time and frustration later.

After committing to move forward, you will need to gain a clear understanding of the cost of SA for students. Charlotte West rightly acknowledges that the "cost of studying abroad—both real and perceived—is one of the biggest barriers for many students" (33). Know your student demographics and have a sense of what kind of price tag your students are able to pay. In order to do so, learn how program fees are calculated at your institution and what they include. Faculty costs, student housing, activities, and excursions are fairly standard inclusions. But there are items that vary significantly by institution, including group airfare, number of faculty per program, and meal inclusions. Understand if your program fee may be variable (depending on the number of students recruited) or if it will stay the same regardless of enrollment. And be aware of costs for which students will be responsible but that may not be included in the program fee. Examples may include airfare, passport and visa fees, meals, and personal expenses.

With a better understanding of the budget and program fee, the next step is to determine how students can pay for a program. Students and their families will ask detailed questions about how to afford SA, so make sure you can walk them through each line item of the budget and can refer them to resources for funding. Can they use federal financial aid and institutional scholarships to pay their fees (West, 34)? Do students have access to departmental and external scholarship opportunities? What guidance do they receive for creative fundraising opportunities? There may be institutional resources available to students, but, if not, developing a frequently-asked questions (FAQ) page or a funding tips sheet for interested students could be a huge help during the recruitment period. Money is a significant barrier for many students who wish to participate in SA and receiving funding resources early may allow more students to consider such an opportunity.

One final—and extremely important—preliminary consideration is your institution's policy on insurance and liability. Will students and faculty be covered under a comprehensive medical insurance policy for the duration of their program? Are there certain locations to which your institution prohibits travel? What steps must you take prior to recruiting to ensure that any liability concerns have been mitigated? Find out if there is someone who can help you understand any liability issues or concerns associated with developing and leading a SA program at your institution and be sure to ask if there are any legal issues to be aware of, particularly for your institutional context.

Logistics

Now that you have done the hard work of understanding your institutional context, finding your SA champions, learning how a SA budget works, and investigating important liability and legal issues, we turn our attention to program design. Truly, the opportunities are limitless; getting started will require that you make a few key decisions to necessarily limit your options. Who is your target audience, and how can you tailor your program to their needs? What term will you offer your program, and what is the optimal length? What is your program location(s)? How many students will you take abroad, and how will that number impact the logistics of on-site travel? Do you need a minimum number of students to make the program viable?

Once you have the initial answers to these questions (and remember, the answers may change as you delve deeper into program design!), you can start to flesh out your program. As cost will likely be a consideration, ask yourself early: what components are absolutely necessary to the integrity of the program? While it may be disappointing to cut activities or locations, costs may mandate it. Simply put, your SA program should meet the learning objectives of the course while adhering to the constraints (time, money, location, etc.) of your particular context.

Whether you have limited or substantial institutional resources, using a provider to help you plan the logistics of the program can be extremely beneficial (Eckert et al., 442). Providers are companies whose task it is to provide logistical support for SA programs. This includes arrangements for accommodation, airport pickup and drop-off, and in-country transportation, to name a few. In addition, providers offer on-site staff that can accompany a group, take care of day-to-day logistics, translate if necessary, provide cultural explanation and context, and navigate an unfamiliar location for the group. Finally, and perhaps most important, most providers offer 24/7 emergency support. Regardless of the time of day or night, faculty leaders and their students have access to someone on-site who knows the language, understands the hospital and legal systems, and can garner additional support and resources in the case of an emergency.

Faculty may be leery of using a provider for a number of reasons. First, they worry about price increases (Marine, 181). While the price usually does go up when using a provider, the increase is often much less significant than faculty anticipate, and it is almost always worth the time savings for you. Second, some faculty worry they will lose control over their program. As the faculty director, it is up to you to communicate your wishes clearly to the provider and engage in a dialogue as you work together to hone an itinerary and list of activities that can be safely and effectively facilitated by the provider while meeting the student learning outcomes of the course you have created (Eckert et al., 442). Communication is key, and when you and the provider communicate, both before the program and on-site, the likelihood of a successful and impactful program increases exponentially. Finally, it is important to remember that you can use a provider as much or as little as your program—and your international experience and contacts—demands (Eckert et al., 442). If you already have great contacts abroad, you might schedule the lecturers and ask the provider to arrange transportation. If you are unfamiliar with the location, you can rely on the provider for quality logistical, cultural, and academic support. Using a provider takes much of the logistical pressure off your shoulders, allowing you to concentrate on delivering the academic content and ensuring that students have an impactful and formative experience abroad.

If your institution has an education abroad office, consult with them on the use of providers. Many institutions require that first-time faculty leaders use one. At other institutions, even if using a provider is not required, it will be highly recommended because of the health and safety coverage that comes with such a decision. Your education abroad office or contacts from other institutions may be able to recommend providers in the region to which you are traveling that could be a good fit for your program. In general, it is always wise to request bids from multiple providers so that you can see the functions that each provides, and the costs associated with those services. Shop around, do

Experiential learning through faculty-led study abroad programs 83

your research, and make sure that you are getting the best program (logistics, academics, health and safety) for the price.

As you develop your program, the logistical decisions you make will significantly shape your program and contribute to its structure. The curriculum is of equal importance and will likewise influence the structure of your program. We discuss academic considerations in the next section.

Curriculum

Designing the curricular components of your program might be where you began your brainstorming session, and it is important to ensure our curricula are purposefully and holistically designed in order to have the positive impact we desire (Bell et al.; Tarrant and Lyons). If lessons and activities are not well-planned, they may not reach all students equally or could facilitate culturally problematic interactions. As with campus courses, begin with learning objectives and outcomes. What do you want your students to learn? Consider subject matter content, new perspectives on issues, cross-cultural understanding, field research experience, and personal growth.

As you begin to formulate your learning objectives, ask yourself the following questions. Will your program be centered on a particular event or theme via an IR lens? Or will it be interdisciplinary or multidisciplinary? How will you balance discipline-specific academic content and cultural learning? Are your objectives specific to undergraduate students or can they accommodate graduate students? How might graduate students be engaged to support their research? Will there be a language component (either as a core objective or as part of larger cultural objectives)? Will you incorporate service learning and/or research? As the literature has shown, SA is a rich opportunity to utilize active learning techniques to help you meet your various objectives. Your answers should affect everything from course texts and materials to on-site activities and how you recruit students.

One of the greatest rewards of SA is that it presents opportunities to incorporate new methods of innovative teaching and learning. For example, faculty may be comfortable adopting a familiar IR lens, but multi- and interdisciplinary approaches can facilitate rich conversations and learning experiences and can attract students from across campus (potentially increasing enrollment). Additional benefits include incorporating a variety of in-country experts and stakeholders and encouraging co-teaching with faculty across your home institution. Having two (or more) faculty on-the-ground can also divide faculty responsibilities and provide students additional support outlets, especially if faculty are of different ages, genders, and races/ethnicities.

Another important set of concerns regards the balance between academic and cultural competency, the latter having become increasingly important for our students, our universities, and our globalized world (P. Anderson et al.). Faculty must decide how to weave cultural contexts, histories, and contemporary discussions into their discipline-specific objectives. A similar concern is that of relationality or positionality. How will you discuss your students' role and behavior in the host country? As Pipitone writes, we should be wary of "problematic trends in SA that reproduce hierarchies of power and colonialism, perpetuate views of an exotic cultural 'other' and privilege tourism over education" (55).

It is also important to consider the demographics and backgrounds of your students, understanding that each comes to your program with different lived experiences, racial backgrounds, and cultural competencies that affect their SA experiences (Mitchell and Maloff). Malewski and Phillion encourage faculty to reconfigure "formal curricula to account for the ways different lived histories, outlooks on the world, and self-understandings innately affect experiences studying in another country" (63). These factors apply to how our students interact with course material, each other, and with the people and groups they encounter on-site and learn from and with.

Having considered broad academic and cultural objectives, a next step is to think about the pedagogical tools used to meet these objectives. One "tool" especially worthy of thoughtful attention is time. Thus, ask yourself: Will you have regularly scheduled class sessions? How much free time will students be given? Will there be parameters for that free time? Will you schedule excursions? If so, where in the duration of the trip will they be scheduled? Most of your answers will depend on the length of the program, but all programs should balance structure and flexibility. On the one hand, given the amount of change and adjustment students will be undergoing, continuity and a clear set of daily expectations can be extremely helpful and appreciated. On the other hand, keeping the schedule dynamic and flexible is a must. SA is full of unforeseen events and circumstances for which both faculty and students should always be prepared.

The types of assignments and activities are also a key factor, as they will help you attain your learning objectives. Can any pedagogical tools be adapted from your on-campus courses? Common assignments such as group work, presentations, and reflection pieces can translate well. Another is journaling (Gough at al.). Journals can be guided or free-form, formal or informal, graded or not. They provide important time for student reflection, individualized learning, and personal growth. Also, consider the use of daily student leaders. They would be in charge of leading group discussions, introducing the group to guest speakers, or making sure everyone is on the bus on time, for example. While this has logistical benefits, interactions with locals and public speaking opportunities can provide both cultural and personal growth for your students. Other engaging and impactful assignments uniquely tailored to SA include assigning student leaders to share a "Word of the Day" in the host-country's language(s), scavenger hunts or mapping exercises where students are asked to investigate their new surroundings, or photography assignments asking students to select a recent photo that highlights a particular theme or feeling from that day. Such activities can meet a number of linguistic, cultural, and academic learning objectives simultaneously.

Teaching students abroad also provides endless opportunities to meet learning objectives through experiential and active learning, addressing both content learning goals and cross-cultural learning. We offer several examples from programs we have led, which can be modified for other settings. A sustainable development program in Morocco included a week-long stay at a girls' boarding school where students ate meals and participated in activities with the Moroccan girls, experiencing their lives, perspectives, and priorities (cultural understanding). During the same program, students were asked to take one picture of something they considered "unsustainable" and another of an example of "development." This exercise vividly revealed to students how their own assumptions influenced how they identified and evaluated other societies (contextualized cross-cultural perspective). On a program to Ecuador, the group spent several days in a remote community, staying with local families, hearing their perspectives, and writing narratives (awareness of political and community perceptions).

On a program in the Dominican Republic, the faculty implemented a role-playing simulation to represent local sectors, volunteers, and communities. At the same time, students conducted preliminary field research as they worked alongside local citizens. The final deliverable of this week-long program was a proposal for funding to fit a perceived community need. The role-playing exercise gave students the chance to interact with funders and local citizens, which led to stronger written proposals, a clearer understanding of local community needs, and the complex dynamics of development work (community engagement in development projects).

Finally, a critically important activity unique to SA is holding daily debriefing sessions (Coryell, Mills et al.). Students will appreciate the time to digest and reflect on recent experiences. Sessions work nicely as free-flowing, comfortable spaces where students can share emotions, interactions, and observations. This is also a useful way for students to learn from each other's experiences and expand the scope of everyone's learning. The focus of such sessions can be academic but will often result in personal and cultural learning as well. Such "check-ins" can even serve as your "regularly scheduled" group sessions suggested previously, providing continuity and community learning.

FACULTY EXPECTATIONS

Once you have worked through some of the nuts and bolts of your program, it is important to focus on your role as a faculty member and to be realistic in your expectations, in terms of both potential challenges and benefits. This may be simultaneously one of the most arduous and rewarding teaching experiences you will ever have. You are no longer "just" the person charged with educating students and providing academic and career advice. You will wear many additional hats ranging from mental health professional to activities coordinator, from triage nurse to university liaison. How will you mentally prepare for being on call 24 hours a day? Will you stay in the same accommodation as your students? How will they be able to contact you? What is your responsibility during free time? How will you successfully convey that to students? In what ways are you willing to step into a parenting/familial role? Boundaries are important (and students will also want time away from faculty), but students will appreciate knowing they can turn to you when they need to.

This relates to a critical faculty responsibility—ensuring student mental health. In what ways will you be prepared to react to distressed or misbehaving students? In these scenarios, prevention is key. The aforementioned debriefing sessions can have the additional benefit of helping students acclimate to their new environment, the intense time demands, challenging interpersonal dynamics, or homesickness. Be aware that some students may require additional support and one-on-one time beyond group sessions. It is also possible that faculty will need to attend to students who have been disruptive or who have found themselves in legal trouble (potentially the result of mental health challenges). The above concerns provide additional argumentation for having two faculty leaders and/or the additional support personnel from a service provider.

Finally, here are more additions to your list of "things to be prepared for": lost passports; inebriation, missing students; missing/forgotten medication; roommate conflicts; disruptive group dynamics; challenging situations due to student identity (i.e., gender, ethnicity, LGBTQIA+ [lesbian, gay, bisexual, transgender, queer (or questioning), intersex, and asexual (or allies)] status, religion); student issues that were not disclosed in the pre-departure phase; anti-American sentiment; and even terror attacks, the outbreak of global pandemics, or other international incidents.

BOOKENDS: BEFORE AND AFTER THE SA PROGRAM

Now that we have explored key components for designing a quality SA program that can result in transformative learning, we turn to important programming considerations for before and after the SA experience: pre-departure and re-entry orientations. The innovations in pedagogy for a transformative SA program begin with the pre-departure orientation (PDO), which can range from a single meeting to a complete pre-departure course. The literature emphasizes the necessity of providing students with a PDO, and agrees that the effectiveness of the orientation depends on how it is designed and how well it prepares students for the experience they are about to undertake (Forbes-Mewett; Engle; Giedt et al.; Campbell and Walta; Bai et al.; Paras et al.). PDOs are also upheld as an ethical professional standard by the Forum for Education Abroad ("Standards").

So, what does a quality orientation include? Cross-cultural awareness and culture-specific preparation are essential, along with program and academic content and country-specific information. Topics should include health and safety in the host country, arrival information, academic expectations, packing lists and accommodation details, currency and finances, use of electronics, and host-country information. In addition, your PDO provides an opportunity to build a student learning community which will create a better team from the moment you arrive in-country. Students who have met and gotten acquainted can help each other prepare for the program and support and learn from one another more effectively abroad.

While the time allotted depends upon your schedule and the material you need to cover, we recommend a for-credit pre-departure course if possible. This type of course allows plenty of room for active learning; preliminary research can be done by students on selected topics, and class meetings can cover history, culture, politics, and other current events in the host country for which students should be prepared. Students, either individually or in groups, can be made responsible for presenting material to the class on various topics related to the program. There is also room to provide, if appropriate, some basic language training. The pre-departure curriculum should correspond to the innovations you have designed into your SA program, such as research projects or service-based experiential learning. If this type of course is feasible, it can be extremely effective, giving faculty time to prepare students for field research and work on local projects as well as ensuring students have a deeper understanding of the host culture and the myriad logistics involved in a SA program.

Regardless of the discipline and central topic of your SA program, preparation for a cross-cultural learning experience is essential to the wellbeing of students and to the potentially transformative nature of studying abroad. While preparing beforehand for functioning in a new culture cannot be done completely (Campbell and Walta; Parmentier and Moore), and indeed continues throughout one's experiences abroad, the PDO should lessen the severity of culture shock and increase the students' ability to communicate, understand,

and empathize with the local community, seeing world events through a different cognitive lens. Moreover, culture is a disciplinary factor, and, while it is well known in the field that culture has not been seriously considered as a variable, it is also recognized more recently as a basis for the construction of enduring IR concepts (Jahn).

In exploring their own cultures in contrast to the host culture beforehand, students are more able and more aware to perceive cultural values, interpret behaviors (and not offend!), and potentially apply cross-cultural perspectives to comparative and international politics. Gaining awareness of how they will be perceived is also important; US students represent a diversity of backgrounds and identities and will not necessarily be perceived and understood by the host culture in the same way. Potential reactions should be directly addressed in orientation, ideally as a group, to properly prepare students, both for cross-cultural learning, and for safety in some contexts.

Finally, an orientation at the end of the program, called "re-entry," is also highly recommended (Forbes-Mewett; Engle; Giedt et al.; Campbell and Walta; Bai et al.; Paras et al.). The reasons why returning home can often produce emotional and adjustment difficulties are thought to center on several assumptions (Sorti). First, it is assumed that returning to one's own country is easy—after all, you are going home. Yet, students invariably experience changes abroad, and the SA experience can feel surreal, or even unreal, as students struggle to integrate back to "normal" life after such an adventure. Moreover, family and friends often have a limited capacity for listening to stories about the experience, making it painful and dislocating for the returning student (and faculty). The re-entry process should begin while still in-country, to prepare students for what they might feel when they return home. Follow up meetings to de-brief, have a reunion, and provide professional development on how the SA experience can enhance a resumé are all standard re-entry components. You might even have students present posters from the program, sharing with other students in a post-program symposium. This serves as a re-entry device, a marketing tool, and a learning opportunity for other IR courses.

CONCLUSION

You do not plan and lead a SA program primarily because you want to travel. However, you must love to travel in order to lead students abroad. A love of travel and cultural learning, together with a love of teaching, can provide a sound basis for developing SA programs with innovative ways to address IR curriculum and teaching. Short-term faculty-led programs allow a larger number of students to have this transformative experience, and, with careful design and marketing, these numbers can reflect more diversity in US students abroad (Below; Yuksel and Nascimento). Building in a research and/

or service-learning component increases the possibility of sparking critical thinking amongst students as they work alongside host-country citizens to gain local perspectives and think critically about standard approaches to the study of IR and related disciplines. If designed and executed carefully, a short-term faculty-led SA program can contribute significantly to students' understanding of other cultures and national contexts, and potentially impact a substantial number of students with an experience that they will carry with them throughout their lives.

8. Using Statecraft in the classroom

Eric Cox

INTRODUCTION

Statecraft is a turn-based, online international relations (IR) simulation used for the teaching of international politics. Statecraft provides a number of tools for instructors to use in customizing the simulation for particular class needs, and it scales well to different class sizes. Moreover, the simulation includes a number of built-in assessment tools that assist in evaluating students. That said, to be most effective, the simulation requires active monitoring and participation by the instructor.

While it may be unusual to discuss a particular educational product in a volume on teaching, Statecraft has become a popular tool. In fact, the IR simulation is now one of several simulations offered by Statecraft Simulations LLC; its other offerings include American Government, International Security, Foreign Policy, International Organizations, and International Political Economy. This article is specific to the IR simulation, but much of the discussion regarding the mechanics and inclusion in class will apply to all the simulations. The company claims to be used by more than 300 universities (Statecraft) and has generated several pedagogical articles (E. Cox; Epley; Linantud and Kaftan; Raymond; Saiya 2016, 2017; Smith and Michelsen).

Statecraft is an interesting addition to the world of active learning. While there is a rich literature on using simulations to teach lessons on particular topics such as the environment and sustainable development (Brown; Crossley-Frolick), foreign policy processes (Butcher; Shaw 2016), international security (Chasek; Sears), and international organizations, including Model UN and the European Union (Clark, et al.; Engel, et al.; Shannon), Statecraft is somewhat different. Statecraft is not a simulation designed to teach about one situation or a particular process; rather it is a complex simulation that touches on almost every aspect of IR, including tradeoffs between domestic and foreign policy.

This article proceeds as follows. It begins with a general description of the IR simulation itself, followed by a discussion of research on the effectiveness of the simulation. It will then move to a discussion of best practices for using the Statecraft simulation in class. While general lessons regarding simulations, as will be discussed in Chapter 9 by Amanda Rosen and Victor Asal, apply to the use of Statecraft, the nature of the simulation requires certain special considerations.

THE SIMULATION

Statecraft is a turn-based, online simulation of interactions between countries in a fictional world. When setting up the simulation, instructors are faced with some basic options, including how many countries will be in the simulation (from six to 12), which affects how many students will serve in each country (from one to nine), how many turns to use (Statecraft recommends seven to ten), when the turns begin and end (usually a turn lasts one week, but can be much shorter), and how students are assigned to teams (they can be assigned according to a foreign policy attitude test or can be manually assigned by the instructor).

During the first week of the simulation (known as Turn Zero), students are able to elect a president, name their country and cities, choose their government type from an array of options (Democracy, Constitutional Monarchy, Communist Totalitarian, and Military Dictatorship), and select two attributes for their country (Industrial, Green, Militaristic, Pacifist, or Scientific). Each government type and attribute has certain benefits and drawbacks as the game progresses. After the first turn is complete, the president is able to assign the other members of the team to certain roles, including Secretary of State, United Nations (UN) Representative, and Secretary of the Interior.

From that basic beginning, students must then make a number of decisions for their country. They can pursue a wide array of domestic construction projects, build up their military, build nuclear weapons, and compete for big projects. To do so, they must accumulate natural resources (gold, food, steel, scientific knowledge, and oil) and political capital. All natural resources can be traded through standard means or on a black market. Externally, students can exchange diplomats, engage in espionage, join international organizations, create treaties, and engage in war. Many actions take multiple turns to complete, and students must always be aware of how much of each resource is required for each move. Moreover, each action the student takes affects domestic quality of life and political approval from a variety of factions within the country. In addition to items that any country can purchase as long as they have sufficient resources such as schools, military equipment, hospitals, and museums, students can also compete for "big projects" that include items such as a national railway system, the CIA (US Central Intelligence Agency), and the Manhattan Project. These big projects require countries to bid against one another, and only one country can acquire them.

In addition to the actions students can take, the game itself throws a number of scenarios at students. Each semester pirates engage in raids on coastal areas; while the pirates would be easy to defeat, they pay tribute to one or more countries in the game. Similarly, terrorist organizations operate in other parts of the world, and students begin to receive warnings about the melting of "Ice Mountain" and the potential disaster it represents early in the game. Many of those problems could be solved by cooperative action or, if no action is taken, continue to worsen until resource production begins to fall. Moreover, one island in the simulation is occupied by a small indigenous population. Seizing the island greatly increases resource production for the country that seizes it, but also leads the indigenous population to begin an insurgency against the occupying power and to carry out other attacks during the game.

If all of this sounds complex, it is. To assist students (and the instructor) in understanding how to plan actions during the game and to make sense of the array of options, the simulation includes an extensive Student Manual detailing all options available to students and how to acquire various technologies. The system also tries to guide students through the steps necessary to acquire each good; very little can be done in one turn. Most actions require careful planning. Students are pursuing four primary types of goals: (1) a world without nuclear war; (2) cooperative goals (such as ending world hunger or solving environmental problems); (3) country development goals based on quality of life; and (4) competitive country goals in which countries compete in categories such as most educated, most scientific, or most militarily powerful (Statecraft Student Manual). At the end of the simulation, each team is rewarded based on accomplishments made during the game; some of these are mutually exclusive.

The system itself provides a number of additional tools to assist the instructor and students. Students are expected to complete two manual quizzes during Turns Zero and One – these quizzes help encourage students to read the manual. Each week, students also complete a memo regarding actions taken during the week or their plans for the upcoming week. These memos are visible to the instructor and to the other students on the team. Instructors are able to download a spreadsheet at any point during the semester that includes quiz grades and the percentage of memos each student completes.

The simulation has a number of other useful tools as well. An internal messaging system allows students to message one another or other teams; the system utilizes the message system to distribute news alerts. Instructors can view all the messages sent by students or the system. Fully describing everything in the game would require many, many more pages. Suffice it to say the game includes the balancing of internal and external politics, lessons on environmental destruction, the challenge of confronting non-state actors, deciding how heavily to invest in military resources, all while trying to maintain political support at home. All of this begs the question: how effectively does it work?

RESEARCH ON STATECRAFT

Statecraft has been the subject of a number of pedagogical studies measuring different aspects of its effectiveness as a teaching tool. One of the first published studies found that, although students enjoyed the simulation, they did not believe that it was particularly effective at helping them learn major concepts from the class (Carvalho, 549–550). In response, Keller, who wrote the material on which the simulation is based and designed many of the teaching tools available to professors who use the simulation, lays out a number of ways in which Carvalho did not use the simulation as intended, including a failure to use the system's gradebook, manual quizzes, or included notes on how to incorporate the simulation into lectures (Keller, 558–559).

This debate spawned a research note that used questions drawn from Carvalho's study to measure student perceptions of the Statecraft simulation (Saiya, "How Dangerous are Virtual Worlds"). Saiya found that his students not only enjoyed the simulation, but also found Statecraft to be helpful in understanding course material (291–292). Saiya argues that the difference in the two results are likely due to the way the simulation was used – Saiya more carefully integrated the simulation into his class than Carvalho reported doing – and the larger sample size. While Carvalho only measured one class, Saiya examined six classes over the course of three semesters (293–294). Epley had similar findings, arguing that students enjoyed the simulation and, when combined with other teaching tools, that the simulation improved student learning (214–215). Raymond examined the effect of Statecraft on student perceptions of their own decision-making; he concluded that student perceptions of their own decision-making did not change, but that they did greatly enjoy the simulation experience (310–311).

Several scholars have used Statecraft to perform comparative analysis, either of different ways of running the Statecraft simulation or looking at Statecraft in comparison to other teaching methods. Smith and Michelsen manipulated ten instances of the simulation across two campuses by giving their own survey to students and then grouping students in countries by ideology. They wanted to see how the Statecraft world varied based on the number of idealist countries versus the number of realist countries. What they found was that student ideology mattered in simulation outcomes; worlds dominated by realists had more attacks. One world populated entirely by idealist countries experienced no attacks (323–324). They conclude that the simulation itself was quite useful to teach a number of concepts in their introductory classes (328).

Cox ("Does Statecraft Improve Student Learning") used a comparative analysis of two sections of international politics, one using Statecraft as an additional assignment and one using a traditional research paper, to examine the effect of Statecraft on student-learning outcomes. He found that while students in the research paper class did perform better on exams and on the final grade, once incoming student grade point average (GPA) was controlled for, no other factors were statistically significant in explaining student grades, including major, classification and Statecraft. Saiya ("The Statecraft Simulation") used a pre/post-test to measure change in student foreign policy attitudes after participating in Statecraft and compared those findings to students who did not participate in Statecraft. While he found no meaningful shift in attitudes overall, he did find that students who participated in Statecraft tended to moderate their views (64). Linantud and Kaftan also conducted a comparative study of students over the course of three years that examined their academic honesty and engagement, changes in their political beliefs, and their perception of assessments. Their findings were that Statecraft was viewed very positively relative to other assignments (71). They also found that student attitudes as a whole became more hawkish regardless of participation in Statecraft, but that Statecraft students showed a stronger reduction in support for pacifism (75–77). The nature of the Statecraft assignments also led to reduced academic integrity issues (78).

Excluding Carvalho, the one consistent finding across these articles was that, when well-integrated into classes, students enjoyed Statecraft and believed it helped them learn. The key, however, appears to be successful integration within the course itself.

USING STATECRAFT EFFECTIVELY

The effective use of Statecraft in the classroom requires consideration both of how Statecraft will be integrated into course learning objectives and how to navigate the mechanics of the simulation. As Raymond and Usherwood warn regarding simulations in general:

> simulations can negatively affect student-learning outcomes if they lack clarity in their learning objectives, replace other, more effective teaching methods, require an inordinately complex application of skills or technology, do not incorporate adequate levels of presimulation training or lack meaningful postsimulation assessment mechanisms. (158)

Considering each of these factors when using Statecraft is very important as the simulation itself is extremely complex. It has an array of possible learning outcomes, can potentially take a great deal of class time, and has rather complex mechanics that can be challenging for students. Each of these issues will be discussed in turn.

Integrating Statecraft into Course Learning Outcomes

While professors may often design a simulation to teach one specific learning outcome (see Shaw and Switky), the Statecraft simulation is unique in that the world is basically a sandbox. No two Statecraft simulations will progress in exactly the same way, though some common lessons can emerge. To leverage Statecraft in achieving learning objectives, one has to consider the different elements of the simulation and how they can be used. Statecraft truly develops an entire world with multiple countries that have active domestic political situations and no restraints regarding their interactions with one another. The possible applications are numerous. As noted by Smith and Michelsen, students are often not all familiar with real-world examples or historical situations that instructors often use to illustrate points. The complexity of Statecraft allows for common reference points for teaching a wide variety of issues; comparing what happens in Statecraft to historical examples or current events can potentially help students better relate to and analyze the real world (326).

What follows are some examples of how the Statecraft simulation can be used to aid in teaching a number of concepts in international politics.

Understanding theory

The simulation itself gives students significant freedom to interact with one another however they like. It does, however, incentivize certain behavior through its cooperative and competitive rewards. So certain awards, such as "The Historian's Verdict" require countries to refrain from engaging in nuclear war; other awards such as "most powerful military" are inherently competitive. While students have significant freedom, the system often adds complications for the students. The "Statecraft Rumor Mill" sends periodic messages regarding things that may or may not be happening in other countries, including military buildups, troop movements, and domestic unrest. As noted above, certain scenarios always play out, including pirates who pay tribute to some countries, terrorists engaging in attacks from one country into another, and the melting of Ice Mountain, which leads to global flooding. Often times, elements of multiple theoretical perspectives are present. In particular, however, the game is very good at illustrating mainstream IR theories.

Realism

The Statecraft world is anarchic; nothing prevents students from building their militaries and attacking one another. In my classes, a constant comment from students is that Statecraft truly makes them understand the security dilemma.

Countries that aspire to be more peaceful are often concerned that they are going to be attacked by someone else in the game. This often leads to alliance formation as different blocs of countries square off against one another. As the Statecraft Rumor Mill kicks into high gear, countries that resisted growing their militaries will often reverse that decision. That the game allows for espionage and covert actions also contributes to students gaining an appreciation for state behavior in an anarchic system in which all states seek security.

Liberalism

The game also incentivizes cooperation. While most countries start off with similar levels of resources in the aggregate, countries are able to acquire valuable resources at different rates and are able to trade them. Moreover, countries are able to make treaties, join international organizations, and take other steps to facilitate cooperation. As students discover over the course of the game, certain actions are greatly facilitated by cooperative action. The one solution to the melting of Ice Mountain is to build the Globe of Frost. While it is possible for one country to build it alone, doing so takes so many resources that it requires that country to trust that other states will not exploit it, and the process is greatly facilitated if everyone works together on it. If a country becomes aggressive, it is also possible for countries to vote to expel the offending country from the UN.

Constructivism

If anarchy is what states make of it, Statecraft affords students the opportunity to design a world in the image of their choosing. While constructivists are quite varied in their approaches, Statecraft is quite good at teaching intersubjective meanings and mutually constituted identities. Students are able to set a tone in the world early on and are often able to identify the nature of particular countries within a few weeks of the simulation starting. Students are also able to see that one country can greatly affect the world; if all the countries in the simulation pursue peaceful relations but one chooses to build its military and threaten others, a peaceful world can quickly transition into one with a lack of trust.

The game also allows students to consider the impact of multiple identities on outcomes. Countries that are bound together through pre-existing friendships (or discord) often affect the simulation. The best example I had of this phenomenon came during a semester in which a number of students who formed a cohort in another program at Texas Christian University all took my introductory class the same semester to fulfill a university requirement. All of these students knew each other well and took all of their classes together. They made up approximately one-fourth of the class. As students are assigned to countries randomly, every country had at least one of these students in it.

Their friendship overwhelmed the simulation. All the countries got along and worked cooperatively to solve global issues. It was in many regards an illustration of overlapping identities shaping relationships.

I have now incorporated this last lesson more explicitly into discussing the simulation, using Johnston "Treating International Institutions as Social Environments" as a theoretical guide. As we debrief the simulation, I ask students to reflect on connections they have with other students in the class, whether it is a shared status as veterans or members of Reserve Officer Training Corps (ROTC) (a frequent occurrence in my introductory classes), membership in organizations, and/or geographic connections. As we have discussed these connections, other aspects of constructivist thinking have emerged. A desire to maintain amicable relationships outside the class leads some individuals to avoid conflict in the game, while others are more comfortable treating it as a game, particularly if they do not believe the game will have an impact on their relationships. These observations all lend themselves to a discussion of how identity and beliefs may shape interactions.

Liberal feminism
While an imperfect illustration of feminist IR theory in the simulation itself, particularly critical IR theory, Statecraft often affords the opportunity for students to consider liberal feminist theory and differential aspects of decision-making in female- versus male-dominated countries. While I personally do not assign students to countries, invariably I have at least one country formed either entirely of women or mostly women. As we discuss feminist IR theory in class, students can reflect on differences in decision-making between countries in the simulation. This also allows for a deeper conversation of critical feminist theories as we examine underlying issues and structures outside Statecraft that may affect the way decision-making occurs.

Non-state actors
The game has a number of non-state actors that affect countries. The Typhoon Pirates engage in numerous raids while paying tributes to some of the states. Similarly, the Orion Liberation Front (OLF) engages in terrorist attacks throughout the world. As with the pirates, some states benefit from the action of the OLF. If anyone attacks an island in the center of the Statecraft world known as Sapphire Island, a liberation organization known as the Sword of the Amaru (SOTA) begins carrying out attacks.

Something that is clear to students if they read the Student Manual is that any country which hosts these groups can eliminate their presence in their country with the simple click of a button. While this is much easier than dealing with terrorist organizations in the real world, this tool demonstrates that some states may benefit from the presence of such actors. If the host countries will not act against these actors, other countries can use covert actions to destroy terrorist and pirate bases. From these examples, students are able to learn a great deal about the complexity of addressing terrorism. The lesson is not just that different countries will view the same groups in different ways, but also that efforts to attack terrorists within another country invariably involves an act of war.

Coalitional politics

One interesting aspect of the game is that students receive constant updates on their approval ratings as well as news bulletins regarding prominent political factions in their country (capitalists, socialists, environmentalists, nationalists, civil libertarians, and intellectuals). If a faction's approval of the government drops low enough, it will engage in demonstrations and potentially riots. Not surprisingly, actions that please one faction often upset another. Students quickly learn that while they must build a coalition, it is not possible to keep all factions happy all the time. They begin to examine the relative size of factions to help determine how to improve their overall approval rating.

The environment

The primary environmental issue in the game is the melting of Ice Mountain. While the simulation is only a few weeks long, it does an effective job of modeling many of the real challenges of the addressing global environmental problems such as global warming.

Shadow of the future

Early warnings about the melting of Ice Mountain are somewhat speculative. Scientists are very concerned that it is melting, but the effects are not present. As the simulation progresses, if no action is taken the warnings not only get more dire, the effects continue to accumulate. The effects include harming resource production and, eventually, global flooding.

Cost / benefit analysis

Building the Globe of Frost project to save Ice Mountain requires accumulating technologies over several turns at a significant resource cost. Any country choosing to take on the project on its own will face a significant cost that can prevent it from carrying out a number of other projects, leaving it economically and militarily vulnerable.

Collective action problems

In the system, Globe of Frost research and construction must be based in one country. However, other countries in the simulation will often agree to contribute resources toward its construction. While this has worked at times, frequently at least one country will decide to free ride by not making its contributions. If this happens early on, other countries will often stop paying as well until insufficient resources are dedicated to building Globe of Frost, leading to global flooding. Alternatively, countries contribute resources to the host of Globe of Frost, only to see that country take the resources and dedicate them to other priorities, reneging on its agreement to build the Globe of Frost.

Foreign policy analysis
While the game does not address foreign policy analysis in great detail – a separate simulation addresses US foreign policy making – the simulation does allow for the illustration of some concepts.

Bureaucratic politics
The success of addressing bureaucratic politics depends in part on how seriously students take the simulation. Students are assigned one or more roles in their country; they receive special notification depending on their role and will frequently advocate on behalf of their position. As each allocation of resources is zero-sum – no deficit spending exists in the game – different advisors must compete for resources as the government sets policies.

Groupthink and polythink
Intergroup dynamics are often fascinating in Statecraft. As countries must set priorities early on, ample opportunity exists for students to agree (or disagree) on the direction the country should take. If a team has a particularly strong personality, that student can frequently drive the team forward to take positions that not all students necessarily agree with. The opposite problem can also occur when teams lack clear leadership or have a number of strong personalities who have such diverging views that the country is unable to move forward with decision-making.

Beyond these examples, Statecraft offers numerous other ways to illustrate concepts in international politics. The website includes a number of sample teaching materials that instructors can use to get started in using the simulation to explore major themes in class. In concluding the section, the most important takeaway is that Statecraft differs from other simulations used to illustrate one aspect of international politics; the complexity of the world and the ways in which students interact in the world provides each instructor with a myriad of ways to incorporate the simulation into their learning objectives.

Incorporating Statecraft into Course Design and Assessment

This section will look at practical incorporation of Statecraft into an overall course design and assessment strategies. In considering how to incorporate

Statecraft, instructors should consider a number of questions, including how much of the final grade Statecraft should comprise, how participation will be assessed, how many weeks the simulation should last, and how much class time should be dedicated to the simulation. Given the complexity of the simulation, it should not be used unless faculty are willing to dedicate a fair amount of time to the simulation – for a semester based class, instructors should plan on using the simulation over 8–10 weeks. I have found that early in the simulation, students need 20–25 minutes to meet with their teams; as the semester progresses, this can be reduced to 15–20 minutes.

Incorporating into assessment
Instructors must determine how much weight to give the assessment on their own. Too much, and it becomes the only focus of the class and too little leads students not to take it seriously. The weight of the overall simulation also affects how long the simulation should run and how much class time to dedicate to it. For my classes, I weight it at 20% of the class grade overall. In terms of calculating the grade, Statecraft offers a number of in-system options.

Manual quizzes
The Student Manual details all aspects of the options available to students as well as the various scenarios that will occur. The manual is 41 pages long; the quizzes occur during the first two turns of the simulation, Turn Zero and Turn One. Using the manual quizzes helps a great deal, as knowledge of the manual helps students navigate the simulation. The system has a gradebook function which provides quiz scores to the instructor.

Memos
Each student can write one weekly memo – the system allows one memo per turn per student (to be discussed further below). The memo can be viewed by a student's team members and by the instructor. To be accepted, the system requires memos to be at least 300 words. Beyond that, any requirements are up to the instructor. Once the simulation ends, instructors can view the completion percentage for each student using the gradebook function in Statecraft. If professors wish to use the memos to assess writing, or prefer to specify content, they can do so outside the system.

The system also gives each country points based on accomplishments it reaches during the course of the simulation. As discussed above, some of these points/awards are competitive, while others are cooperative. The points can be used as part of student grades or as bonus points.

Within the system, there is no final, summative assignment. Various options for instructors include incorporating exam questions that ask students to reflect on certain situations in Statecraft, class discussions on how theories and issues discussed in class relate to Statecraft, and a final paper that incorporates Statecraft into the class.

Number of weeks

Instructors can choose the number of turns that the simulation lasts within certain constraints. The simulation will normally run for seven to ten turns, but instructors can control how long the turns last. When setting up the simulation for class, instructors can choose which day of the week turns normally begin and when turns normally end. Each turn can be customized to be shorter or longer, and the system can automatically account for holidays. Normally, a turn runs for one week, with bidding on "big projects" occurring on Wednesdays. The end of the turn is important for system-controlled assessments: quizzes and memos are tied to turns; once the system closes for a turn, the instructor cannot reopen it to allow additional submissions.

Amount of class time

While the simulation can be used purely online, if a class is meeting in person or synchronously online, it is important to provide time for students to meet. This time should be apportioned according to how much the simulation will count towards a student's final grade. If the overall simulation accounts for 20–25% of a student's grade, class time should be apportioned accordingly. During Turns Zero and One, as students begin to become more familiar with the simulation mechanics, students will normally need 20–25 minutes to meet together to plan aspects of the simulation. Dedicating time in class to these meetings conveys the seriousness of the simulation. As the simulation progresses and students get more comfortable with it, less class time can be dedicated to allowing students to meet.

My model

I count Statecraft as 20% of a student's final grade, broken down as follows:

- 10% Manual Quizzes.
- 30% Memo Completion Grade: I have no requirements other than students make a good faith effort to summarize their team strategy and react to what is happening in the game.
- 60% Statecraft Paper: Students write a four–five page paper in which they use one or more of the theories discussed in class to explain a major occurrence (or occurrences) in the simulation and compare that situation to some real-world event.
- Bonus: I normalize the points students receive for receiving various awards. The top team receives 10 bonus points, with the other teams' points calculated from there. For example, if the top team receives 33 points in

the game, its bonus would be 10 points. Every other teams' in-game points would be divided by 3.3 to calculate their bonus.

Class Mechanics

The final consideration of how to incorporate Statecraft is the actual mechanics of using the simulation. This consideration is distinct from the amount of time to dedicate to the simulation; rather it is how to use it in class.

Setting up the simulation
Once you have determined how long to run the simulation, setting it up is relatively quick process. The website includes step-by-step instructions, including setting up a unique class code to give students to sign up, setting the turn schedule, entering the number of expected students, and entering the number of desired countries. The number of students and countries and details regarding turns can be updated until Turn Zero begins, and turns can be modified as the simulation progresses.

Introducing the simulation
While the simulation will not normally begin during the first week of class, it is a good idea to introduce the basic concept of the simulation, show students the simulation website, and clarify expectation regarding the assessment of the simulation. If you are electing to have students sign up for the simulation individually, setting a clear deadline prior to the beginning of Turn Zero is recommended, as is monitoring student sign-ups. Encourage students to read the Student Manual prior to the beginning of Turn Zero.

Turn Zero
Turn Zero can be very complicated. After dividing students into their assigned countries (which both the instructor and students can see in the system), it is important to remind students that they will need to select a government type, two attributes, elect a president, and name the country and cities. If they do not complete the naming of the country prior to the end of Turn Zero, they will be stuck with the system generated name (Country [number]).

In electing the president, remind students that the president is typically responsible for entering moves into the system; the president will set a decision key – a code that is required to make any changes or take any actions. The president can share this key but is not required by the system to do so. In selecting government type and attributes, students should begin to think about their long-range objectives in the simulation; the Student Manual is very useful in this regard.

At the end of Turn Zero, the first manual quiz is due. Students who do not complete it will not have the option to make it up.

Turn One
Turn One is the first turn when students can begin negotiating with other countries, signing treaties, and start purchasing items. At the outset of class, remind students that major purchases require significant resources and careful planning, as very little can be accomplished in one turn. Their country attributes allow them to "rush" certain purchases; they should consider the best time to use that ability.

As the countries meet, the instructor can monitor messages students send to one another, read the "news" updates the system sends students regarding events in the world, and be available to answer questions.

At the end of Turn One, the second manual quiz is due, as is the first student memo. Once the turn ends, it cannot be reopened to make up a missed quiz or memo.

Remaining turns
As the game progresses, instructors are able to monitor major events that occur in the simulation, including combat, news reports about each country and the Statecraft world, Quality of Life and resource rankings for each country, and student memos. Even if the instructor is treating memos as a completion grade, it is a good idea to read the weekly memos. They can be read outside class or while students are meeting in class.

As the meeting time for Statecraft ends, a brief discussion of what is happening in the Statecraft world can serve as a nice transition to the class topic. As discussed, the Statecraft world is exceedingly complex; invariably something has happened in each turn that lends itself as a jumping off point for the day's class.

Other tools
The Statecraft system affords instructors other ways to stay abreast of the simulation. When viewing the student list in the simulation, students can view student messages, log in as a student to view the game from a student perspective, view the gradebook, and monitor troop movements from the game's central map. Students and instructors can also take advantage of the in-game chat system that allows instant communication between countries.

CONCLUSION

The Statecraft simulation is a powerful teaching tool. While it is complex, students typically learn the system very quickly. It has proven quite popular in my classes. Since 2014 I have included two questions related to Statecraft on my anonymous electronic student evaluations. The first question asks students if they felt Statecraft was a useful tool in the class while the second asks if it should be used in the future. From 2014 on, the most frequent response has been that students believe that the simulation should remain in class and that they appreciate its inclusion in class.[1] While researchers have not been able to definitively demonstrate that Statecraft changes student perceptions of global politics, or that students completing Statecraft perform better on assessments, with the exception of Carvalho's work, professors have found that students appreciate and enjoy the simulation. This suggests that, if instructors are looking to increase student satisfaction and engagement with material, Statecraft is a useful tool. Moreover, Statecraft may make teaching certain concepts easier for instructors by providing common reference points for all students in the class.

The first semester of Statecraft often involves a steep learning curve and may require changes to adapt the simulation to the instructor's needs and teaching style. Once incorporated, it is a useful pedagogical instrument for instructors.

NOTE

1. The Likert scale language has changed over time; the most frequent response has been the top category.

9. Teaching political violence with games and simulations

Amanda Rosen and Victor Asal

INTRODUCTION

Political violence is an area of international relations that lends itself exceptionally well to the use of games and simulations. Political violence is more than just the causes and consequences of war—it is about the political decision of states and their leaders to use force against individuals or groups of people, often members of their own population. There are great games and simulations that deal with these problems in the abstract (Haynes; Jimenez; Brynen and Milante; Siegel and Young). Giving students concrete experience in this decision-making process, where their individual decisions result in their classmates losing their "lives," can be even more powerful in teaching students the concepts and theories of political violence.

Games and simulations have a largely successful history as methods of teaching political science. While their use in the classroom dates back decades (Shaw and Rosen), interest more recently has exploded with games and simulations used to teach a wide variety of topics, particularly in international relations and comparative politics (Asal; Asal, Sin, Fahrenkopf and She; Baranowski and Weir). At a minimum, simulations can lead to an increase in student engagement with the material as well as providing opportunities for skill development (Linantud and Kaftan; Rosen). When facilitated well and debriefed effectively, simulations and games can generate at least as much learning as more traditional teaching techniques, often with a longer time frame for retention (Nishikawa and Jaeger; Levin-Banchik). In short, simulations and games are firmly rooted in the pedagogical toolbox available to instructors, and it is appropriate to draw them out in service of teaching topics in political violence.

In the remainder of this chapter, we outline the concepts, theories, and approaches to teaching a course in political violence. We then present ten games and simulations that help teach these core aspects of the field, focusing on games where the decisions students make result in the immediate life or

105

death of their fellow students, and activities that require students to reflect on their own identities and decision making in times of crisis. This therefore creates a starting toolkit for instructors eager to tackle this tough subject with engaging and effective active learning techniques.

SIMULATIONS AND GAMES IN POLITICAL VIOLENCE

Political violence is a subject that lends itself well to active approaches such as simulations and games. Simulating violence in the form of "using" nuclear weapons, "killing" another player, "attacking" an ally, or seeking cease fires, peace, and counterterrorism operations can be an effective way to have students engage in experiential learning while not actually experiencing any real physical danger. So much of international relations focuses on security and violence, and yet most syllabi approach these topics from a theoretical or historical lens. While such approaches are valuable, they risk keeping these topics very abstract, leading to lost opportunities for students to understand why political violence occurs. Turning students into actors in situations of political violence can help them understand issues facing decision makers, military leaders, and individual actors, and perhaps even realize that they themselves, when put into positions of power or powerlessness, might choose to engage in violent actions.

The key concern for choosing games and simulations is the types of violent political conflict the course is going to cover. Specifically, instructors must decide if the course is going to cover interstate conflict, intrastate conflict, or both. Doing both together provides a very useful overview but has its own challenges. For example, while interstate conflict tends to take an international relations theory lens that is less applicable to intrastate conflict, the comparative politics perspective of the latter tends not to jibe well with the former. This means that a class that teaches both needs to take the time to teach two sets of theories. It also means that the games used in each are likely to be different. For example, the Avalon Hill game Diplomacy (discussed below) is a game that fits very strongly within the context of the international relations realist perspective (Asal), while the identity and poetry exercises (Asal and Griffith) we will also discuss below fit very strongly into a cultural comparative politics perspective (Lichbach and Zuckerman).

Once instructors settle on an overall theoretical lens, they must decide how to approach the material and which specific topics to cover. Some people start with the key meta-theories that will relate to the focus of international relations or comparative politics or both. Another approach is to start by looking at conflict from the perspective of history (Lawler) or human nature (Wilson 2012, 99–120) or psychology (Cashman, 49–114) or some combination thereof and then bringing in political science theories. Some instructors also discuss the difference between violent and nonviolent contention (negotiations and protests). One can also examine the actual mechanics of political violence on the ground. Many political violence courses in political science and international relations do not do this, but it can be very useful for the students to get a somewhat better idea of what is involved on the ground when it comes to organized political violence. The Dalig and Vadan game (Asal, Griffith, and Schulzke) discussed below relates directly to this by dividing the class into two warring sides and having them go outside and physically fight a battle of sorts. All of this can lead into a very useful discussion of the components of political violence at the international or domestic level or both applying the key theoretical meta-theoretical arguments to the different components of conflict. We should note that at least for intrastate political violence it is important to include state violence against their population which is not always covered in civil war syllabi.

One way to approach a course is to start with the link that has been made between human nature and the use of violence (Hobbes; Wilson 2012), the psychology of violence (Cashman), and what is the base of social conflict and contention (Rubin et al.). Then you can move into the basics of negotiation as well as the basics of tactics on the battlefield—something that often is left out of courses on political violence—and pivot to the causes of both domestic and international conflict, touching on topics like power politics at the international level and culture, inequality and identity and grievance at the domestic level. Then give a specific focus on the issue of targeting and killing civilians and the factors that make certain states and organizations more likely to do so. The games and simulations we discuss below relate directly to many of these areas.

There are two other topics which are not always covered in conflict syllabi that are important to help the students understand conflict and its ramifications on politics and people. One of these topics, often excluded from syllabi, is the ethics of political violence. Helping students understand the moral challenges of political violence and the choices that soldiers, leaders and rebels need to make—and how hard those choices can be—is, we believe, extremely important. Below we discuss an exercise that situates students in ethical dilemmas in the realm of political violence and asks them to make decisions about what to do (Asal and Schulzke). Another area often overlooked in the discussion of political violence is the place of gender in understanding political violence. Adding this to a class can be very useful for opening the eyes of students to how gender impacts war and political violence generally.

In the section below we will discuss a variety of exercises and simulations you can add to your class to help your students actively experience important aspects of these challenging environments.

GAMES AND SIMULATIONS FOR TEACHING POLITICAL VIOLENCE

There are many games and simulations that can be used to teach theories, concepts, and cases of political violence in the college classroom. Some are created explicitly to do so, like the Dalig and Vadan game, Identity and Poetry Exercises, and mini ethical case studies. Other games and simulations—such as the Hobbes Game, Model Diplomacy, and Statecraft—can be used to teach a variety of concepts in political science, and present opportunities for instructors to tailor their focus and debrief on issues in political violence. Still other games are not designed with an educational purpose at all, but can be adapted to teach concepts of political violence, like the board game Diplomacy or the party game Werewolf, sometimes known as Mafia. Here, we synthesize a non-exhaustive list of such games and simulations, drawing from published articles in the scholarship of teaching and learning as well as touting several games that have not yet been explored in the literature. Table 9.1 lists all the games, simulations and exercises we talk about in this chapter and the concepts and theories they address.

Table 9.1   Exercises discussed and related concepts and theories

Exercise	Concepts and theories
Dalig and Vadan	Clausewitzian theory of war; friction and fog; basic tactics
Identity and poetry exercises	Culture and conflict; identity and conflict; nationalism
Mini ethical case studies	Kant; utilitarianism, and Aristotelian Virtue Ethics; military ethics
The Hobbes Game	Realism; Hobbes; individual choices of violence
Statecraft	Realism, nationalism, international conflict, terrorism, negotiation, deterrence
Diplomacy	Realism; power competition; international conflict; negotiation and deceit
Werewolf, Red Card game, and social deception games	State propaganda; atomization; civil conflict; ethics

Dalig and Vadan

For most students, their only "experience" with the battlefield (if any) are video games where one often gets right back up after being shot. In such games, many real-world challenges of that environment are often minimized, as communication between teammates is easily achieved through their headphones, and the game continually provides you with key information to track your progress. You generally know, for example, if you managed to shoot your enemy as you track their health bar on your screen, and you know just how much damage your own forces have sustained. If one wishes students to have some sense of the challenges that soldiers face on the battlefield and to have a much better sense of what Clausewitz calls "friction and fog," the Dalig and Vadan game (Asal, Griffith, and Schulzke) can be very useful. The game provides students with a first-person perspective on the challenge of actual conflict with people thinking that their comrades are going in one direction while they actually go in the other. The game is similar to the Capture the Flag game but with some changes that make it more challenging. A class is divided into two sides and each side has a commander. The game is played outside and each commander is on one side of the area where the game is played. Each side is also given two production centers placed midway between where the commander is and where the border between the two sides is located. Each side can win by killing their opponent's commander or capturing both of their production centers. Before the game starts the commander is given a certain number of points that they can assign to each player in one of three attributes: movement, defense and offense. The commander is not allowed to move and must use their voice to communicate to their fighters.

Moves are simultaneous and the attacker is determined by touch: Anyone who touches someone else first becomes an attacker and uses their offense score against the person they touched, who will use their defense score. Attackers and defenders compare points, and whoever has the most points lives, and the other person dies. Fighters can stack their defense and offense points by holding hands with their compatriots. As the game goes on fighters often end up not doing what the commander wants and communication from their fixed position can often be not heard or understood. The game can be very helpful for highlighting how hard and confusing combat can be—an experiential version of the famous Leeroy Jenkins video, where a team of 40 people carefully plots out a strategy to defeat an encounter in the game World of Warcraft, only for Leeroy to just run straight into combat with no warning and no plan. As one student said about Dalig and Vadan: "Damn that was a hell of a lot harder than a video game." One can see a short video of the game being played and students discussing the game here: https://www.youtube.com/watch?v=tJoiAlxqgME (accessed November 10, 2020).

Identity and Poetry Exercises

The identity and poetry exercises (Asal and Griffith) are very useful for getting students to think about identity and identity salience and how this can impact how they feel about the world and various groups—which can then be applied to how connections and people's cultural milieu can impact their involvement in conflict (Lichbach and Zuckerman). The identity exercise is one that is very personal and it is very important that the instructor make clear that they will request from the class as a whole to share what they have written—if they are comfortable doing so—but no student will be asked specifically or forced to share. The students are then asked to write down their five top identities that make them part of a larger group. Examples are given such as a woman, an American or a Christian. Students write them down on a piece of paper or on their computer. The students are then asked, if they had to give one up, which one would it be? Then they are asked to give up another one by one until they are left with only one identity. This can often be very challenging for students but it is important to push them to make their own choice and pick what they would not give up under any circumstance.

The instructor then requests the categories of identities that were written down and writes down all the different categories that students volunteer. These almost always include gender, national identity, religious identity, sports fan of a particular team and others. The instructor can then ask if people are comfortable to ask who listed a particular identity. Often the results are important for a discussion of identity. Generally, men are much less likely to say gender, white people are much less likely to say race, and so on. The students then are asked to raise their hand as each identity category is read if it was their last one—and, if no one raises their hand, it is crossed off. This usually reduces a list of 20 to four or five identities. The students are then asked: Why are these the identities you wouldn't give up? For many students the reasoning is similar and either one where they felt discriminated for being part of that group or it is an identity that their parents pushed very hard for them to focus on. This can lead to a very powerful discussion about how identity and discrimination can lead to mobilization and violence.

The poetry exercise should follow the identity exercise and is another way for the students to relate the identity exercise directly to the use of identity to mobilize people into nationalist and other kinds of identity conflicts. In this exercise you can either ask students to find one or two nationalist poems or songs to share with the class or you can assign them poems or songs. One good way to demonstrate to the students what kind of poem or song they should be looking for is to share with them The Proclaimers song "Cap in Hand" which can be found here: https://www.youtube.com/results?search_query=cap+in+hand+ (accessed November 10, 2020). A poem that can be useful for demonstrating what you are asking them to look for is "Easter 1916" (Stanza IV) by William Butler Yates. Once the students have brought in their poems, they are asked to break into smaller groups and discuss the poems and talk about different questions like how the poem makes you feel and how the poem could be used to mobilize or incite. We have found this to be a very effective tool for getting the students to understand the uses of nationalism and the impact of it on a personal level.

Mini Ethical Case Studies

While some classes on political violence specifically cover the ethical challenges that war and insurgency can create, many do not. The mini ethical case studies (Asal and Schulzke) are a way to push your students not only to understand that ethics is a part of the use of violence, and that many soldiers are trained about the ethics of violence, but also how incredibly hard making ethical decisions can be under short time constraints and the threat of death or destruction. Students are first briefed on the moral perspectives of Kant, utilitarianism and Aristotelian Virtue Ethics. The exercise breaks the students in a class into smaller groups. All the groups are simultaneously told a brief scenario related to a real life situation on the battle field, and they have a short time to decide what the right move is for them to do. Once they have done so they are asked to explain to the class what their choice was and what ethical perspective motivated them to go in that direction. The discussions in both the smaller groups and the larger class are very useful and help the students understand very different perspectives on violence and morals and the tremendous challenges that political violence often creates for individuals.

There are three scenarios to be used, one related to state and nonstate violence, one related to a decision to bomb or not bomb a village where terrorists might be hiding, and one related to torture and a potential ticking time bomb. This exercise is extremely useful for helping students to see the impact of political violence through their own eyes more directly as well as making them much more aware of how hard it can be to try be ethical and humane when political violence is being used and the challenge that is there and that needs to be addressed by soldiers, commanders and leaders on a regular basis. Students have said repeatedly how powerful and important they have found this exercise. They have also said that the exercise is one of the first where they have actually learned about the ethical approaches used in the simulation and the importance of learning about these approaches to morality—particularly within the context of political violence.

The Hobbes Game

The Hobbes Game (Asal) is one that can be used in Introduction to International Relations classes as well as political violence classes, and therefore is one of those versatile games that can be adapted for teaching these concepts. It gives students a very personal view into the realist perspective and the logic of international conflict by giving them the choice of whether or not to "kill" their fellow students in order to win a prize. This game can be used in the first class of the semester to introduce students to the basics of conflict from a realist perspective or later in the semester when discussing international conflict and realist theory. More importantly, the game is a strong fit for a political violence class because it creates a situation where students are placed in a situation where many choose to be violent with their compatriots—and can then discuss after the game from a personal perspective the different motivating factors driving someone to choose (simulated) violence as the right course of action.

In this game each student is given a random playing card and told if they have a playing card at the end of the game they will get a half grade bonus on the next quiz (or some other reward the instructor deems appropriate). The students are also told that they can challenge their classmates to a Rock Paper Scissors game and whoever wins gets all of the other person's cards. A student does not need to challenge but if challenged the student must fight. For a short period of time they can get another card from the instructor if they die but, at some point, if they lose their cards, they are dead and must sit down. They are not told at any time that more cards gives you more power—it doesn't—or that more cards gives you a bigger reward. Invariably most of the students fight until all the students are dead but two or three. The instructor can then stop the game and ask the living students what the point of the game is. The answers vary but regularly there are answers such as:

"Killing everyone else to win."

"To get the most cards."

"Protecting myself by getting more cards."

The professor can then ask the dead students sitting down what the point of the game is—to which at least some of the students will respond: not to fight. Some students will insist that there can be only one winner but that was never the case but an assumption, but many students will have realized that they all could have gotten the bonus if they had just cooperated. The instructor can then show them this quote from Hobbes:

> In the nature of man, we find three principal causes of quarrel: First, competition; secondly, diffidence (fear), thirdly, glory. The first maketh man invade for gain; the second, for safety; and the third, for reputation. (Hobbes, 220)

This leads to a very productive conversation about the reasons for political violence and the motives of leaders—as well as the application of various theories to the exercise. The Hobbes Game can be played in as little as 15 minutes,

Teaching political violence with games and simulations

although iterating the game (and adding in new elements such as power or culture) can stretch the game out to an hour or more.

Statecraft

Statecraft is a fully online simulation (www.statecraftsims.com [accessed April 15, 2021]) that positions students as leaders of a country in a fictional world that faces real-world problems such as civil unrest, terrorism, climate change, and improving quality of life for their people. Working in teams, students select their country's form of government and key characteristics, and then research technologies and build improvements in education, health care, military, and other key policy areas. As they do this, they can choose to cooperate with or fight their fellow students, but if they ignore certain areas of global cooperation (such as climate change), all their other efforts will be wasted. Gameplay proceeds in turns, with students having a set amount of time to negotiate with other teams, manage their resources and choose their actions, often responding to news reports that clue them in on world events and upcoming crises.

Like Model Diplomacy, Statecraft has utility as an educational game beyond teaching political violence. Through careful priming and debriefing, students can use their own experience in the game to better understand concepts of terrorism and counterterrorism, deterrence, negotiation and diplomacy, the causes of conflict and nationalism. Some studies have shown that playing Statecraft can impact student attitudes toward foreign policy, although Saiya (2017) found that it moderated both hawks and doves while Linantud and Kaftan found that it increased hawkish tendencies in students. This raises the suggestion that instructor focus can matter in how students interpret the simulation or game. Generally, Statecraft is played over the course of an entire semester, but could also be condensed to play over a single week or two if multiple hours are devoted to it.

Diplomacy

Diplomacy is a classic board game that can be used in class to highlight classical realism as well as the challenges that negotiation and trust can present in a very conflictual world. This game has been used both in its current format (Asal) and with a variety of extensions (Mattlin) and online (Bridge and Radford; Arnold) to teach about realism, war, great power conflict and negotiations. The game is set in 1900 Europe with seven countries taking part. There are 35 supply centers spread throughout the map both in countries under the control of a player and some in open spaces. Each turn is either a fall turn or a spring turn. A country wins by controlling 18 supply centers at the end of a spring turn. Every spring turn the number of supply centers are counted up and players lose forces if they have fewer supply centers than forces or gain forces if they have more—if they have an open supply center in their home country. It is a game that is supposed to be won by one player (although many players will accept coalition wins) but no one can progress without alliances throughout the game. Besides which country a player is assigned, there is no luck in the game—no dice or any other luck manufacturer. Winning and losing is determined totally by effective negotiation, effective alliances and the use of force judiciously and hopefully in the right direction at the right time.

The game can be played in a variety of modalities. If played entirely in class, the instructor should plan to use at least four classes for the game to develop properly. The game can also be played entirely online over the course of a semester using one of many platforms such as Play Diplomacy Online (https://www.playdiplomacy.com [accessed April 15, 2021]). A third alternative is a hybrid style. Students negotiate outside class time and turn their moves in at the start of class. The instructor adjudicates, creates a writeup of the results along with an updated map (easily created in PowerPoint), and emails that to the students, who prepare their next moves. We should note that students can either be teamed up in groups of two, three or four for each country, or multiple games can be played in the class so that the game can be used in classes of up to 30+ students. Even though the game Diplomacy takes a significant amount of time, many students have said that it has had a huge impact on their understanding of international relations and the realist perspective. Beyond an understanding of realism and its views on international conflict, the game gives students an excellent understanding of several key aspects of political violence at the international level. The game shines a light on why states will launch attacks against others related to the desire for power as well as the fear of attack. It makes clear how powerful deceit can be in starting conflicts and how useful deceit can sometimes be in triumphing in international conflict. It also sheds an important light on the impact that the personality of leaders can have on state-to-state interactions and how clashing perspectives can lead some to be allied while leading others to be enemies.

Werewolf, Red Card Game, and Social Deception Games

One final style of game that is effective at teaching political violence is the broad category of social deception games, where players to deceive each other about their assigned role within the game. One type of social deception game is a cooperative game of social deduction where the players work together as a team to find and disable the traitors or villains in their midst, who are pretending to be regular players. There are many commercial games that use this kind of mechanic, including Resistance, Avalon and Secret Hitler, but the version most people might know is called Werewolf or Mafia. In this game, most players are ordinary villagers, tasked with finding the werewolves (or mafia members) in their midst. Simple playing cards are given to each student, the values of which determine whether they are villager or villain. Each "night," the villagers go to sleep, closing their eyes while those students secretly assigned the villain role—werewolves or mafia—indicate to the moderator their chosen victim. The villagers awaken, find out which of their own has been killed, and then discuss amongst themselves whodunnit. They must choose the person they think guilty and kill them. That person reveals their true identity, and the game continues until either all the werewolves or villagers are eliminated.

This game can be very effective at teaching students about how states can atomize their citizens, whip up paranoia and encourage violence. From a meta perspective, the only reason students believe that either a werewolf exists or that they must kill one of their own each round is because the instructor tells them so. This can be a very effective way of showing students about how some will accept the word of an authority figure without question and engage in acts of violence without evidence. On the flimsiest of excuses a person can be chosen at the end of the round as the "werewolf" and, even as the entire village dies, students never try to stop the game on the grounds that they don't want to kill each other anymore. Granted, part of that is that the game is fun and students enjoy playing it, but the lesson remains, and opens up the class for discussion of similar circumstances in the "real world" where the stakes of disobedience are much higher.

You can actually play Werewolf or Mafia without ever designating anyone to play the villainous role. As the moderator, the instructor (alongside any "dead" students) is the only one with their eyes open, so you can just select the victims yourself, perhaps by choosing those most vocally accusing others, to send a message that staying quiet can buy you your life.

Another game, the Red Card game, is based on this premise. In this game, divide students into small groups and give each group a pack of playing cards. Ask them to build a card tower, with a prize going to whoever has the tallest tower at the end of the allotted time. Pass out a separate playing card to each student, telling them that on each team, someone will secretly get a "red card" that means their fortunes rise and fall with the team *next* to them—meaning they have every incentive to betray the team they are working with. As card towers are built and topple over, accusations of betrayal will fly between the students. And at the end of the game, you of course reveal that there were no red cards—just a Red Scare.

Werewolf, Mafia, and Red Card can be played in classes as small as eight and as large as several hundred, depending on your supply of playing cards. With large classes, you can divide up the students into several different "worlds" of about 20 students, with a teaching assistant (TA) moderating each group. While Red Card does not adapt well to online play, Werewolf can be played completely online via teleconferencing or on a discussion board or chatting app. Players can use the private chat or email to communicate with the moderator about roles and victims. A single game can take as little as 30 minutes to play.

CONCLUSION

In conclusion, political violence is an area of political science that particularly benefits from the use of games and simulations. By putting students in the role of decision makers, they have to grapple with whether or not to use force against their fellow students. Sometimes this takes the role of using the rules of the game to make students question their eagerness to "kill" each other when seemingly told to by their instructor, as in the Hobbes Game or Werewolf. In other cases, students are placed on the battlefield, making decisions under conditions of fog and friction, as in Dalig and Vadan. At other times, they have to use skills in diplomacy and negotiation as they decide whether to respond to crises or aggression with military action, as in Diplomacy, Statecraft or Model Diplomacy. Or perhaps you just ask them to think deeply about how their own identity and ethical outlooks might affect their perspective and ideology when it comes to decisions to use force against others, as in the identity exercise or mini ethical case studies.

This chapter does not attempt to provide an exhaustive list of games that can be used to teach core concepts, theories or issues of political violence, but to give instructors a starting kit as they move into this space. Some of the games we review here take just 15 minutes while others require an entire semester's investment. All of them have educational value, however, making the investment in time worthwhile in the outcomes of raising student engagement and deepening learning.

10. Teaching with the IR theory toolkit
Eric K. Leonard

THE IMPORTANCE OF PROCESS, NOT JUST CONTENT

Teaching international relations (IR) theory to undergraduate, non-majors in a survey-level class is difficult. That seems to be a statement that most instructors can agree upon. This chapter is about the journey to make that topic more accessible to students and the rationale as to why the teaching of IR theory is so important to the introductory level student. The primary idea behind the building your IR theory toolkit method is that at the survey level it is often more important to help students develop a set of skills (process) rather than ascertain a detailed understanding of the course material (content). Such an approach draws on much of the Association of American Colleges & Universities (AAC&U 2020) literature on liberal education (AAC&U). Liberal education is defined as, "an approach to undergraduate education that promotes integration of learning across the curriculum and cocurriculum, and between academic and experiential learning, in order to develop specific learning outcomes that are essential for work, citizenship, and life" (AAC&U 2020). In short, liberal education involves students, in the process of their education, creating a place where they can own that process and work on skills that will assist in their educational journey, their future career, and their place in a democratic society. It is an approach to higher education that is active, engaged, and challenging, but also necessitates a different approach to the classroom. It entails an approach that softens the emphasis on content and, instead, uses content as a means to emphasize process and skill building.

Two words that are an integral part of the liberal education literature are *active* and *engaged*. These terms are also an essential part of building your IR theory toolkit. The scholarship of teaching and learning (SOTL) has shown that an active and engaged environment is one that benefits the students for a variety of reasons (Johnson et al.; Omelicheva and Avdeyeva). The introductory chapter to this book provides a wonderful summary of these different advantages, but with this chapter's focus on process building, the main benefit of the active engaged classroom is student ownership over course material

(Pintrich). Active students must be engaged in the course material. As a result, they must take greater control or ownership over their education. They cannot act as empty vessels that show up for class ready for the instructor to fill them with knowledge while they passively listen, take notes, and regurgitate information. Instead, they must engage the course material, their peers, the instructor, and the process by which they gain knowledge. The result is independent, critical thinkers who can articulate their thoughts and work through these problems within a group. In short, the result is a productive member of a democratic society who will succeed within their chosen profession (Davidson). And, as I will show throughout this chapter, that process can occur in a multiplicity of pedagogical delivery methods. The key is to stay true to what you are trying to achieve and the overall goals of your pedagogical approach. Building your IR theory toolkit is one example of how an instructor may embrace this set of outcomes.

MY JOURNEY TO THE TOOLKIT METHOD

To illuminate how I came to this moment of pedagogical enlightenment, let's begin with a story about how the phrase, "building your IR theory toolbox" came about. It was years and years ago at an annual International Studies Association (ISA) conference, and I was having a discussion with several of my colleagues about teaching the Introduction to IR course. During this conversation, several of my colleagues mentioned the difficult nature of teaching IR theory to survey-level students, many of whom are not IR or political science majors. For some of my colleagues, their frustrations resulted in dropping that content from the course. They believed that instead of struggling and fighting an uphill battle of teaching an intellectually difficult set of concepts that has no real bearing on the students' future career goals (since most of these students were non-majors), they decided that course time was better spent on other topics. Although I sympathized with their frustrations, noting that teaching IR theory to non-majors was difficult, I refused to submit to the idea that this theoretical content should be jettisoned from the class. It seemed that something about this content was essential to the student's education, but I wasn't quite sure why. What I did realize was that, if IR theory was going to be accessible to the typical non-major undergraduate, I had to rethink my approach to the introductory level course, in terms of both my own pedagogical style and the outcomes that I adopted for the course. This was also the moment that the idea of building a student's "toolkit" began to take hold.

At about the same time as this conversation occurred, two of my other colleagues were publishing a wonderful article on how to teach social constructivism to the introductory level student. Alice Ba and Matt Hoffman's article, "Making and Remaking the World for IR 101: A Resource for Teaching Social

Constructivism in Introductory Classes," was a pedagogical game changer in terms of how they approached teaching the difficult subject of social constructivism to a survey-level course. In short, this article was a roadmap for how to make social constructivism accessible to the introductory level student. I employed the tactics discussed in this article and even had students read the article, although the authors did not necessarily intend it for student consumption, and I noticed that it resulted in greater understanding of the theory and its applications. It created a technique for teaching IR theory that was accessible and engaging for the students. Simply put, it personalized the theory rather than discussing it solely from an abstract, academic perspective.

But what exactly was it about this article and its tactics that had worked? Was it simply the roadmap that Ba and Hoffmann had provided or was there more to students understanding IR theory? And how could I take these tactics and apply them to the other theoretical perspectives and other course material? The last piece of the puzzle came about in the conversations with my soon to be editor. I would meet with Susan McEachern at most ISA conferences to discuss pedagogy and it was during one of these conversations that the notion of students building their IR theory toolkit came about (Leonard). After several discussion about a possible IR theory textbook it occurred to me that there was more to teaching theory than simply teaching theory. Students could benefit greatly from the exploration and application of IR theory, but those benefits extended well beyond the content of the topic. In short, I realized survey-level students, that were typically non-majors, should absolutely learn IR theory. However, in order to make that content accessible and relevant for the students, I would have to reorient my course and its outcomes. The focus of this chapter is that reorientation of outcomes and what that meant for not only my Introduction to IR course, but my general pedagogical approach.

BACKWARD DESIGN TO ENGAGE PROCESS

When I first began teaching Introduction to IR survey courses, I felt the most important aspect of the course was to provide my students with knowledge about the field. I think that is typical of newly minted PhDs that have spent years studying the intricacies of the discipline and now feel it is their mandate to give that knowledge to their students. Many of you may still think that such a content-oriented approach to the course is the proper one. And you wouldn't be wrong, if that is the desired goal for your course. It is important to recognize at the outset of this chapter that there is no one-size fits all in terms of teaching the Introduction to IR course. I am going to lay out the rationale for why I transformed my course and provide justification for such an approach. However, I think it is important to understand that professors must determine what the purpose of their course is going to be. With that said, professors should start with an understanding of what it is they want to achieve in their course. This may seem intuitive and simple, but I have reviewed many a course syllabus where the absence of course outcomes is the norm, not the exception. When I fully embraced this notion of course design, my pedagogical approach changed.

To talk about course design as starting with learning outcomes is to talk about a learner-centered approach (Barr and Tagg), coupled with backward design (Wiggins and McTighe). For many professors, the way to set up your course is to think about the learning activities that you will employ in your course first, then develop assessments for those activities, and finally connect this to a set of learning outcomes. This "forward design" process is, admittedly, how I would set up my courses during the early part of my career. I was so concerned with what my students would do in class and how I would assess them, I did not consider if these activities fit a pre-determined set of course outcomes. Instead, I would create the course activities and then connect them to a set of outcomes that I constructed as an afterthought.

Backward design implores the instructor to create the learning goals or outcomes first, then create the assessment of those goals, and finally work on the activities or experiences that students engage to achieve these goals. According to Davidovitch:

Backward design answers three questions:

- What will the student know and be able to do, in general, by the end of the course, independent of the activities and texts used?
- What evidence is there of such abilities?
- Which texts, activities, and methods will best serve the desired results?

When applying this form of course design to an Introduction to IR course, the instructor should start by considering Davidovitch's first question: What will the students learn, not only in the course, but also in each module? This necessitates a learner-centered approach to pedagogy, as well as an increased focus on intentionality when constructing your course (Gannon). But when thinking about IR theory, it also necessitates a rethinking of the purpose of teaching IR theory. Is the purpose of teaching IR theory to provide students with a detailed understanding of the main theories and their application in studying global politics? And is this even an attainable outcome for non-political science students in a survey-level course? But if the point isn't a detailed understanding of the content, then why teach IR theory? This is the dilemma that I and my colleagues were debating and why instructors often give up on teaching theory. Those that give up on teaching theory tend to believe that the purpose of teaching theory is content driven, meaning that students study IR theory solely to understand the intricacies of the theories themselves. A learning outcome based on this perspective might look like this: "At the conclusion of this course students will be able to detail the foundational principles of the main theories of the discipline." There is nothing wrong with this outcome and, in fact, my own module outcomes often contain similar goals. But for the typical non-major undergraduate sitting in your introductory level course, is this outcome attainable or even desirable? And even if it is attainable, what benefit will this outcome provide the non-major? To take this questioning a step further, how much of this content-oriented information will students retain after taking your class? If you were to meet your student five years in the future and ask them to explain the co-constitutive nature of social constructivism, could they do it? I seriously doubt it, unless they went to graduate school to study international politics.

So, what to do? I decided that IR theory was something that I wanted to maintain in my course, but the reason for teaching theory had to change. Instead of teaching theory for the sake of theory, I decided to teach theory because of all the other skills that it provides students. At its core, a theoretical assessment of the global community requires that students engage in critical thinking. This becomes evident when reviewing the AAC&U definition of critical thinking as "a habit of mind characterized by the comprehensive exploration of issues, ideas, artifacts, and events before accepting or formulating an opinion or conclusion." Further exploration of their rubric shows that engagement of IR theory is an exercise in critical thinking due to its emphasis on comprehensive explanations of issues/events, the need to provide evidence to support own's perspective, an understanding of the context, and the formation of logical conclusions concerning that issue or event (AAC&U n.d.b). By having students read articles and chapters discussing these theories, they are engaging in critical reading and, by applying to these theories to global events, they are engaged in critical thinking. Finally, I also feel it important to have students work on communication skills and information literacy, along with the ability to collaborate with their peers. All these process-oriented outcomes can occur in the study of IR theory, if you start with the understanding that these are the desired outcomes. In fact, these skills are a big part of the IR theory toolkit because, without these skills, the ability to apply the actual theories to situations within the global community is difficult if not impossible. These skills also establish a foundation that IR students can use to gain future employment and perform as productive citizens within a democratic society (Lightfoot).

This approach to a broader process-oriented undergraduate education has always been part of the pedagogical debate concerning higher education, but its recent revitalization appears to be in response to the latest attempts to devalue a university degree (Davidson; Gannon) and the forfeiture of liberal education values in our higher education curriculum (Nussbaum). In my courses the movement to process-oriented outcomes was a result of a need I saw in my students and that need was not content-oriented. In fact, as I saw it, the focus of the debate on whether to teach IR theory to non-major undergraduates was faulty because it centered on the content of the material. In considering whether to teach IR theory in an introductory course, the primary question that instructors were asking was, could non-majors in a survey-level course understand the intricacies of IR theory? However, that was the wrong question. The question instructors should ask is, if students learn about IR theory, what can that knowledge provide in terms of their overall education, their job preparedness, and their role as a productive member of a democratic society? The premise of building your IR theory toolkit is about providing students with the tools to employ when trying to understand and evaluate the actions of global actors, but also to fulfill all the premises listed in the refined question.

FLIP IT TO CREATE AN ENGAGED CLASSROOM

Once I realized that my outcomes were more process-oriented and less content driven I had to adjust the assessment plan and the course activities. This brings me to the final means of building the student's toolkit—flipped learning. Flipped learning is an approach to teaching that reorients how a professor uses the students' time outside the classroom and the face-to-face (F2F) time (Talbert). In a typical classroom (the traditional model), the class meeting time is used to introduce students to new material and disseminate information typically through a lecture. The out of class time or the non-F2F time is when students engage in higher-level learning activities that require them to analyze, evaluate, and create. The rationale behind this model is that professors would use the initial F2F time to "fill up" the students with information via a lecture. In essence, professors have the knowledge and they will give this knowledge to the students. Only when students have this information, as disseminated by the professor, can they apply that material and evaluate a situation or topic. But the flipped learning method turns this model on its head (Mazur et al.).

In flipped learning the initial interaction or first contact with the course material occurs outside of the F2F classroom (individual space time). In most instances this occurs in an asynchronous format with students possibly engaging a short lecture on the topic, along with the other requisite course materials (readings, videos, statistics, etc.). It is during this first contact that students begin to understand and accurately describe the content. This is a form of low-level learning that requires less intensive faculty guidance. Once students ascertain, or at least work through this low-level of learning, they come to class and engage in higher-level learning. The students spend their F2F time (or groups space time) analyzing, evaluating, and creating, rather than passively listening to a lecture (Bergmann and Sams). If one were to flip their class, the instructor should follow these five steps for the flipped module:

1. Set the objectives/outcomes for the module or the topic.
2. Establish what the group space exercise will entail.
3. Determine what individual space material students require so that they are prepared for the group space activity.
4. Create an assessment tool about what knowledge students gained in the individual space.
5. Follow up and debrief the students.

But what is the benefit of flipping the classroom from a traditional course to a flipped course? And how does this fit with the method of building your IR theory toolkit? For those that advocate for the flipped learning method, the benefits are numerous. First, the students must take "ownership" of their work. As described earlier, what is meant by that phrase is that students must take greater responsibility for their studies and their initial interaction with the course material. Because the flipped classroom employs the individual space as the initial contact with new material, students must take control of their learning process and the sources that constitute the foundation for their knowledge (Talbert). This control over lower-level learning teaches students to regulate their preparation for higher-level learning. Flipped learning scholars often referred to this as self-regulated learning (Talbert). A self-regulated learner sees learning "as an activity that students do for themselves in a proactive way rather than as a covert event that happens to them in reaction to teaching" (Zimmerman, 65). Thus, self-regulated learners control their learning process and engage in that process with an understanding of what is necessary to succeed and how to achieve success (Pintrich). This form of learning is a quintessential skill of the IR theory toolkit because it provides students with the ability to learn how to learn. If they don't take this portion of the flipped classroom seriously, they will struggle in the group space.

Second, flipped learning allows faculty to be present when students are engaged in higher-level learning and the cultivation of the skills that are necessary when students are analyzing, evaluating, and creating. In the traditional model, the group space would be a time of lecture and passive learning. It would be a moment when the sage on the stage (the instructor) would give students the knowledge that was necessary to pass the course. Students would then carry the knowledge that they had memorized and describe it into the individual space where they would attempt to apply this knowledge or appraise its value to the academic discipline. In the flipped learning model, we flip both the relationship between the instructor and student, and the student and course material. The instructor's role is not to fill the student with facts to memorize

124 *Teaching international relations*

or an understanding of cognitive knowledge that they could acquire, albeit with some guidance from the instructor, on their own. The instructor's role is to be present when students take that initial knowledge and apply it, evaluate it, assess it, and even create new knowledge.

Third, flipped learning allows for a greater emphasis on active learning and, in particular, active learning within the group space. Several studies have shown that active learning is a more beneficial method of learning than passive, lecture-based learning (Freeman et al.; Johnson et al. 1998; Omelicheva and Avdeyeva). What these studies have shown is that students engaged in an active learning environment, regardless of the form of active learning, understand the material at a higher level and retain more information. This is not to say that all studies show an increase in learning when active learning is present (Lawrence and Lester). However, most studies appear to support this link. In flipped learning, the focus of the group space is on active learning. In fact, flipped learning only works when the instructor creates an environment that embraces the basic pedagogical method of active learning.

PUTTING THIS INTO PRACTICE

So far, this chapter has described the rationale for the building your toolkit approach to teaching. Now is the time to provide a more practical view of this approach. In this section, I describe an actual course module that exemplifies this approach. Just as it is important that we model for our students, it is also important to model for our colleagues and the goal of this discussion is to provide that model of how this approach works in practice.

After providing an overview of IR theory and having students investigate the purpose of theory, the course moves to a module on the foundational principles of realism. Per the principle of backward design, prior to setting up the assignments or the exercises I establish the module outcomes. There are four outcomes:

1. Describe the foundational principles of realism.
2. Explain how a neorealist alters the classical principles of realism.
3. Demonstrate how realism would assess a real-world situation.
4. Appraise the ability of realism to understand twenty-first century world politics.

Notice that the outcomes progress from low-level learning (remembering and understanding) to higher-level learning (analysis and evaluation). In order to fulfill the lower-level learning outcomes, students begin the module in an online asynchronous mode. At this time, they will read the chapter on realism, watch a 15-minute Panopto lecture, and complete a short assignment that will ask them to accomplish both outcomes #1 and #2. This assignment is due the morning of our F2F class time. It is important that the instructor has time to review the students' answers and assess their basic understanding of the theory prior to the group space. The F2F time is spent engaging a collaborative learning exercise. In base groups of three to five students, the class engages in an analysis of a hypothetical global politics situation of the instructor's choosing. During the spring of 2020, I provided students with a situation like the Myanmar crisis and the mass atrocities being committed in that territory. I then asked them to evaluate how realism would assess this situation and whether they felt this was an accurate understanding of the situation. In these base groups, every student must provide an initial answer to the question. This provides a means by which to facilitate universal participation in the conversation. After that initial response, the group engages in a discussion about the scenario and then crafts a short summary of their assessment that they will share with the entire class. One key aspect of this discussion is that a few minutes into the exercise I pause the conversation and ask if the groups have any questions of clarification concerning the hypothetical. This is crucial moment in the assessment process because their questions tell me a lot about their initial assessment and evaluation of the situation. After the groups have all shared the evaluation of the situation, the class engages in a debriefing discussion in which clarification of key points can occur and students can ask further questions.

If performing this in an online class, the discussions detailed above would occur within either a Google doc discussion board or a discussion board within my learning management system. The class can perform this exercise synchronously or asynchronously, but the key is to create an organic discussion amongst the group's members and a summary of that conversation so that the rest of the students can see the conclusions of the other groups. The instructor would also be involved in those discussions, in order to answer questions, and provide a short debrief video that engages the groups' summaries.

One of the important things to recognize about the exercises in this module is that they connect back to the broader outcomes encompassed in the notion of building your IR theory toolkit. Earlier in this chapter I stated that content-oriented outcomes were not quintessential to my courses. Yet, these four outcomes have a solid basis in the content of IR theory. But the course outcomes that these module-level outcomes feed into are much broader and more process-oriented. If students can achieve the four outcomes for the realism module, they have started down the path of being able to achieve the course outcomes. These include an improvement of students' critical reading skills, a capacity to think critically, the ability to articulate their ideas in both a written and oral format, and, most important, the capability to learn how to learn. These process-oriented skills are the tools within the IR theory toolbox, not just the specifics of the theories themselves.

Thus far, I have mentioned the positives of this exercise, but there are plenty of pitfalls that can and will emerge as you try to implement a flipped classroom. Let me begin this discussion by stating that failures are not a reason to abandon the flipped learning model. In fact, failure is part of the process and instructors must be willing to fail. I will detail a few obstacles and issues in this exercise because these are all issues I have dealt with in my classroom. But those failures allowed me to learn, adjust, and improve. The result is a better structured group space exercise with a strong foundational individual space assignment.

The first issue that many professors encounter is a lack of participation within the group space, whether that group space occurs face-to-face or online. The most common reason for this lack of participation is inadequate preparation by the students. We have all run into the issue of students not reading or engaging the required course material. The easiest way to cope with this issue is a formative assessment exercise that tests their understanding of the course material. These assignments do not need to be high stakes and can often take the format of complete/incomplete. This minimizes instructor grading time, but, if constructed properly, also provides a sense of what students are understanding prior to the group space exercise.

Second, at times a lack of participation can be the result of either your extrovert students dominating the conversation or the introvert ones not wanting to participate. I have employed two solutions to this issue. First, make sure that students begin talking early in the semester to build a community. This means early introductions, whether face-to-face or via video, and an early collaborative learning exercise that does not entail a lot of content knowledge. This will decenter the classroom and put the emphasis on the students and not the instructor (Shinko; Burch). You want students to "break the seal" on their voice so that they reach a comfort level with their peers. Second, it is also important to divide the class into small groups; three or four students per group is best. The purpose of small groups is that students in this small group setting cannot hide from the conversation (Johnson et al. 1998). I have found this particularly important in the online setting. I would recommend against trying to run an online discussion board with 20, 30, 40, or more students. If you break the students into small groups, they can engage in a more organic conversation where everyone in the group must be an active and engaged participant. In the end, that is the primary goal of this approach.

Another issue you may encounter is a failure of students to make the most of the group space activity and the collaborative learning environment. What I mean by this is that the conversations in these exercises don't always remain focused on the topic. Even if you engage in the most basic of best practices for collaborative learning, that is walking the room and engaging the groups during their conversations, at times the students get off track. This can be a real issue when using Zoom breakout rooms. One easy fix for this issue is to have students produce something from their discussion. The production of a Google doc is a wonderful means of keeping them on track and checking on their progress in the collaborative learning exercise. It allows the instructor to see, in real time, the progress students are making on the exercise and provides summary material that the instructor can share with the rest of the class.

These are just three issues that I have encountered and that may arise in your attempt to flip the classroom. It is important to reiterate that failure must be an option when moving to a flipped learning environment and employing the building your IR theory toolkit approach. Just as your students will learn from this approach, the instructor should learn as well. One thing that I have gleaned from implementing this approach in my course is that good pedagogy is always intentional. If backward design becomes a part of how you structure not only your course, but each module within the course, you should see greater success. And if you succeed, your students will succeed as well.

CONCLUDING THOUGHTS

In the end, what exactly is the IR theory toolkit method? It is a pedagogical approach to teaching survey-level courses to non-majors that assists them in more than just learning the content of the course. This approach allows students to fill a toolkit full of skills that help them in both their academic and professional career, regardless of their major. It also assists them in being productive members of a democratic society. It accomplishes these goals by creating an environment that not only allows students to take ownership of the course and their learning experience, but also puts them into an active learning environment.

To conclude this chapter, let's bring it back full circle to the SOTL literature that is foundational to the IR theory toolkit approach. An active and engaged classroom is the best classroom. It is beneficial to students in terms of their learning the course content, but also advantageous in terms of their skill building. Rather than creating passive students that are waiting for instructors to give them information, the building your IR theory toolkit takes a difficult topic, IR theory, and provides a means by which students can make it their own. It allows students the opportunity to work on their understanding of this topic initially in the individual space, and then with the assistance of their peers and the instructor in the group space. Such an approach gives students greater ownership over their education. It as a result of this ownership that students gain critical reading skills, critical thinking skills, communication skills, ethical reasoning skills, and the ability to work collaboratively. But most importantly, students learn how to learn. The result is that when you meet that student five years after graduation and ask them to explain the co-constitutive nature of social constructivism, they still won't be able to recall that content from memory. However, what they can do is employ the tools that your course provided them to find that answer. If they can accomplish that goal, then the IR theory toolkit approach has fulfilled its primary outcome.

11. Teaching IR with literature and film

Gigi Gokcek and Patrick James

College students in the twenty-first century have grown up in the digital age. These students overwhelmingly have been exposed to many forms of technology, facilitated through computers, tablets, video games, and smart phones. Studies suggest that constant exposure to technology and social networking (via Facebook, Twitter, Instagram, TikTok, etc.) from birth may have wired the brains of this new generation differently from previous ones (Becker, 11). Their attitudes, behaviors, and learning styles have been shaped by the way they view the world through this technological lens. Whereas lectures and readings served as primary modes of education for centuries in higher education, the text literacy of current students raised in the information age appears to be relatively less well developed (Kuzma and Haney, 10; Oblinger and Oblinger, 14). In addition, this generation's ability to access information at record speeds from multiple sources may actually inhibit their ability to properly evaluate what they have gathered (Becker, 11).

Professors need to consider how best to approach undergraduate courses with a generation of students who are not only less inclined to read large amounts of text, but also routinely bring iPads and laptops into the classroom. Efforts to avoid such distractions as texting, checking social media, and surfing the Internet have led some professors to shy away from incorporating the use of technology into the classroom. But this chapter suggests that we should embrace certain technologies and offers innovative approaches to incorporating multimedia including film and literature into international relations (IR) courses. It examines themes including: What types of fictional movies and novels are appropriate for educating students of IR? What kinds of pedagogical approaches may work best for using literature versus film? What are the benefits and drawbacks of relying on film and literature in an IR course? We grapple with such questions based on direct experiences with active learning and insights from the larger scholarship on teaching and learning.

The chapter proceeds as follows. First, it introduces Bloom's Taxonomy as a framework for better integrating fictional movies and novels into the classroom as an appropriate pedagogical technique for educating students of IR. Second, the chapter reviews scholarship on why popular culture media are an effective resource to access when teaching undergraduates in the twenty-first century. Next, we show how fictional franchises like *James Bond* and *The Lord of the Rings* work well in teaching a variety of IR content ranging from theoretical paradigms to levels of analysis. The final section reflects on what can be accomplished with these approaches and identifies a few priorities for further work.

BLOOM'S TAXONOMY FOR TEACHING WITH LITERATURE AND FILM

Our approach to effective teaching with film and literature has been inspired by Bloom's (1956) Taxonomy of Learning Cognitive Domain (and its revised form) as a pedagogical framework. This framework, a classic within pedagogical studies, provides an effective way for instructors to engage students with IR content and promote *active* learning. According to Krain (2010), "[active] learning is a pedagogical approach that attempts to move classroom instruction from traditional lecture oriented 'instructional paradigm' to a new 'learning paradigm.' It is conceived of as a holistic, student-centered approach designed to produce learning, develop critical thinking skills, and elicit discovery and construction of knowledge." Bloom's Cognitive Domain taxonomy consists of six categories, which educators may access to facilitate the meeting of student learning objectives in the preceding context. These categories in the original taxonomy provide measurable terms to describe as well as classify observable knowledge.[1] They also provide pathways for effective teaching and learning using films and literature.

In its updated form, the taxonomy begins with *remembering* (knowledge) at the lowest level, which entails the learner's ability to "define, memorize, recite, recall" information or retrieve knowledge from memory. Lectures, course readings, and class discussions fulfill this category by introducing students to the information they will need to learn and recall later. The second category is *understanding* (comprehension), which is the ability to "interpret, describe, explain, discuss" the meaning of course material that is learned (Anderson et al. 2001). To satisfy this category, instructors can use a worksheet that asks students to define, explain, and discuss theories, concepts, terms, and questions associated with the course prior to the start of the film or reading a novel. Third, *applying* (application), involves processing something learned about novel situations through "practice, demonstration, execution, illustration" (Anderson et al. 2001). Students can use the worksheet to identify scenes from televisions shows and movies, along with scenarios in novels and short stories, which illustrate theories, concepts, terms, and even problem scenarios. *Analyzing* (analysis) is the fourth category, which involves separating the concepts learned "into component parts so that [their] organizational structure may be understood" (Bloom et al.). A concept mapping exercise can fulfill this category. Concept mapping enables students to interpret the information in an active and "non-linear" format. Whereas the worksheet can provide a linear structure for students to define specific theories and concepts, a definition alone does not provide a complete picture, nor does it allow students to understand the complexity of international studies or global topics. Much of the course material is built on a web of theories, as well as concepts, and the construction of a "concept map" illustrates their inter-relatedness. As Halpern and Hakel (39) explain, when students engage in concept mapping, they focus on identifying "different types of relationships or links among concepts. Many students report that concept mapping is a challenging experience, but that it pays off in [the] long-term."

The final two categories from the taxonomy are the most demanding. Bloom's fifth category is *evaluating* (synthesis), which calls for using previously learned knowledge to "argue, evaluate, judge, criticize" (Halpern and Hakel, 139). The classroom activity assigns students to work in small groups to complete the worksheet before and during the movie or novel. When the movie is complete or everyone has finished reading the novel, students can engage in a large group debate and discussion to determine if the scenes in the film or scenarios in the novel they have identified illustrate the theories/concepts covered in the course. The sixth and final category is *creating* (evaluation), which requires one to "generate, produce, construct, and formulate." In essence, the sixth and highest category entails the creation of a new idea based on the combining and reorganizing of everything already learned. To ensure that this step is covered, students could find a current news item that portrays those same theories and concepts associated with the course content. In addition, this category of *creating* is assessed through students' learning, critical thinking skills, and knowledge with an exam, or a paper assignment, at the end of the course.

Taken together, the categories from Bloom represent ascending steps toward expert-level knowledge – a progression that greatly informs our approach to instruction with film and literature. Deeper learning goes well beyond retention of material or even the ability to explain it in a basic way. Cross-referencing and links distinguish knowledge organization by an expert, who in turn can draw upon such material more effectively (Ambrose et al., 51). While expert status may not be a realistic goal for students in a single class, everything should be done to move students along in that direction and set the stage for its achievement after sufficient exposure to the subject matter in increasingly advanced courses.

Application of the taxonomy and interactive media can greatly enhance student engagement with subjects in traditional IR classes like realism, liberalism, and radicalism. Put simply, readings and lectures may not be enough to illustrate IR theories or concepts effectively enough for today's generation of students to make maximum progress along the categories from Bloom. This is because students may not be able to relate as well to the examples drawn from the past, especially involving people and events long before they were alive. While more timely examples may be effective in showing how the theories play out in the real world, an illustration fitting nicely into each tradition may not always be readily available when a professor needs it to make an important instructional point. Moreover, consider also thinking "outside of the box" via analytic eclecticism (Sil and Katzenstein). This approach urges a quest for explanation that goes beyond paradigms. Analytic eclecticism is pragmatic; it focuses on solving problems and encourages a combination of ideas from different schools of thought. With an orientation toward policy relevance, analytic eclecticism finds a natural place in a classroom that seeks active and innovative learning. Thus, it is appropriate, in the quest for expert-level knowledge, to grasp both paradigmatic thinking and ideas that exist independently. Otherwise, the most advanced categories from Bloom, synthesis and evaluation, ultimately may remain elusive to students.

Relational reasoning of four types – analogy, anomaly, antinomy and antithesis – can help further in processing text and graphic material in tandem with each other.[2] Experimental evidence from Danielson and Sinatra (68) supports the idea that visual and verbal expositions, coupled with a stimulant toward relational reasoning, work effectively together. Applications of relational reasoning will appear in later sections that focus on learning about IR through the characters and contents of major movie franchises.

SCHOLARSHIP ON TEACHING AND LEARNING

Teaching IR through film and literature can help students attain greater understanding and retention of knowledge. As noted earlier, today's students are visually intuitive, yearn for group activity, prefer to be proactive (as opposed to passive), and seek general versus specific instructions. These digital natives "learn better through discovery than by being told" and are "intuitive visual communicators" (Kuzma and Haney, 9). More broadly, Oblinger and Oblinger contend that post-millennial students prefer to learn and work in teams and thereby "gravitate toward group activity" (14). As evidence shows "students on average retain 10% of what they read but closer to 30% of what they see" (Oblinger and Oblinger, 14).

These approaches speak more broadly to the scholarship on teaching and learning, as well. According to Halpern and Hakel, "the purpose of formal education is transfer." When teaching writing and mathematics, it is assumed that these learned skills will be transferrable and useful for students at a time and a place beyond school (Halpern and Hakel, 38). Educators constantly need to keep in mind that they "are teaching toward sometime in the future" when these students are no longer in their classrooms (Halpern and Hakel, 38). How and what professors teach has to enable students to transfer what they have learned from their teachers to the unpredictable real-world "tests" that they will not be examined on in an academic way but still must "pass" to maintain employment and function well as citizens (Halpern and Hakel, 38). In order to optimize their learning potential to achieve student success, professors must build interaction in the classroom after laying down "a solid foundation of skills and concepts" through lectures, selected readings, and other assignments (Hoover). Over and beyond performance in the classroom, learning can contribute to citizenship through an enhanced ability to seek out and filter information from the vast amount that is available through virtually countless sources to those who live in the twenty-first century.

Our study also contributes to the scholarship of teaching and learning focused on visual media and "alternative texts."[3] Indeed, a number of teacher–scholars have recommended the use of different movies to teach political science and IR. Simpson and Kaussler provide a list of appropriate films to teach about different scenarios in world politics (including the Cuban Missile Crisis, terrorism, Middle East politics, and nuclear weapons) as well as theories and concepts in IR (such as realism, idealism, constructivism, Marxism, and nationalism). Some films are specifically identified for scenarios, such as *Thirteen Days* for the Cuban Missile Crisis (CMC), *Munich* for terrorism, and *Dr. Strangelove* for nuclear weapons. While these are longstanding staples, other less conventional films include *300* for realism, *Remains of the Day* for idealism, the *Matrix* trilogy for constructivism, and *Braveheart* for nationalism (Simpson and Kaussler). To that list could be added *Seven Days in May* for civil–military relations and a host of other possibilities (see, for example: Gerner; Combs; Simpson and Kaussler; Van Belle 2018; Lobasz and Valeriano; Campbell and Gokcek).

Inspired by Bloom's Taxonomy, we recommend that instructors cover the theories and concepts they want students to learn through the readings and lectures prior to film viewing. Additional discussions during a break in the film or certainly afterward are also good ways to engage the students in a large group discussion using concept mapping. Whereas Sunderland et al. suggest distributing discussion questions before the viewing, we recommend relying on an assignment with a list of the key IR theories and concepts for students to define. This can help students identify the scenes in the film (or novel) that best illustrate the IR content they are learning about in the course (Sunderland et al., 544). The next two sections provide a sampling of our pedagogical approaches using two well-known franchises, *James Bond* and *The Lord of the Rings*.

JAMES BOND: *DIE ANOTHER DAY* (2002) AND *QUANTUM OF SOLACE* (2008)

The *James Bond* movie franchise is full of rich plotlines to teach theories and concepts from IR. James Bond started out as character in an Ian Fleming novel published at the end of the Korean War and, seven decades later, the character possesses iconic status. James Bond, AKA 007, is an intelligence officer in the British Secret Service (MI6), and is often, on behalf of "queen and country," trying to take down international criminal organizations. This activity takes place under the order of his boss, known by the single letter, "M". The Fleming novels were adapted for the big screen beginning in 1962, and, by 2012, the franchise had produced 23 movies; further iterations have a virtually guaranteed audience for years to come.[4]

Real-world events seem to be the inspiration for storylines in nearly all of the 23 fictional films, with each production reflecting the time period in which it appeared. Although some of the films contain elements of science fiction, notably gadgets used by Bond or his adversaries, nothing is all that far-fetched in relation to current technology. If someone wants to use James Bond movies to teach about the Cold War to a generation of students that never lived through it, there are approximately 17 films to choose from in the period between 1962 and 1989.[5] For example, in the 1963 film *From Russia with Love*, Bond courts a Russian Counselor Officer stationed in Turkey so that she will betray her country and help him get his hands on a Soviet encryption device. Given that this movie came out soon after the 1962 Cuban Missile Crisis (CMC), the plot's focus on a Soviet encryption device and a Western spy trying to acquire it in Turkey (a country where American Jupiter missiles had been hidden prior to the CMC) made a lot of sense. Jockeying for position in Istanbul, the principal setting in the movie, is quite realistic for the adversaries in the Cold War. In the 1977 film *The Spy Who Loved Me*, Bond works with a KGB agent Amasova to investigate the disappearance of British and Soviet submarines. The plot for this movie also makes sense because of détente, which was an easing of tensions between the United States and Soviet Union from 1969 to 1980.

After the collapse of the Soviet bloc and end of the Cold War, the Bond franchise evolved in response to the emergence of multiple axes of cooperation and conflict in world politics. For example, in the 1997 movie *Tomorrow Never Dies*, the plot once again reflects the times. The focus shifts to relations between China and the West that are not filtered through the previously paramount Soviet–American rivalry. In this movie Bond aligns with a Chinese Agent, Wai Lin, to stop a global media mogul from using the 24/7 news cycle and forum to manipulate each side into starting a war with each other. As one considers US efforts in the mid-1990s to engage a rising China by supporting its membership into the World Trade Organization, this story line makes sense as well.

The *James Bond* franchise represents a good example of fictional material that can be employed in IR classes to enhance learning. Its range and intricacy of its story lines, spanning more than four decades, works well to teach the paradigms of realism, liberalism, Marxism, constructivism, feminism, and concepts like anarchy, sovereignty, balance of power, alliances, collective security, cooperation, imperialism, and interdependence, to a name just a few. Through engagement of such concepts with novels and films, students also learn how paradigms can guide but also sometimes limit thinking about IR. While perhaps not relevant to the logic of confirmation, fictional story lines and characters come into play with the logic of discovery. Students may think of existing concepts and paradigms differently or even come up with new perspectives about IR after encountering material from the world of James Bond or other fictional settings.

There are 26 Bond movies to select from (between 1962 and 2020), so the problem for the instructor is not finding a movie but instead trying to figure out which one to show to best illustrate select theories and concepts in IR to enhance student learning. This probably is a nuanced matter that will be influenced by the choice of textbook(s), among other things. Both *Die Another Day* (2002) and *Quantum of Solace* (2008), when viewed as fictional narratives, provide concrete and visual examples that enable collegians to understand how abstract IR theories and concepts make better sense of real-world events.

Die Another Day begins with the North Korean Government capturing James Bond. Bond is released 14 months later in exchange for a North Korean terrorist, Zao, who was captured by the West. As James Bond sets out to investigate what led to his own capture, this brings him right back to Zao and his associate in the West, millionaire Gustav Graves. Bond and another MI6 officer, Miranda Frost, along with Jinx of the US National Security Agency, set out to uncover the connection between Zao and Graves. Soon it becomes clear that Graves is a former North Korean officer, posing as a diamond mogul to develop an international space weapon to use against South Korea and the West. In *Quantum of Solace*, James Bond sets out to uncover who tried to assassinate his boss, M. This leads him to a wealthy pseudo-environmentalist, Dominic Greene, who belongs to a mysterious international criminal organization known as Quantum, which is determined to back a coup in Bolivia in order to take control of its water supply. As Bond investigates, he meets a former Bolivian intelligence officer, Camille, who appears to be a friend of Greene's. But he quickly learns that Camille is only using Greene to gain access to a Bolivian General named Medrano, to exact vengeance for murdering her family. While the CIA looks away, hoping to reap the benefits of any oil discovery in the country by Greene's so-called environmental group, Bond and Camille try to stop Greene and General Medrano. The movie concludes, similar to *Die Another Day*, with Bond successfully stopping Greene and Medrano from carrying out their plot to take over Bolivia.

Each movie plot lends itself very fittingly to many of the theories and concepts in IR. Relational reasoning – through analogy, anomaly, antinomy, and antithesis – can be applied to great benefit in moving students forward along Bloom's Taxonomy. For example, in *Die Another Day* students look at the alliance between Bond and Jinx as cooperation and illustration of collective security as they fight off Graves and Frost. Note that Frost, as a double-agent, represents an anomaly in the tightly monitored world of intelligence. Moreover, in the scene near the end where Bond is engaged in a fistfight with Graves, and Jinx in a sword fight with Frost, students might see connections to a balance of power as well as feminist IR theory in the case of the latter. In each instance, students are reasoning through analogy.[6] They may also pick up on an interesting juxtaposition of the North–South Gap, as well as concepts like core, periphery, and imperialism/colonialism, in *Quantum of Solace*. These scenes include MI6 Headquarters in England, as opposed to Haiti, from which Greene is operating. The opulent headquarters and impoverished island are antithetical to each other. Another apt observation of antithesis is the performance of the Opera Tosca in Austria, where members of Quantum are holding their secret meeting, versus Bolivia, where the poor citizens are struggling to find water in a manufactured drought.

In summary, the world of James Bond, with its mysteriously disappearing submarines (*The Spy Who Loved me*), or an international space weapon (*Die Another Day*), or a media mogul using a stealth boat to manufacture another world war (*Tomorrow Never Dies*), provides an excellent pedagogical tool for professors aiming to reach those higher levels of the cognitive process identified in Bloom's Taxonomy. Synthesis and evaluation from that taxonomy, in particular, can be enhanced through analysis of story lines and characters from the *James Bond* franchise.

THE LORD OF THE RINGS

Since J. R. R. Tolkien published *The Lord of the Rings* over a half-century ago, it has become one of the most popular novel series of all time.[7] Its major themes – good versus evil, human agency versus determinism, and various others – remain just as relevant today to the human condition in general and IR in particular. *The Lord of the Rings* is a timeless story set in the imaginary world of Middle-earth, but with enough parallels for us to see the great questions of our time asked in different and thought-provoking ways. In the new millennium, *The Lord of the Rings* is more prominent than ever, with all three

Teaching IR with literature and film 137

of Peter Jackson's movies standing among the top 100 of all time in box office revenue.

How can the fantasy world of Middle-earth assist with learning about IR? This question is answered at length in Ruane and James (2008, 2012), so only a brief summary is provided here. The foundation for a pedagogical approach based on alternative worlds from literature and film is in educational psychology. A mixture of written and graphic material is ideal for understanding and retention of material. Thus, a character or story line from Middle-earth – a very complex world – can assist in the process of learning social scientific material, such as IR. A few illustrations follow, with a concentration on the characters and story lines from *The Lord of the Rings*.

Consider an essential concept in IR, levels of analysis, which for students does not generate much interest because it is abstract and seems distant from the concerns of the day. A conventional presentation for levels of analysis would focus on a historical event, with the First World War as the most common choice in the textbooks on IR, and combine variables from the system, state and international levels to form a comprehensive explanation for how things turned out in August 1914. Carried out for the War of the Ring in Middle-earth, this same process can stimulate relational reasoning – analogy, anomaly, antinomy and antithesis – among students and increase comprehension of fundamental ideas.

Take, for example, the individual level of analysis. One contributing factor to both the First World War and the War of the Ring is highly questionable and even incompetent leadership under intense crisis conditions – an anomaly in the practice of politics that creates a massive potential for escalation. Incompetence was similarly manifest in various ways for the Kaiser of Germany, Tsar of Russia, and Emperor of Austria-Hungary on the eve of war in August 1914. These problematic leaders can be compared to King Theoden of Rohan and Steward Denethor of Gondor in *The Lord of the Rings* (Ruane and James 2012, 76–112). Theoden had fallen under a spell from the villainous Saruman of Isengard, while Denethor went mad as a result of looking into a dangerous seeing stone. Errors by these leaders, which contributed to the outbreak of war under dire circumstances, took place in both Middle-earth and our world just over a century ago. Lessons about the individual level of analysis are reinforced by a comparative assessment of the respective cases.

Next, consider the Ring of Power as an antinomy that can be used to help students grasp the nature of Weapons of Mass Destruction (WMD). If the villainous Sauron can obtain the Ring of Power, he will possess absolute power and cast Middle-earth into a permanent darkness. The Ring of Power can serve as an antinomy in various ways with respect to WMD. In other words. understanding of what a WMD *is* can be enhanced by a grasp of what it is *not*. Wielding the Ring of Power does resemble use of WMD in one way because, for instance, detonation of a sufficient number of nuclear weapons could bring on devastating climate change and possibly even extinction of life on this planet. However, WMD can be used by anyone with the right combination of material and expertise and a massive deployment would not lead to victory but instead annihilation. The Ring of Power, as pointed out by the wisest characters in Middle-earth, such as the wizard Gandalf (chief strategist for the free peoples of Middle-earth), and Aragorn (the eventual King of Gondor after the adventure story is concluded), cannot be wielded by anyone but Sauron *and* can make him absolute ruler of Middle-earth.

Many theories co-exist in IR, even if the subject matter is restricted to war. Imagine trying to communicate predation theory, which focuses on choices of strategy among the peers of a great power in significant decline, to a classroom. Predation theory puts forward the idea that multiple strategies are available to great powers; these options range from predation (intense and negative) through to bolstering (intensive and positive) in relation to one of them in decline (Shifrinson). Like other theories, predation contains a significant amount of unfamiliar terminology and may not be easily comprehensible when encountered by students. At the same time, the theory has performed well under testing and possesses significant policy relevance, so it is worthwhile to convey even if somewhat challenging in composition. What, then, to do?

One approach is to work through an analogy based on a story line from Middle-earth. For thousands of years, Gondor had been the greatest power in Middle-earth. Gondor assumed that position after the defeat of Mordor, led by Sauron, thousands of years before the story of *The Lord of the Rings* gets underway. How do other entities in Middle-earth react to the decline of Gondor? In the language of predation theory, Mordor, which itself is on the rise, engages in predation. The specific properties of implementation for the strategy can be compared across the two worlds, Middle-earth and ours, with the analogy helping to grasp both terminology and the functioning of cause and effect. The other great powers in Middle-earth, Isengard and Rohan, can also be assessed in terms of strategic responses to the downward shift in power for Gondor.

CONCLUSION

Life in the new millennium offers both opportunities and challenges for pedagogy. This study has looked beyond conventional approaches to teaching and learning to consider the pedagogical value of pop culture to connect with today's college students. A balance of visual and verbal communication is ideal in moving through the categories from Bloom's Taxonomy in the quest for expert-level knowledge. This chapter has explored two major movie franchises – the Middle-earth *Lord of the Rings* franchise from Tolkien and the *James Bond* franchise from Ian Fleming – for their potential in conveying concepts and theories from IR to students more effectively than otherwise. Each of these franchises, and undoubtedly many others, can assist students in moving forward along Bloom's Taxonomy in their encounter with the curriculum of IR.

Finally, we would also offer a few points of caution. There is a risk that relying on movies could cause students to become passive viewers (Sunderland et al.). There might be an inherent bias depending on who produces a movie (or documentary), or where it is made, most notably a "West-centric bias" (Kuzma and Haney, 545). Consider also a certain type of identity-based mythology that can stand in the way of learning if left unchecked. While self-stated study preferences exist, the same research just noted does *not* affirm the existence of individual learning styles that favor visual learning. Put differently, at least some students may hold inaccurate beliefs about what will help them learn best and that can cause problems and lead to suboptimal choices regarding instruction (Pashler et al.). Finally, while much more can be learned from the franchises noted so far, so many other multi-film series have great potential utility in teaching IR. The online appendix for this chapter offers an initial list of possibilities in addition to *The Lord of the Rings* and *James Bond*.

NOTES

1. Anderson et al. (2001) revised Bloom's taxonomy so that the terms used for the cognitive domain are redefined in correspondence to a knowledge dimension.
2. While beyond the scope of the present exposition, a further survey of findings from educational psychology would reinforce the results from the preceding study.
3. We also recognize the potential value of teaching with popular streaming platforms and television shows. For example, Beavers used the *Daily Show* in class to teach politics; Centellas turned to *American Idol* to teach about political philosophy; and Becker relied on both the *Daily Show* to illustrate significant concepts about politics and media and politics and *Office Space* to show aspects of bureaucratic dysfunction. Note that both comedy and drama, along with reality TV, can be accessed to enhance learning.
4. Ian Fleming was a British Naval Intelligence Officer and author. His first novel on James Bond, *Casino Royale*, was published in 1953. Altogether he published 12 novels about James Bond.
5. The list includes *Dr. No* (1962); *From Russia with Love* (1963); *Goldfinger* (1964); *Thunderball* (1965); *You Only Live Twice* (1967); *On Her Majesty's Secret Service* (1969); *Diamonds are Forever* (1971); *Live and Let Die* (1973); *The Man with the Golden Gun* (1974); *The Spy Who Loved Me* (1977); *Moonraker* (1979); *For Your Eyes Only* (1981); *Octopussy* (1983); *Never Say Never Again* (1983); *A View to A Kill* (1985); *The Living Daylights* (1987); *License to Kill* (1989).
6. Moreover, the latter observation also identifies an antithesis to the early days of the *James Bond* franchise, in which women tended to play stereotypical roles.

140 *Teaching international relations*

7. *The Hobbit*, which Tolkien published in 1937, became a very popular children's novel and introduced readers to some of the characters and story lines that later would appear in *The Lord of the Rings*.

APPENDIX: SAMPLE OF FRANCHISE MOVIES AVAILABLE FOR PEDAGOGICAL APPLICATION

DC Comics/Warner Brothers
Batman (1989)
Batman Returns (1992)
Batman Forever (1995)
Batman & Robin (1997)
Batman Begins (2005)
The Dark Knight (2008)
The Dark Knight Rises (2012)
Man of Steel (2013)
Batman v Superman: Dawn of Justice (2016)
Suicide Squad (2016)
Justice League (2017)
Wonder Woman (2017)
Aquaman (2018)
Wonder Woman 1984 (2020)

Fast and Furious
The Fast and The Furious (2001)
2 Fast 2 Furious (2003)
The Fast and The Furious: Tokyo Drift (2006)
Fast and Furious (2009)
Fast Five (2011)
Fast and Furious 6 (2013)
Furious Seven (2015)
The Fate of the Furious (2017)
F9 (2021)

James Bond
Dr. No (1962)
From Russia with Love (1963)
Goldfinger (1964)
Thunderball (1965)
You Only Live Twice (1967)
On Her Majesty's Secret Service (1969)
Diamonds are Forever (1971)
Live and Let Die (1973)
The Man with the Golden Gun (1974)

142

The Spy Who Loved Me (1977)
Moonraker (1979)
For Your Eyes Only (1981)
Octopussy (1983)
Never Say Never Again (1983)
A View to A Kill (1985)
The Living Daylights (1987)
License to Kill (1989)
Goldeneye (1995)
Tomorrow Never Dies (1997)
The World is Not Enough (1999)
Die Another Day (2002)
Casino Royale (2006)
Quantum of Solace (2008)
Skyfall (2012)
Spectre (2015)
No Time to Die (2020)

J. R. R. Tolkien's Lord of the Rings
The Lord of the Rings: The Fellowship of the Ring (2001)
The Lord of the Rings: The Two Towers (2002)
The Lord of the Rings: The Return of the King (2003)
The Hobbit: An Unexpected Journey (2012)
The Hobbit: The Desolation of Smaug (2013)
The Hobbit: The Battle of the Five Armies (2014)

Marvel Universe Infinity Saga
Ironman (2008)
The Incredible Hulk (2008)
Ironman 2 (2010)
Thor (2011)
Captain America: The First Avenger (2011)
The Avengers (2013)
Ironman 3 (2013)
Thor: The Dark World (2013)
Captain America: Winter Soldier (2014)
Guardians of the Galaxy (2014)
Avengers: Age of Ultron (2015)
Ant-Man (2015)
Captain America: Civil War (2016)

Doctor Strange (2016)
Guardians of the Galaxy Vol. 2 (2017)
Spider-Man: Homecoming (2017)
Thor: Ragnarok (2017)
Black Panther (2018)
Avengers: Infinity War (2018)
Ant-Man and the Wasp (2018)
Captain Marvel (2019)
Avengers: Endgame (2019)
Spider-Man: Far From Home (2019)
Black Widow (2020)

Marvel's X-Men
X-Men (2000)
X-Men 2 (2003)
X-Men: The Last Stand (2006)
X-Men Origins: Wolverine (2010)
X-Men: First Class (2011)
The Wolverine (2013)
X-Men: Days of Future Past (2014)
X-Men: Apocalypse (2016)
X-Men: Dark Phoenix (2019)

Mission Impossible
Mission Impossible 2 (2000)
Mission Impossible 3 (2006)
Mission Impossible 4: Ghost Protocol (2011)
Mission Impossible 5: Rogue Nation (2015)
Mission Impossible 6: Fallout (2018)

Star Trek
Star Trek: The Motion Picture (1979)
Star Trek II: The Wrath of Khan (1982)
Star Trek III: The Search for Spock (1984)
Star Trek IV: The Voyage Home (1986)
Star Trek V: The Final Frontier (1989)
Star Trek VI: The Undiscovered Country (1991)
Star Trek Generations (1994)
Star Trek: First Contact (1996)
Star Trek: Insurrection (1998)

144   *Teaching international relations*

Star Trek: Nemesis (2002)
Star Trek (2009)
Star Trek Into Darkness (2013)
Star Trek Beyond (2016)

Star Wars
Episode IV – A New Hope (1977)
Episode V – The Empire Strikes Back (1980)
Episode VI – Return of the Jedi (1983)
Episode I – The Phantom Menace (1999)
Episode II – Attack of the Clones (2002)
Episode III – Revenge of the Sith (2005)
Episode VII – The Force Awakens (2015)
Rogue One: A Star Wars Story (2016)
Episode VIII – The Last Jedi (2017)
Solo: A Star Wars Story (2018)
Episode IX – The Rise of Skywalker (2019)

The Bourne Series
The Bourne Identity (2002)
The Bourne Supremacy (2004)
The Bourne Ultimatum (2007)
The Bourne Legacy (2012)
Jason Bourne (2016)

The Hunger Games
The Hunger Games (2012)
The Hunger Games: Catching Fire (2013)
The Hunger Games: Mockingjay – Part 1 (2014)
The Hunger Games: Mockingjay – Part 2 (2015)

12. Engaging in inquiry: problem-based and research-focused teaching and learning

James M. Scott

Many factors contribute to a rich and successful academic learning experience for undergraduates. As previous chapters in this volume discuss, approaches organized around student engagement and active learning contribute to effective learning experiences and outcomes. In this context, problem-based and research-focused teaching embedded within a course or as the overall course structure and design offers opportunities to advance a student-centered learning experience. They also contribute to a participatory environment where students are engaged in and owners of their learning and a practical and experiential method, where students learn in an active, applied fashion.

This chapter explores approaches to the classroom that incorporate problem-based and research-focused learning strategies. After situating these strategies in relevant literature on active and engaged learning, the chapter lays out key aspects of problem-based and research-focused teaching and learning, and then offers suggestions for incorporating them into classes to promote and enhance student learning outcomes. It concludes with a few observations about the opportunities and challenges of this approach.

FOUNDATIONS: ACTIVE LEARNING

Problem-based and research-focused teaching rest on the foundations of active learning. A central tenet of active and engaged learning gleaned from long years of study is that when students are the owners of learning they learn more and develop faster (e.g., Bean; Bonwell and Eison; Kille, Krain, and Lantis; Nilson). Grounded in constructivist, student-centered pedagogy (Brooks and Brooks), much evidence from many disciplines indicates that this approach improves student learning, mastery of course material, higher-order critical and analytical thinking skills, and preparation for future tasks and challenges (e.g., Anderson et al., 2005; Freeman et al.; Kember and Leung; Kille, Krain and Lantis; McCarthy and Anderson). As the introduction to this volume also indicated, "multi-modal" learning can help promote education and retention of knowledge (Mueller and Oppenheimer; Ward). Finally, substantial evidence shows that active learning more effectively addresses multiple learning styles, applies well across disciplines, and improves inclusiveness in classrooms (Ambrose et al.; Haak et al.; Laws et al.; Lorenzo et al.).

A core goal of active learning is to employ approaches that privilege the production of knowledge and not its passive transmission via the "sage on the stage" approach, in part because the former promotes higher-order thinking and deeper learning (Dubinsky et al.; Blakemore and Frith; Glisczinski). As Bonwell and Eison note in their seminal work on the topic, active learning involves "instructional activities involving students in doing things and thinking about what they are doing" (Bonwell and Eison, iii). Active-learning approaches include a wide range of teaching strategies, many of which receive attention in the chapters of this volume: case-based teaching; "games" and simulations; role-playing; discussion; collaborative and group activities; and many others. At its heart, active learning includes five main characteristics: (a) students do more than listen; (b) emphasis is placed on developing skills rather than transmitting information; (c) higher-order thinking, including analysis, synthesis, and evaluation, is central; (d) students are engaged in activities; (e) emphasis is on student exploration (Bonwell and Eison).

PROBLEM-BASED LEARNING AND RESEARCH-FOCUSED LEARNING

Problem-based learning (PBL) and research-focused learning (RFL) are grounded in the active-learning context. While distinct, the two approaches complement each other, and both are focused on student inquiry and discovery. The heart of both PBL and RFL involves teaching through inquiry and a focus on problems. As such, they derive in part from the work of John Dewey, who noted that "only by wrestling with the condition of the problem at first hand, seeking and finding [his/her/their] own way out, does [the student] think" (Dewey, 188). Key benefits of problem-based/research-focused approaches rest in the diffusion of critical, analytical and research skills, as well as creative, inquiry-oriented thinking. According to Healey and Jenkins' survey of this literature, inquiry-based learning can be: "*structured* – where lecturers provide an issue or problem and an outline for addressing it; *guided* – where lecturers provide questions to stimulate inquiry, but students are self-directed as regards exploring these questions; and *open* – where students formulate the questions themselves as well as going through the full inquiry cycle" (Healey and Jenkins, 22–23, emphasis added). Which form depends in part on instructor preference, course objective and level, and student starting skills.

Problem-Based Learning

PBL is a student-centered approach to teaching/learning in which students tackle a "problem" to be "solved," generally with application of course concepts and/or additional research (e.g., Savery; Jonassen and Hung).[1] Generally, PBL emphasizes real-world problems or puzzles – "why" or "how" questions that are constructed to foster student engagement and promote discovery, student ownership, problem-solving and higher-order thinking skills, and teamwork/group collaboration when those things are incorporated into the approach (Dochy et al.; Gijbels et al.; Kille, Krain, and Lantis; Krain). As Burch explains, "The PBL premise holds that most students will better learn information if they need it; need arises as they try to solve problems" (Burch, 33).

Of course, different kinds of problems will apply to different disciplines. For international studies, the range of potential problems is virtually limitless, and runs the gamut from simple "why" questions generated from a currents events reading to more extensive and elaborate case studies (Burch). For example, asking students: "Why did the US lead efforts to create the International Criminal Court and then refuse to join?" sets up a puzzling situation for students to grapple with and explain (see further discussion below). As Burch explains, "problems may appear in a written case, a video clip, a cartoon, a photo, a journal article, an editorial, or a vignette," among other sources (Burch 33).

However, regardless of discipline, the problems in PBL tend to share some common characteristics (Duch, Groh, and Allen):

- they lead students to understand and apply concepts more deeply;
- they involve making and defending reasoned decisions;
- they are devised to mesh with course learning objectives and establish sequences and laddering from previous objectives/content;
- they are sufficiently complex to require and facilitate group collaboration and disaggregated tasks if structured as a group project;
- they move from open-ended and engaging initial steps to draw students into the endeavor, especially if more complicated and elaborate multistage projects are involved.

Through PBL, "students wrestle to identify learning issues, information they require, resources necessary to gather such information, possible solutions, and a final answer" (Burch, 33). The PBL process proceeds from an open-ended problem about which students proceed to initial analysis of what they know, what they need to know, and what they should do. They then engage in research and evidence/information gathering – which may involve careful

148 *Teaching international relations*

study of required texts or other provided materials, or more elaborate activities such as library/internet searching, data collection, interviews, and others. The PBL process concludes with the production, submission, and often presentation, of some kind of "report" (Burch, 34–36; see also Duch et al.; Allen et al.). As active participants and owners of each part of this process, students learn more deeply and develop core critical and analytical skills more thoroughly.

Research-Focused Learning

RFL is a close cousin to PBL, with emphasis on research assignments and inquiry and discovery. It is also related to undergraduate student research programs and initiatives: both emphasize learning through inquiry and discovery, with undergraduate research programs emphasizing independent student research projects with faculty mentoring and RFL stressing classroom based investigations tied to course objectives and structures (see, e.g., Healey and Jenkins; Hu et al.; Kreber; Lopatto; Scott). When carefully integrated into courses and programs, RFL can foster creativity, intellectual curiosity, and a sense of discovery. Through RFL, undergraduates learn in active ways that both complement and supplement traditional learning in classrooms and coursework. This approach to learning contributes to substantive mastery and application of classroom/course concepts/knowledge that deepens learning and independent thinking (e.g., Healey and Jenkins; Lopatto). Like active learning in general, and PBL more specifically, RFL empowers student ownership of learning, builds student confidence, and develops higher-order thinking skills (e.g., Boyd and Wesemann; Hu et al.; Hunter et al.; Malachowski).

Some of the foundations of RFL stem from the movement toward undergraduate research (Beckham and Hensel, 43; see also Boyd and Wesemann; Hunter et al.; Kreber). A useful way of conceptualizing undergraduate research experiences distinguishes between two dimensions: the role of the student (as audience or as participant) and the research emphasis (on content or on process/problems). Combining these two dimensions produces a simple 2×2 conception of the foundations of undergraduate research and inquiry (Healey and Jenkins, 7). As Figure 12.1 shows, this conceptualization yields four approaches:

- *Research-Led*: learning about current research in the discipline, typically by including scholarly research articles in course reading assignments;
- *Research-Oriented*: developing research skills and techniques, typically through an undergraduate scope and methods course;
- *Research-Tutored*: engaging in research discussions, typically through small, focused seminars intensive examination of a problem, research questions, and scholarly work;

- *Research-Based*: undertaking research and inquiry, with students actively engaged in research projects.

The framework of the undergraduate research experience movement helps to situate RFL approaches. Critical elements of this framework are in the upper quadrants of the framework. Most teaching exposes students to the research of a discipline (research-led), and most Political Science programs have some version of "scope and methods" requirements that teach research methods (research-oriented). Like more elaborate undergraduate research programs (Scott), RFL emphasizes the research-tutored and research-based elements, through which students actively engage in inquiry and investigation, but within the confines of a course or course assignment instead of the independent research project, thesis, or capstone experience common in undergraduate research programs. Instead, research and inquiry are integrated into courses as a pedagogical strategy. The hallmark of this approach involves inquiry-based learning strategies embedded in substantive courses (e.g., Blackmore and Cousin; Huber; Kreber), not simply those designated as research methods or research courses. Strategies include small, carefully

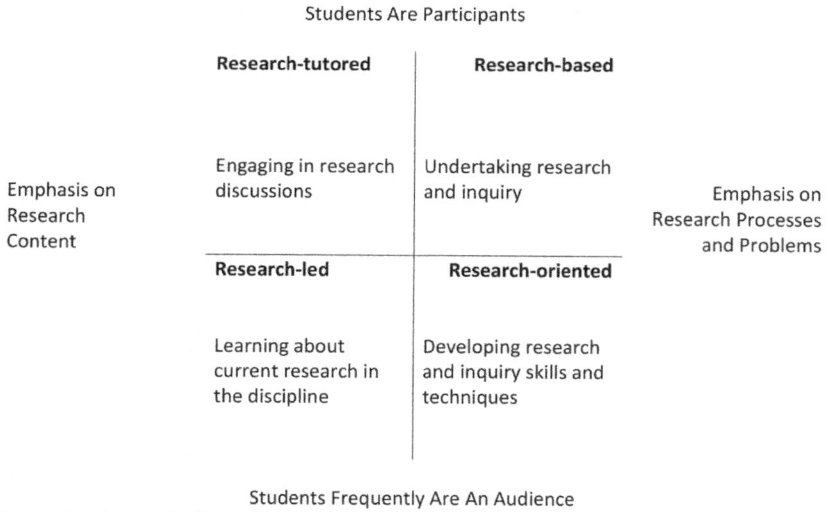

<table>
<tr><td colspan="3" align="center">Students Are Participants</td></tr>
<tr><td>Research-tutored</td><td>Research-based</td><td></td></tr>
<tr><td>Engaging in research discussions</td><td>Undertaking research and inquiry</td><td></td></tr>
<tr><td>Research-led</td><td>Research-oriented</td><td></td></tr>
<tr><td>Learning about current research in the discipline</td><td>Developing research and inquiry skills and techniques</td><td></td></tr>
</table>

Emphasis on Research Content

Emphasis on Research Processes and Problems

Students Frequently Are An Audience

Source: Healey and Jenkins 7.

Figure 12.1   Approaches to undergraduate research

150 *Teaching international relations*

focused "evidence-gathering and analysis" exercises as well as larger, more sweeping research problems, puzzles, and projects.

In RFL, students engage in research and investigation and assume greater responsibility for determining what they need to learn. Implementing RFL involves engaging students in research problems, puzzles, and processes with instructor support. Students identify and use evidence and report on it, and they typically assess their own progress (Roy et al.). As a good summary explains (Roy et al.),[2] RFL:

- begins with a general theme or problem as a starting point for learning;
- emphasizes asking good research questions on the theme/problem;
- builds library, data, and search skills, along with the critical thinking skills necessary for thoughtful review of the information;
- coaches students to report their learning (orally or in writing);
- provides a way (e.g., drafts, benchmark activities, etc.) for students monitor their progress;
- Draws on the instructor as coach, guide, facilitator, mentor, and model.

APPLYING PBL AND RFL FOR STUDENT LEARNING

Implementing a teaching/learning strategy that integrates PBL and RFL can take many forms. In this section, I focus on approaches that combine PBL and RFL in different ways. I present two avenues: in-course assignment strategies – both simple and more elaborate – and whole-course construction strategies. Although obviously not exhaustive, I discuss these broad approaches, provide examples, and offer some description of the kinds of learning outcomes that may occur to suggest illustrative routes for building PBL and/or RFL into courses.

First, a caveat: a starting point for both strategies derives from the "backward design" approach to course development. In this approach, instructors plan out courses by beginning with the learning results they seek, and then work backward to develop activities and assignments that are connected to and achieve those outcomes (Wiggins and McTighe). The first step involves intentional consideration of what the instructor believes students should know, and then (perhaps most importantly for the PBL/RFL approaches) what the instructor wants students to be able to do with what they have learned. For the incorporation of PBL/RFL into courses, this approach prompts instructors to think not only about how to construct well-designed and effective problems and research opportunities, but also to consider carefully why, where, and how to integrate these PBL/RFL activities and assignments into a course.

In-Course Assignment Strategies

A fundamental and underlying premise of in-course strategies is neatly summarized by Burch: "By combining [PBL/RFL] with traditional writing and testing assignments, all students acquire a fuller learning experience. Each student participates in a set of activities that, as a whole, challenge and build upon her or his skills and preferences" (Burch, 36). Here I discuss four general types of assignments that instructors might build into a course to complement and supplement lectures, discussions, writing assignments, and examinations. These types reflect a range of approaches and contribute to a range of learning outcomes:

- evidence-gathering/data collection exercises;
- course-based problems/puzzles;
- open-ended research problems/puzzles;
- case-based problems/puzzles.

By no means exhaustive, these four types nevertheless illustrate key features and choices of PBL/RFL approaches, including varying degrees of open-endedness; simple questions vs. elaborate case contexts; course material-based vs. external research-oriented evidence requirements; and individual vs. group applications.

Evidence-gathering/data collection exercises are a good starting point, falling on the side of simple, predominantly RFL activities. This type of activity directs students to a structured, but relatively open-ended data/evidence/information collection task to encourage the discovery process, stress empirical evidence, and foster a sense of ownership and empowerment. This approach is largely descriptive, but generally leads to more interpretive and explanatory engagement in subsequent class-time opportunities for discussion and "debrief." It can be set up and executed in a single class session, across several sessions, or assigned as an outside-of-class activity that students bring back to the next class session.

As an example, I have routinely used an exercise in introductory international relations and comparative politics courses called "Inequality in the World: The Gap between North and South." This exercise is typically assigned for out-of-class, individual effort, which students bring to a subsequent class session for an in-class discussion but is easily adaptable to in-class and/or group application as well. After some framing language to encourage students

152   *Teaching international relations*

to embrace the role of investigator, the core of the assignment is relatively straightforward:

> Your task is to find empirical evidence that provides good indicators of the nature and scope of inequality in the world. You must prepare a brief, one-page memo in which you:
>
> (1) Identify and briefly describe at least 5 economic and/or social factors in which inequality is evident between the developing and developed world.
> (2) Offer your general assessment of the seriousness of the problem and some measures that could be taken to address it.

For this evidence collection exercise, I specify the sources the students must examine (in this case, World Bank data at http://data.worldbank.org/topic and/or http://hdr.undp.org/en/2019-report [both accessed April 15, 2021]). Students are then set free to explore the data and select evidence. Subsequent class time begins with an inventory of the evidence they collected, followed by an effort to categorize them and a discussion to interpret and explain the causes and consequences of, and potential responses to, the inequality they reveal. In my experiences with this exercise, student engagement is high. Students are eager to share the evidence they "discovered" and to place it into the mosaic we create together in the discussion. I also find that students often return to "their" evidence in subsequent discussion, writing, and examinations.

A second option is a problem/puzzle that turns students back to the assigned text or readings to uncover concepts and information that help them to "solve" a puzzle. Such assignments fall more on the side of PBL activities and direct student attention to assigned reading material to be used for a purpose – solving the problem. These problems thus treat course readings as "evidence" students may harness to an explanation/solution they create. In addition to other outcomes and goals, this approach also increases engagement with and accountability for course material and concepts. I structure my introductory international relations course around a series of such problem themes, each keyed to a specific chapter or chapters, and devote class time to presentation and discussion of student responses.

For example, in introductory international relations courses, I present a simple puzzle to students in the first week. The problem/puzzle prompt states:

> Why is cooperation so hard in world politics? Your task is to review the relevant course materials in chapters 1–2. Then write a clear, concise memo that develops at least three reasons explaining why cooperation is hard in world politics.

Students typically bring their initial hunches and combine them with concepts drawn from the first two textbook chapters such as anarchy, security dilemmas, identity and diversity, stratification, historical legacies, and others.

In the case of this particular problem, I also return to this cooperation puzzle at the end of the course as well.[3] Doing so presents an opportunity for a "pre-test/post-test" experiment in which students "solve" the same problem/puzzle at the end of the course and reflect on how their understanding and explanation evolved. The concluding prompt states in part:

> Your task is to reflect on the relevant course materials in chapters 1–14 ... Then write a clear, concise memo that develops at least three reasons explaining why cooperation is hard in world politics, focusing on the factors and conditions that inhibit and promote it.

To give an example of the learning and self-reflection this offers, consider the responses of this student, who offered the following as the opening paragraph to the initial problem:

> Why is Cooperation so Hard in World Politics? After reading the first chapter of our class textbook, answering the question above doesn't seem so intimidating. There are countless examples to draw from, as well as a never-ending stream of complicated ties and relationships within the realm of world politics. It only makes sense that simple cooperation between states is no quick and simple task, especially when considering the wide variety of players in the game. In my opinion, there are three overarching themes that contribute to the difficulty of cooperation among states and non-state actors in politics: a lack of large-scale empathetic intelligence, blindness associated with extreme security measures, and, most notably, the lack of a binding authority.

At the end of the course, the same student offered the following response:

> Why is Cooperation so Hard in World Politics? In my very first problem theme as a novice international politics student I blamed the difficulty of cooperation in world politics on the following: a lack of large-scale empathetic intelligence, blindness associated with extreme security measures, and the lack of a binding authority. I don't entirely disagree with my past self, but my previous assertions could be refined as a result of studying international politics for a semester. International cooperation is so hard because the stage is innately complex, diverse, and anarchic; it is continually inhibited by a state's pursuit for security and promoted by factors like globalization and interdependence.

Overall, student engagement, learning and progress is further indicated by the average scores on the initial and final responses to these "pre-test/post-test" puzzles. Over the past four semesters in which I taught Introduction to

154 *Teaching international relations*

International Relations, average scores (out of 10) improved from about 7.5 to 9.2 on the opening and closing problems.

In sum, as this example suggests, the basic problem/puzzle approach steers students to the text and incentivizes them to read purposefully and use it practically. The "before-and-after" aspect of this particular problem/puzzle encourages the same but adds a reflective element in which the student ownership of the evidence and solution to the problem/puzzle combine with self-assessment.

A third example is a more open-ended problem/puzzle that blends PBL and RFL, challenging students to seek out (i.e., research) evidence outside course material to understand and solve the problem. The nature of problems like this makes them especially useful for collaborative groups, as students can work in teams to consider what they know, what they need to know, and what they should do (i.e., a research strategy for evidence/information gathering), which is distributed among the members of the group. The group approach contributes to "soft skills" and fosters learning communities of students in which they may be more comfortable participating (Johnson et al. 1991).

I noted a good illustration earlier: "Why did the US lead efforts to create the International Criminal Court and then refuse to join?" The basic problem/puzzle statement remains relatively simple and, after some framing language to set up the problem and ground it in relevant course material (e.g, "review the relevant course materials in chapter ## and the context of preceding course material"), students are directed to engage in research to understand and explain the anomaly presented by the puzzle. My construction of the problem setup directs students to begin at the website for the International Criminal Court (ICC) for foundational information about the ICC (https://www.icc-cpi .int/about [accessed April 15, 2021]). Instructors may also suggest some additional starting points for relevant perspectives and information (e.g., "you may also find the following sources helpful"). However, this problem/puzzle leaves students/groups with the responsibility of devising their own research needs and strategies for their response. Students/groups are asked to prepare a memo with their answer, with some basic content/structure prompts (e.g., "include relevant descriptive information about the ICC" and "at least three reasons"), and subsequent class sessions can be devoted to presentation and discussion of the responses from each group.

Students responded to these PBL/RFL assignments by engaging with the course material and each other and taking responsibility for much of their own learning. A further consequence of these outcomes is a far richer and substantively more engaging set of class discussions across the courses in which I incorporate these activities. Student responses on their course assessments reflected this, emphasizing their own engagement and learning.

A fourth example of assignments that blend PBL/RFL and incorporate them into a course relies on a more elaborate foundation – the use of a case (see

Ralph Carter's chapter on the case approach earlier in this volume) to serve as the basis of a problem for students to solve. Students may work alone or in small groups. They rely on the descriptive case material as the core of their information but devise their own plans for gathering other evidence outside the case and for identifying and applying relevant course material for their explanations/analyses. As in the previous example, this approach may be undertaken as an individual or group assignment, or in some phased sequence of the two.

A good illustration is this example from an upper-division course focused on the politics and processes of American foreign policymaking. Students are provided/assigned a case: *The Clinton Administration and Multilateral Peace Operations* (Daalder). This case describes the Clinton administration's struggle to develop a new policy ("Assertive Multilateralism") to guide US participation in expanded peacekeeping, peacemaking, and peace enforcement operations with other members of the international community in the post-Cold War world, while contending with the immediate challenges of conflict in Somalia, the former Yugoslavia, and, eventually, Rwanda.

The framing for the problem puzzle highlights the starkly diverging comments from key administration officials at the beginning and end of the case, as shown in Figure 12.2. The problem/puzzle presented to students is straightforward: "Why did the Clinton administration change its efforts to develop an 'assertive multilateralism' policy for US support and participation in international peace operations?" Students are guided to prepare a "case memo" that offers their explanation, consisting of three to five points focused on the players and factors that make and shape US foreign policy decisions, presented in cause-and-effect observations, and they are prompted to build their response from case evidence, course material/concepts, and their additional research.

Student feedback and performance indicates that their engagement and learning outcomes from this approach are very positive. I structure my course around a set of seven of these case-based problems. Student engagement on

Source: Healey and Jenkins, 7.

Figure 12.2   The "Assertive Multilateralism" peace operations puzzle

them contributes to broad participation, careful attention to and use of course material, and substantively good discussion/analysis. Student ownership and progress in learning is also significant. For example, from the most recent four years of teaching this course average scores improved across the iterative sequence of memos from less than 7.5 (out of 10) on the first to almost 9 on the last.

Whole-Course Construction Strategies

In addition to integrating PBL/RFL activities and exercises as components of courses, a second general approach is to develop a course in which the overall structure and content of the course is organized around a broad PBL/RFL focus. This approach is a more complex, predominantly RFL approach. Many options for such an approach exist but they range from more structured (where the central problem for the course is established by the instructor and students focus on individual or, more generally, group solutions, supported by instruction, discussion, and mentoring) to more open (where the topic/substantive focus or broad theme is established by the instructor, but the specific puzzles and/or research questions are formulated and investigated by students themselves) (e.g., Healey and Jenkins).

To illustrate, consider the example of an upper-division "Topics in Research" course. In my department, these upper-division courses are required of Political Science majors in the Bachelor of Science degree track, following their completion of an intermediate-level scope and methods course. For context, instructors of such courses situate them somewhere on a spectrum between focusing on advanced training in specific research methodologies (e.g., survey research; experimental research; text analysis; case methods; game theory; etc.) and focusing on an opportunity for RFL and a research experience.

In my course, the emphasis was toward the RFL, research experience emphasis. This course focused on student design and implementation of a research project/proposal employing a "mixed-method" approach combining quantitative and case study research to improve causal inferences on both causal effects and causal mechanisms. The training element focused on the skills and techniques of large-N statistical analysis and small-N case study analysis, and the topical theme of the course focused on problems of conflict, war, and change in international relations. The RFL element stressed student formulation of problems and research questions, the construction of a theoretical explanation to be tested, and the design and execution of empirical tests combining large-n and case study components.

While this course could have involved a more structured approach (designing a problem or problems and directing students to address them), I opted for a more open-ended strategy that placed more responsibility on the students and

Problem-based and research-focused teaching and learning 157

the development of a student research community (e.g., Chang). To provide a common theme, structure and parameters for student problems/puzzles and research questions, I relied on the substantive focus of the course and foundational readings on conflict, war, and change, and on my broad framing of four outcomes that constituted the "meta-problems" on which students could choose to direct their focus: international conflict (inter- or intra-state); terrorism; democracy/democratization; and human rights. I curated a dataset drawn from prominent international relations data for each area for student use (e.g., for terrorism, the Global Terrorism Database from https://www.start.umd.edu/gtd/ [accessed April 15, 2021]).

The course consisted of 16 students and was structured around materials and class sessions that: (a) explored scholarship, evidence, and issues in each of the four outcome areas; (b) tutored students on research project development (i.e., formulating effective research questions; building from relevant literature to establish a theoretical argument and hypotheses; developing a research design – in this case a mixed-method design – to test hypotheses; analyzing results and concluding); (c) trained students in data collection/management, the application of designated statistical techniques, and use of statistical software (STATA); the conduct of case study research (case type and approach, selection, construction, evidence); and the integration of the two methods. With respect to PBL/RFL in particular, in combination with student ranked preferences, I assigned students to one of the four outcome areas (four in each). Building from and on the underlying coursework, students in each group worked together and individually to understand the context of existing scholarship (group); identify puzzles and problems for exploration (group), in part by collaborating to complete some data analysis tasks that explored patterns in the aggregate and disaggregated data I provided in each topical area; and formulate potential research questions for investigation (individual).

Within each group, individuals then focused their attention on developing their own research question, supporting each other as they each constructed a theoretical argument and hypotheses (situated in the context of relevant scholarly literature), and they designed a project to carry out the investigation, applying the mixed-method approach. Their discussions within their groups, with me, and among groups in and out of class helped each of them to: (a) frame a research puzzle and question; (b) build their theoretical argument and hypotheses; (c) model their theoretical argument about their respective dependent variable with their independent variable(s) of interest and three to five control variables; select data to operationalize the variables in their respective models; design a case study component to complement/supplement the large-N element (they proposed, but did not complete the case study component); apply some statistical techniques for preliminary results; and discuss actual and expected results.

Overall, the learning outcomes in this class nicely represented the summary of the benefits of RFL offered by Beckham and Hensel in a summary of studies of learning outcomes derived from undergraduate research experiences:

> For students, the opportunity to define a problem and work toward a solution that might have practical, real-life applications constitutes significant value. Students are more likely to engage actively in the total learning process when their curiosity is stimulated by the research question. Solving research problems can help students to organize their thinking, develop more creative thinking, and gain confidence in their own intellectual abilities ... Opportunities for presenting the results of student research can lead to improvement in their oral and written communications skills. [RFL] research can foster both collaborative and independent skills. Researchers learn to handle ambiguity, to accept the fact that the research project doesn't always work out as expected. And perhaps most importantly, undergraduates will develop the habit of asking 'what if' and 'why not' questions that can lead to new discoveries or new ways of improving the practice of their careers. (Beckham and Hensel, 43)

CONCLUSION

Well-designed PBL/RFL assignments and courses both promise and deliver on student engagement, beneficial learning outcomes, and positive classroom experiences and dynamics. To be sure, instructors surrender some control and direction of course content, but the role of facilitator, guide, and mentor supports student-centered learning experiences; a participatory environment where students are engaged in and owners of their learning; and a practical and experiential method, where students learn in an active, applied fashion. Challenges include taking care to develop the PBL/RFL exercises and structures carefully to ensure that they are engaging, linked to desired course and learning outcomes, and woven into a context of support and empowerment. Balancing the student-centered approaches with instructor facilitation and engagement to ensure that important issues and concepts are adequately addressed is important to the overall success of the courses employing PBL/RFL. However, PBL/RFL is highly flexible and adaptable as an organizing approach or as a complement to other, more traditional components of pedagogy. It may involve simple, small assignments, larger, more complex ones, and it may engage individuals, groups, or a combination. Assignments such as the ones described here can be layered, tiered, and sequenced to achieve multiple goals and both individual and group participation. These strategies are more learner-centered approaches to making sense of world politics. They help to foster discovery and encourage inquiry as students are engaged in asking questions and seeking answers. Constructing courses and teaching/learning activities around these approaches increases the effectiveness of teaching and learning, with students developing substantive mastery, critical and analytical thinking abilities, and research and writing skills.

NOTES

1. There is an extensive literature into inquiry-based and problem-based teaching. For entry points, see Blackmore and Cousin; Brew; Burch; Huber; Kreber; and Spronken-Smith and Harland.
2. Roy et al. includes a table that compares PBL and RFL approaches, providing a clear summary of their shared aspects and their distinct characteristics.
3. Note: I use (and am co-author of) Scott et al., *IR: Seeking Security, Prosperity, and Quality of Life in a Changing World* (now in its 4th edition, with CQ Press), which incorporates this and other problems/puzzles in end-of-chapter features called "Think About This."

13. Engaging with diversity through technology

Yasemin Akbaba and Filiz Başkan

INTRODUCTION

We have been connecting our courses offered in Gettysburg College (GC) in the United States and Izmir University of Economics (IUE) in Turkey since the spring of 2011. Our students work in pairs on various assignments across two continents using information technology. Merging our courses diversifies the student body by connecting college students in Turkey and the United States in virtual platforms and opens our courses to a dynamic cross-national learning environment. In this study, we reflect on our almost a decade old collaboration with the help of student performance and survey data to locate our work in the larger pedagogical research on the benefits of diversity and internationalization. We explore the following questions: How does internationalization of assignments and diversifying the student body influence learning environment of our students? In what ways has this project contributed to student learning outcomes? How do students perform when they are expected to work with international teammates in comparison to other course work such as team assignments that only include their local classmates? Due to the absence of a control group, we won't be able to map the answers out precisely here or elsewhere, but we see an opportunity to reflect on this long-running collaboration using direct and indirect assessment methods. According to our exploratory analysis, GC students performed well in the assignments that required collaboration with international counterparts. In addition, GC and IUE students perceive cross-cultural collaboration to be a positive learning experience. While GC students appreciate the "new perspective" of their international peers, IUE students report benefits such as advancement of skills and increased motivation to learn more about the themes of the course.

This chapter proceeds as follows. In the next section, we provide a summary of our broader philosophical approach that guided this project. Next, we review the scholarship on diversity and internationalization in higher education. After a project overview, we report the results of our exploratory analysis on per-

Engaging with diversity through technology 161

formance of GC students in three semesters and survey responses of GC and IUE students from fall of 2019. The final section includes concluding remarks.

TEACHING PHILOSOPHY

In traditional "teacher–student" roles, where the teacher is perceived to be the source of knowledge and the student is the recipient, students are discouraged from developing their inner expert, since they are given the message that they do not know enough on the subject matter. Teaching methods that solely focus on bombarding students with facts interrupt the learning process, as they marginalize the student with a role that limits exploration. The student is perceived to be the receiver, who lacks the ability to lead their learning environment as a non-expert. This project aims to invite students to be curious and creative by generating more space for them to connect with the course material through international peer learning. Since pairs are unique, students understand that there will be variation in their interactions. So they become "experts" of their own learning space. This encourages them to explore the content freely.

During various iterations of this project, we identified three learning steps that help students engage with the subject matter: (1) creating opportunities to understand differing perceptions of various actors; (2) exploring common threads; (3) embracing the unique nature of the content through similarities and differences. The following examples from the fall 2019 semester aim to expand on each step.

Understanding perceptions, goals and priorities of various international actors is a shared learning goal for many international relations (IR) courses. With this project we wanted to lift the curtain on perceptions of some of the prominent actors in Turkish politics. For instance, initially we explored the role of religion in the politics and culture of Turkey though lectures, reading and visual material. We identified various actors with different preferences and vision on the role of religion in institutions of the state. Once students developed an understanding of the historical and contemporary actors, we connected students with their international counterparts. Students explored the meaning of religion in various contexts through discussion sessions. This process helped students identify differences in actors' perception on religion in Turkish politics.

We also wanted students to observe similarities. For instance, as our students discussed populism, they observed common threads running across political discourse of the US and Turkey. Many of them also pointed out examples from other parts of the world. Exploration of this global trend encouraged our students to revisit their thoughts on populism in their country of residence.

These two opposing learning processes (identifying differences and similarities) in some ways pave the way for searching for unique components of the subject matter. Exploration of differences helps students to see their blind spots. Similarities connect students with the bigger picture. Collectively, these encourage students to identify distinctive features of Turkish politics.

DIVERSITY AND INTERNATIONALIZATION

IR courses tend to explore complex problems such as climate change, food security and civil wars, which many students are interested in and somewhat familiar with. However, students rarely explore international issues in their immediate social circles. In a classroom setting, most of the time students have a similar set of experiences. Connecting diversity and internationalization initiatives is a productive way of bringing in the unexpected, unknown and out of reach to IR classrooms.

Educational benefits of diversity (Gurin et al.; Packard) created a common thread among curricular goals of various institutions. For instance, as Forest suggests diversity-related learning goals of the United States Military Academy in some ways resemble learning goals of many seemingly different colleges. While diversity and inclusion alongside global citizenship frequently appear in websites and mission statements of various universities, these concepts are moving targets for students and educators. From "teaching race and social justice at a predominantly white institution" (Bauer and Clancy, 72) to "student biases about the Middle East" (Cavdar et al. 2), research reveals challenges faced by educators in various settings. It also shows the importance of paying attention to ever evolving cultural dynamics between students and faculty members as well as the cultural background of students (Bertrand and Lee; Waldron-Moore; Abboud).

Diversity and internationalization in higher education are evolving concepts with seemingly separate origins (Wong; Braskamp). This separation is rather surprising since both concepts are about the inherent value of understanding variation in human experience. While inclusion of previously excluded identity groups and social justice are central in diversity initiatives[1] (Smith, 2009; Wong), internationalization[2] highlights the value of understanding diversity at global scale. This difference is also connected to historical evolution of both concepts. Smith (2009, 51) suggests, "[t]he earliest efforts toward diversity were attempts to open doors to those who were excluded by law from educational institutions." According to de Wit (1999, 2) "in the European medieval university and in the Arab university even earlier, academic and social/cultural rationales for internationalization were dominant: the wandering scholar looking for knowledge and an understanding of other cultures." Wong's (3) research argues while "[d]iversity ... arose out of concerns for civil rights, racism and issues of empowerment," internationalization was mostly on "promoting international understanding and economic competition." Olson et al., with a focus on unveiling "the overlap between internationalization and multicultural education" explains the separate origins of these two concepts with the following:

> Available research does not provide a consensus on what is meant by these concepts, beyond a general recognition that, in the U.S. context at least, multicultural education focuses largely on domestic diversity, while internationalization focuses on knowledge of cultures outside the United States, on relationships between nation-states, and on global trends and systems. (Olson et al., v)

In the same vein, Braskamp (3) suggests "[i]nternationalization is often viewed in terms of a global international perspective rather than a domestic concern" and discusses importance of finding "a common ground" with reference to Olson et al. Similarly, Wong (4) points to possibilities of "reconciliation" between internationalization and diversity. Smith (2009, 63) explores how identity-based exclusion created an identity-based outlook at diversity and proposes "rather than engaging diversity as a list of identities or creating a uniform set of policies and practices, framing diversity in terms of how the institution's mission and goals can be improved through the lens of different groups or issues provides an opportunity for both inclusiveness and differentiation." Smith's (2009, 63–64) diversity framework engages with both "global" and "local context" with "four dimensions"[3] and "shifts the focus from groups to the institutions." This diversity framework creates space for internationalization with its emphasis on the global context.

In our project, we hope to bridge the gap that is outlined in the works of Wong, Olson et al., Braskamp, Killick and Smith (2009). In IR courses, where international focus is a given, teachers have the opportunity to highlight the global dynamics of inequality, racism, discrimination and repression. For example, when our students compared violence against women in Turkey and the US, they discussed global dynamics of gender-based violence. As they explored political discourse on Kurds, they discussed social justice and inclusion in both countries.[4] Being able to focus on these issues with an international peer, who is unapologetically different, created an impactful teaching environment that takes advantage of both diversity and internationalization.

PROJECT OVERVIEW

Evolution

Our collaboration dates back to the spring of 2011.[5] Initially, we connected our courses, both titled *Contemporary Issues in Turkish Politics* (CITP), through a series of blended learning activities. We had the opportunity to repeat this project three times (spring 2011, fall 2011 and fall 2012). In our previous article, we explained how we used technology "in a bi-national context as a blended teaching tool in an upper-level college course for instructors pursuing a similar exercise" (Akbaba and Başkan, 1).[6] Our original goal was to expand the horizons of our courses with the assumption that connecting our students via video chat technology, by itself, would elevate the learning environment. When we started almost a decade ago, the use of video conferencing was not a common practice in our institutions. Therefore, we centered our learning goals on exploring the benefits of technology in international projects. Over these three semesters, we engaged more than 90 students by merging our courses via Skype™ to conduct classroom-to-classroom discussion sessions and assignments that required students to work in pairs.

Due to various professional reasons, we no longer offer the CITP course at GC. We transplanted part of this project to a senior seminar in rotation to ensure continuity and regularity. In this second phase, we connected a GC senior seminar (*Religion, Democracy and Foreign Policy* – RDFP) and the IUE upper-level course CITP three times (fall 2015, fall 2017 and fall 2019). This change was an opportunity for us to revisit our initial learning outcomes and make adjustments to the requirements of each course.

This chapter focuses on changes we've made since this transition. Our observations suggested that one-on-one discussion sessions provided high-impact learning opportunities for students of both institutions. What appeared to be innovative in the early stages, i.e. use of technology, took a backseat as we observed it was the international peer learning that was leading the learning process. With this in mind, we decided to focus more on one-on-one team-project assignments and support them with locally led discussions. We expanded in-class discussions that branched out of one-on-one sessions and created space in our weekly sessions for reflection on international team assignments.[7] The benefits of peer learning kept shining though in our observations. Peer learning refers to "the acquisition of knowledge and skill through active helping and supporting among status equals or matched companions. It involves people from similar social groupings who are not professional teachers helping each other to learn and learning themselves by so doing" (Topping, 631). Among the peer-learning models, our approach is closest to "cooperative learning." Topping (632), with reference to the work of Slavin, suggests in cooperative learning, students do not simply work on a task in groups, but collaborate with a sense of "positive interdependence." Topping adds that (632) this process tends to "involve the specification of goals, tasks, resources, roles, and rewards by the teacher, who facilitates or more firmly guides the interactive process." We established a sense of "positive interdependence" though joint assignments. All student reports required contributions from both sides. As teachers, we had guided them closely in the process. What students needed to accomplish was outlined in detail. In addition, the performance of students contributed to their overall course grade.

Assignment Design

The GC senior seminar, RDFP, examines the role of religion in IR with a focus on foreign policy analysis and democratization. Turkey is examined as a case study. Professor Başkan continues to offer CITP as an upper-level course in IUE that fulfills one of the major requirements of the Political Science and International Relations department. This course seeks to familiarize students with the main issues that have considerable impact on Turkish political life in the post-1980 period. Drawing upon academic studies conducted on different dimensions of politics in Turkey, special attention is paid to the discussion of the issues of the Turkish modernization project, consolidation of democracy, civil society, secularism, the rise of Islam, ethnic nationalism, political parties, socio-political changes, and modernity in order to capture the essence of the changing nature of Turkish politics.

We connect these two courses with three projects and a common set of course materials on the themes of the project.[8] GC students start the project in the second part of the semester, after spending roughly eight weeks exploring Muslim democracies in general and Turkish politics in particular. IUE students come in with a strong foundation in Turkish politics due to the scope of their course and their country of residence. Joint assignments aim to reveal different strengths of students as learners in the context of each course and as global citizens experiencing higher education in different countries. These assignments send the message that they need the other student to connect the dots and complete the assignment. We present a diverse composition of teams, in and of itself, as a resource to be used.

Students collaborated with their international counterparts to complete three team assignments on secularism, populism and elections.[9] While the questions of two assignments aimed to produce a discussion on topics specific to the Turkish case (secularism and elections), one assignment encouraged students to talk about a dominant political trend (populism) in the United States and Turkey.[10] Students were asked to describe the recent political climate in the United States and Turkey and compare the manifestations of populism to figure out similarities and differences between experiences in two countries. This assignment showed the rise of populism in the United States, an established democracy, and in Turkey, which has been trying to achieve democratization since the transition to a multi-party system in 1946. Each assignment required students to have a one-on-one discussion session with their international counterparts. We encouraged students to use video chat systems, such as Skype, for their virtual meetings. Although we call these "Skype projects," since Skype was commonly used when we started in 2011, over the years students customized their software use with the help of advancement in video chat applications. After their international meetings, students were asked to share their experience with their classmates.

ASSESSMENT

In this section, we report direct (student performance) and indirect (survey) assessment results.

Direct Assessment: Performance

As part of direct assessment, we report on anonymized performance data of GC students, who had taken RDFP in the last three iterations.[11] Students engage in various assignments, one of which is a research project. We compare Skype project papers with seminar leadership, short papers and overall (scaled) course grade.[12] Our rationale of comparison with these assignments is explained below.

Skype projects
GC students are paired up with IUE students at the beginning of the semester. Students had three Skype (or any other video call application) meetings with their international teammate to talk about specific discussion questions.[13] GC students wrote a report for each session. Reports are graded as full credit, (that is 100 out of 100) or no credit (that is 0 out of 100). There was an in-class discussion on each set as well. During these sessions, students were asked to reflect on their discussions on their individual experiences. Skype projects, as the assignments that included international counterparts, will be compared with other performance data.

Seminar leadership
Seminar leadership consists of preparing a presentation and a series of questions for class discussion based on that week's course material and facilitating a discussion using those questions. Students work as part of a team of two or three. This assignment is compared with the Skype projects since it requires students to work with other students. The main difference is they work with their classmates, not with international counterparts. So, in some ways we can observe differences in performance with "local" and "international" teammates. By nature, this assignment is different from Skype projects since it is presentation/discussion based. The only written material provided are discussion questions and presentation slides. Seminar leadership is graded from 0 to 100.

Short papers

All students are required to write one short paper for each seminar leadership session using the course material. Each paper answers a general question on the themes of the course. Short papers are graded as full credit, (that is 100 out of 100) or no credit (that is 0 out of 100). This assignment is compared with Skype projects since the grading style (full or no credit) and frequency (multiple assignments embedded in one category) are similar to Skype projects.

Results and Discussion of Performance Data

Table 13.1 outlines the performance comparison of students. We included all students (47), who had enrolled to the course offered in GC in the last three iterations of this project. Students' data are anonymized by removing all names and replacing them with a number. We used the average of the assignments with multiples such as Skype projects and short papers. Out of 47, 11 students performed worse in the Skype projects in comparison to the seminar leadership assignment of the course. The median value for this comparison is 8, that is the median student performed 8 points higher in Skype projects than seminar leadership. Out of 47, 36 students performed better in Skype projects than seminar leadership.

Out of 47, ten performed worse in in Skype projects in comparison to short papers. The median value for this comparison is zero, meaning no difference among compared assignments for the median. It is important to add that many

Table 13.1   Course assignment performance comparison

Course	Number of students with a negative value (number of students that performed worse in Skype projects)	Median value for the comparison	Number of students that performed the same in Skype projects	Number of students with a positive value (number of students that performed better in Skype projects)	Total number of students
Skype projects and Seminar leadership	11	8	0	36	47
Skype projects and Short papers	10	0	28	9	47
Skype projects and course grade (scaled)	10	10.79	0	37	47

students performed similarly in these assignments, i.e. 28 students performed the same while 9 performed better. This is the only comparison that reveals such a broad neutral zone. There might be various reasons for this. Maybe it is the rubric and/or students' approach towards the course or their learning style that determines performance here, meaning, both of these assignments required consistent, frequent engagement with course material. There are multiple assignments in each category. In other words, there are multiple Skype projects and short papers. Both groups of assignments aim to engage students frequently throughout the semester. Nine students performed better in the Skype project when compared with short papers.

Out of 47 students, 10 performed worse in the Skype project in comparison to the scaled overall course grade. The median value for this comparison is 10.79, meaning the median student performed 10.79 points higher in Skype papers in comparison to their scaled course grade. Thirty-seven students received a higher grade for their Skype project in comparison to their scaled course grade.

This exploratory analysis suggests that many students performed well in their Skype project in comparison to some of the other assignments as well as the overall (scaled) course grade. This analysis does not provide definite answers to the question of why this might be taking place and/or if this is due to the diversity components of the Skype project assignments. There are additional limitations to this analysis. First of all, it is impossible to know why students performed better or worse in a particular assignment with the performance data available for these courses. In addition, reported comparisons are not apples-to-apples. Either the rubric or the type of the compared assignment is different. For example, seminar leadership is an oral presentation/discussion assignment while Skype papers report on one-on-one meetings of students with their international counterparts about a set of questions. Short papers, on the other side, has a similar grading rubric, but does not rely on collaboration with anyone. Also, students might have performed better simply because the Skype assignments were easier. (We didn't design them to be easier, but this could be an unintended consequence.) This exploratory analysis aims to reveal a general, anonymous look at students' performance to complement survey data as well as our observations and reflections. Skype projects required students to spend many hours to complete a relatively small contribution to their overall course grade. Time-zone difference, language barrier and general time pressure of the semester make this assignment an unappealing one to pursue unless students think they will gain something out of it. While there are exceptions, students rarely decided not to participate in the project and they rarely gave negative feedback on the experience.

Over the years, we have witnessed something unusual taking place with these projects.[14] Seeing how students light up when they report on their meet-

Engaging with diversity through technology 169

ings during our discussions, and how they connect the dots on the subject matter of the course, we think there is high-impact learning taking place during these sessions. We suspect weaving international and diverse peer-learning experience into other course material is the secret ingredient. Over the years, many students have indicated their enthusiasm for this project. However, we are also limited by our own biases and prefer to think students benefit from this collaboration. Although we will never know for sure in the absence of a comparison, we are planning to hold on to the spark we observe in our classrooms. Survey results, which are discussed in the next section, provide ample support for this.

INDIRECT ASSESSMENT: SURVEY

Broad View

At the end of fall 2019 semester, we administered an anonymous survey to capture IUE and GC students' take on the Skype sessions. This survey included two questions on the project and one open-ended question that is welcoming any additional comments. Questions aimed to encourage students to think and reflect on their experiences broadly.[15] The following questions were asked:

- Did you find Skype projects helpful?
- What were the most intriguing/interesting/eye-opening parts of the Skype sessions? (If there were none, please write "none.")
- Anything else?

Although we didn't ask about the previous experience of students to keep the survey anonymous, we know many of GC students who participated in the survey had studied abroad. Almost "60% of Gettysburg students study globally for at least one-semester."[16] Both GC and IUE strive to provide education in small classrooms. Students are not strangers to active learning methods. Many courses take advantage of innovative pedagogical techniques. In other words, students came to us with experience in discussion sessions, global interactions and active learning methods.

Sixteen out of 17 students from each course answered the survey questions, bringing the total number of respondents up to 32. The students of these two courses unanimously found the project to be a positive learning experience. For some GC students, the project offered a new perspective and a "unique insight of the politics of Turkey." Only two GC students stated that the idea was great but they encountered some scheduling and connection problems, and additional issues due to the language barrier. We know that more students had scheduling problems. It was interesting that only a few brought this up

170   *Teaching international relations*

as a concern. We identified the following themes across the comments: jux-taposition of differences and similarities in learning environments, reflection on self-growth, observations on skill development, thoughts on identity in the presence of a new "other" and increased engagement with the course content in the form of curiosity or additional research.

Closer Look

When we examined the details of students' responses, we observed various positive notes. Students suggest that assignments motivated them to carry out further research on the project themes, enhanced their critical thinking skills, created peer-learning opportunities, exposed them to different perspectives, helped them exchange their ideas with a student from another country and improved their English language skills.

IUE students wrote comments that suggest a sense of responsibility to provide accurate information on Turkish politics. It seems like they were moti-vated to do additional research on the course material to be able to explain the content well and provide accurate information to their counterparts.

An IUE student underlined the significance of international teamwork in expanding their motivation to learn more on the subject matter:

> It is a great advantage for both foreign students and for us. Because there is a mutual interaction. Also, even though we have information about the issues, we are not very good at it. For this reason, it is beneficial for us to have a research process in order to provide more information.

Critical thinking is known to be one of the significant components of higher order thinking (Miri, David and Uri; Brookhart). Through conversations with their teammates, some IUE students realized that they had not been examining the topics of Turkish political life in a critical manner. In other words, they had become aware of their uncritical stance when they discussed with their team-mates various contemporary issues of Turkish politics. One writes "talking about Turkish politics with a non-Turkish person and looking at the events through the eyes of someone from outside made me think more critically and objectively." Similarly, another IUE student stated that:

> while working with my partner and answering questions about political climate in Turkey, I realized that I have never truly been objectively thinking and criticizing everything regarding politics. These Skype sessions made me question my knowl-edge about current issues in Turkey and motivated me to research them much more, in order to be an objective and reliable person as much as I can be in the future.

GC students, on the other side, didn't mention development of critical thinking in their responses. They identified different benefits. One theme that emerges in their responses is appreciation of a different perspective. It was helpful for GC students to have access to the first-hand accounts of people who are experiencing the topics of the course. As one of them put: "The skype projects were really interesting because they allowed us to get the perspective of someone who is actually living through the events we are learning about." In addition, one GC student stated that during the Skype sessions they realized the inconsistency between the media coverage and the experience of people on a particular issue.

Students' perception on peer learning surfaces with various positive associations. Three GC and two IUE students remarked that learning from each other through team assignments was a unique opportunity. One IUE student underlined that "It was nice to talk with an American about Turkish politics and learn more about American politics. I learned the general idea of Americans about Trump and his policies and American laws. It was an informative activity for me," while a GC student stated that "I really enjoyed talking to someone my age about issues relevant to both of us. It was also a nice break from the classroom and a different way of learning."

When students do not have an opportunity to participate in a study-abroad program or in a cross-cultural collaboration, they are not "able to make real connections with people in different places" (Shaw 2016, 354). Even when they get to study abroad, these experiences do not necessarily overlap with the content of the course material. As internationalization scholarship suggests, there is a variation in the scope of international projects. Engaging students internationally on the elements of the course could add on even when students have global experiences.

Having conducted this project in a Global North country and in one from the Global South, we have provided an opportunity for our students to engage with an aspect of diversity that is not commonly explored. As mentioned earlier, many of both GC and IUE students have global experience through study-abroad and exchange programs. However, their experience might not be connected to the themes of the course. For instance, for a GC student, who studied internationally, but did not travel to the Global South, this project could be their first exposure to some ideas/perspectives from the Global South. In other words, for some GC students, whose global experiences are limited to Western Europe, a simple conversation with a student from Turkey could be a high-impact learning experience by simply revealing a novel point of view. This might explain why many GC students highlighted the benefit of "new perspectives." For IUE students, novelty could be as simple as GC students' questions on Turkish politics. This could help IUE students distinguish what they have simply accepted to be the truth without question as part of their upbringing, and what they have built as an opinion through critical thinking. As one of the IUE students put it, this could be quite a revelation:

> I found Skype project helpful. Because talking about Turkish politics with a non-Turkish person and looking at the events through the eyes of someone from outside made me think more critically and objectively. Also it was a chance to inform them more accurately about Turkish politics.

GC students reported that participating in this project was a unique experience in helping to humanize the concepts of the course. A GC student remarked that "I thought it was a great way to personalize the study of IR, which is something that is difficult to do if you are not in a study-abroad program." For GC students, it is also important to hear the personal stories of Turkish students. This gives a glimpse of Turkey that is not available through research books and articles, or even documentaries. Furthermore, when they were discussing completing the team assignment on populism in the United States and Turkey, four IUE students and two GC students mentioned that they were surprised that there are several similarities between these two countries. One of the IUE students expressed their feelings as:

> The thing that was surprising for me was that the similarities among the young populations' problems and dissatisfactions with the current political situations in both United States and Turkey. I strongly felt that my partner and I were very displeased with the fact that we were unable to participate in shaping our future. Both of us had so many ideas and desires of "ideal Turkey" and "ideal United States" but with our discussions in the Skype sessions made me realize that as two individuals living in different parts of the world, neither of us truly believed that we could achieve our ideal states.

Another student also emphasized a common thread running across their lives as: "it is really interesting to see the similarity of worries of Turkish and American youth about their future in that kind of a political environment." Similarly, a GC student remarked that "it was very interesting learning from people in another region of the world and how similar our viewpoints."

Our students found value in the opportunity to exchange their ideas with a student from another country. For an IUE student, this project was "interesting and eye-opening because I had the opportunity to share my ideas with people from another country and also learned her ideas." Three IUE students and a GC student were surprised that their teammates knew about the details of Turkish politics or US politics. One IUE student remarked that their teammate:

> knew all the political developments regarding the authoritarian tendencies of the current government. But, the shocking part was that, he also knew what public opinion thinks on recent events. For example, he knew about the success of Ekrem

İmamoğlu and gave many details regarding the role that İmamoğlu played as a political figure. To be honest, I was not expecting him to know such details about Turkish politicians.

Similarly, for a GC student, "it was really interesting to see how much people in other countries know about US."

Similar to other cross-cultural collaborations, which have underlined the importance of these projects in language development for non-native English students (Shaw 2016; Wang) the most visible skill development input from IUE students is improvement in their communication skills in English. Five out of 16 IUE students believed that this project provided a ground for them to practice English. Their survey responses and informal feedback suggest this project increased their confidence as non-native English speakers. One of them underlined it as follows: "I don't trust my speaking skill, so thanks to this project I am more comfortable." This is intriguing since students perceive improvement in their language skills by simply engaging with a peer on three projects.

Student perception as captured in survey responses reveals a shift in the thought process that goes beyond the scope of the course. We suggest this could be due to diverse composition of the groups. The transformative nature of the comments suggests bringing people with different experiences together to solve puzzles and find answers might be unlocking learning processes effortlessly. We are aware of the fact that not having a control group limits our findings in this part as well. We also understand surveys are perception-based assessment tools. In other words, although as teachers we value perception of our students tremendously, what students perceive to be positive might not reflect realization of the learning outcomes. Therefore, we remain cautious regarding our results.

CONCLUSION

This chapter examined the benefits of diversity and internationalization in the context of a cross-cultural collaboration project. Exploratory analysis of performance data and survey responses suggest a productive learning environment and encourages us to think further about ways to diversify our IR courses.

General IR courses as well as more specific courses on a country or theme could benefit from similar initiatives. At the design stage, we found connecting the learning outcomes of each course to the goals of project to be important. For implementation, an excellent professional relationship among instructors is the key. This is not an off-the-shelf project. Instructors will need to remain in touch to facilitate joint activities, and to identify logistic issues. Looking back, we realize remaining in contact was central for the longevity of our partnership. It might be helpful to note that we didn't actually know each other prior to this project. It all started with a brief email. By grafting two courses offered in two different counties, we expanded learning possibilities not only for our students, but for ourselves as teacher scholars.

NOTES

1. Smith (2009) provides a lengthy definition of diversity and evolution of its principles in Chapter 3.
2. Knight's early definition of internationalization, which refers to "The process of integrating an international, intercultural or global dimension into the purpose, functions and delivery of post-secondary education" is frequently used by other scholars. For detailed look at evolution of the concept see de Wit (2020) and Qiang.
3. Four dimensions include "climate and intergroup relations"; "access and success"; "education and scholarship" and "institutional viability" (Smith 2009, 64).
4. These examples are from different iterations of the project.
5. The first iteration of this project was supported by the Mellon Foundation's Embedding Research in the Gettysburg Curriculum grant.
6. Our previous publication, which analyzed different data and referred to different set of iterations (Spring 2011 and Fall 2011 semesters), aimed to describe what we had done, how we did it and lessons learned. In this chapter, our focus is on the impact of diversity and internationalization. In addition, our previous publication focused on a different GC course. In other words, this project, using new data sources examines our experiences from a different set of course offerings.
7. Due to scheduling problems we have encountered in the past, we have abandoned classroom-to-classroom discussion sessions.
8. Although the reading materials of the two courses did not completely overlap, team assignments were identical for both groups. We independently prepared our students for the upcoming project through lectures.
9. CITP, as a required course, tends to have higher enrollment than RDFP, which is limited to 16 students. To balance enrollments, we only included CITP students who volunteered to participate in this project. We paired up students and kept track of their progress.
10. These are examples from fall of 2019. Over the three iterations, we updated the assignments regularly. All team assignments are available upon request.
11. Gettysburg College's IRB reviewed this project and decided that it is exempt from IRB review. Listed topics are from the last semester (fall of 2019).
12. Weighted value of some of the reported assignments changed over time. We kept the Skype project report numbers the same, but questions changed over time. In other words, over the three semesters assignment composition of the course changed.
13. Students were strongly encouraged to have at least an audio component in their discussions. There were exceptions. Although rarely, some students communicated through emails or text messages due to the time difference or unusual circumstances.
14. Although the last three iterations are reported here, we have collaborated six times since 2011.

15. Since IUE students are non-native English speakers, some of their comments include grammar and syntax errors. We kept students' comments in original forms.
16. Center for Global Education. Gettysburg College: https://www.gettysburg.edu/offices/center-for-global-education/ (accessed May 30, 2020).

14. Becoming an effective online teacher: five considerations for better teaching and learning in IR courses

Brandy Jolliff Scott

ONLINE EDUCATION: WHERE ARE WE NOW?

In 2018, *Inside Higher Ed* reported that 34.7% of college students were enrolled in at least one online course, a number that has grown exponentially since online education began in the mid-1990s (Perry and Pilati). Although the rate of growth appeared to slow by the following year, 2020 is likely to be a watershed moment. The experience of the COVID-19 epidemic will have lasting effects on online teaching and learning. While the dramatic conversion to online education in the COVID-era is a temporary shift, it is also likely to leave in its wake increased demand for online courses as more students and faculty are exposed to real online education. Indeed, even before the events of 2020, the same *Inside Higher Ed* piece noted that the steady growth of students participating in online education occurred:

> at virtually all types of institutions and at all levels of post-high school learning ... the data show that graduate students are the most likely to take at least some of their courses online (nearly 40 percent do), followed by four-year (34.5 percent) and two-year undergraduates (33.8 percent). (Lederman 2019a)

Thus, not only has online education been growing consistently, it has done so primarily in the types of institutions and programs at which most international relations (IR) faculty teach.

And yet, for the vast majority of IR faculty, online teaching and learning remains a very unfamiliar practice. In 2014, only about 15% of those in tenured or tenure-track positions had taught an online course, as compared to the 21–22% of contingent faculty who had done so (AAC&U 2014). Online teaching also suffers from a host of negative perceptions, namely that it lacks the personal/social connections of the face-to-face (F2F) classroom, that it prioritizes certain skills, such as writing, over others, and that it is an inferior form of teaching and learning (see Singh and Hurley). However, as I show in this chapter, online education in IR need be none of these things. In fact, there is even evidence to suggest that high-quality online education may be at times more effective than traditional F2F models of education (Nilson and Goodson; US Department of Education). Many of the arguments to the contrary come from those with little to no experience with online teaching or from those who have experienced poor quality online teaching, which certainly does exist. In the remainder of this chapter I provide a grounding of online teaching and learning within a pedagogical framework and address five key considerations that, I believe, can help us become better teachers in IR classes online.

PEDAGOGY OF ONLINE INSTRUCTION

The pedagogy of online education developed out of the pedagogy of teaching and learning more broadly. Many of the same things we know about what makes for high-quality teaching and learning in the traditional classroom also applies online (Nilson and Goodson). However, just as online education is a much newer form of instruction than face-to-face (F2F), many of the most innovative pedagogies are ones best suited to online education. The overwhelming consensus is that a constructivist, student-centered pedagogy (Brooks and Brooks, Freire) is the most effective in online classes (Knowlton; Nilson and Goodson; Parker, Maor and Herington; Pelz). Online teaching is best not when the professor performs a positivist, "sage on the stage" role, but when students and faculty engage together in the process of learning. The constructivist pedagogy lends itself to a more social process, whereby classrooms are filled not with professors and students as distinct entities with very divergent roles but with a community of learners working together to understand the complexities of the world. According to Knowlton, such an approach is both ideal and necessary in online instruction. Precisely because one of the criticisms of online education is that it is impersonal and asocial, employing the "student-centered" approach to teaching allows for a dynamic, highly engaging learning experience. We will explore these ideas much more later.

Additionally, other emergent pedagogies are useful in online teaching. The active learning approach is one that can easily be implemented in the online setting and is highly reflective of the constructivist approach (Krain, Kille and Lantis; Lantis, Kille, and Krain; Pelz; Phillips). More recent (and highly necessary) calls for inclusive, transformative, and contemplative pedagogies can be used in the online classroom to potentially great effect (Coombs; Meyers; Miller; Moriarty; Zajonc), as creating online courses prompts faculty to reconsider course design, materials, and accessibility. Using the opportunity when creating a new online course to think purposefully about the types of materials we use and the diverse student audience in online education is key as more students and teachers engage online and as we continually seek new ways to increase the critical thinking, empathy, and civic engagement of our students.

Even more traditional approaches such as Bloom (see also Miller) can be implemented in an online setting as well as we think about the best ways to engage students and appeal to the diverse learning styles and experiences inside the online classroom. Given that the best approaches to online teaching are often very similar to the best approaches to F2F instruction, in the remainder of this chapter I present five considerations which can help IR faculty become better online teachers.

FIVE CONSIDERATIONS FOR BETTER TEACHING AND LEARNING ONLINE

Online Teaching Is Effective Teaching

When done in a pedagogically informed, evidence-based manner, the best online courses are as good as, and sometimes even better than, F2F (Bernard, et al.; Jorgensen; McLaren; Means et al.; Neuhauser; Nguyen; Salter; Silver and Nickel; US Department of Education; Ya Ni). What does it mean to do online teaching well? Best practices rely on asynchronous methods of teaching and learning, which have been shown to increase learning outcomes for students significantly. Collaborative, asynchronous classes require students to actively work with one another, which increases (rather than decreases) the social component of learning (Jorgensen; Palloff and Pratt). They do these things to greater degrees than they would in a F2F setting (Jorgensen; Poole), and, as a result, some studies have shown that students report higher levels of motivation and satisfaction with their courses than in traditional classes (Jorgensen). Most studies show that online teaching which attempts to mirror the lecture-based style of teaching in a synchronous setting is inferior to all other modes of instruction (Bernard et al.; US Department of Education). Thus, this is not to say that all online teaching can compete with F2F. If, however, we become better educated about the best practices of online teaching we can remedy both our negative assumptions and inferior outcomes in the online class and improve learning for our students.

In my own courses, I find that a combination of pre-recorded mini-lectures ranging from 10 to 20 minutes or so, complemented by a series of intentionally designed, immersive activities, to be a highly effective way to structure a course that is both engaging for students and rewarding for me. A typical Introduction to International Relations course for a 16-week semester might be subdivided into weekly modules. Within each weekly module, I combine lecture, readings, and activities to make room for both content delivery and content application. As instructor, I try my best to strike a balance between the faculty-centered and student-centered approaches to teaching and learning. I see my role as that of delivering essential content and my students' role as that of learning to understand and apply content. I use the (video, pre-recorded or live) mini lecture for essential content (key terms, concepts, a few illustrative examples) and weekly reading assignments from an introductory textbook expand upon the content of the mini lecture. A weekly online quiz ensures that students must engage with the reading.

For content application, students engage dynamically with reading or other content as well as with their peers. There are a range of possible types of assignments that can be used for content application. The use of discussion boards, blogs (Allen; Hansen; Mathews and LaTronica-Herb), multimedia (Salter; Mathews and LaTronica-Herb), evidence/data-gathering exercises (Bachner and O'Byrne), and even simulations (Mathews and LaTronica-Herb; Parmentier) are increasingly common, and all reflect an active learning-based pedagogy that employs asynchronous course design to achieve high-quality outcomes and enhance student learning. As more and more universities create online course options, as more data and free access teaching materials are available to instructors, as social media and application use becomes more sophisticated, the options for instructors seeking to create an immersive online course become nearly limitless.

Online Courses Create the Potential for More Dynamic Course Material Use

Because of the asynchronous nature of good online courses, faculty have opportunities to use course materials they may not feel they have time for in a F2F class. Traditional textbook and academic sources still often provide the foundational reading for online classes, especially in the age of eBooks and publisher-provided digital course materials, but online teaching also brings with it even greater opportunities to incorporate immersive content available via the web that has the potential to improve student learning.

The benefits of multimedia use are significant, and instructors may find they can create more space for immersive content in an online class than within the time blocks of F2F courses. While bad practices certainly exist, studies show that if chosen strategically and implemented mindfully, multimedia and other materials can enhance student learning (Hannafin, Hill, and Land; Malik and Agarwal; Miller 2016). There is considerable evidence that much of learning is visual (Miller 2016), and use of video, film, photos, etc. can add critical visual content to complement audio lectures or verbal slides. Illustrative diagrams, charts, interactive websites, YouTube clips, and so on aid in students' efforts to make sense of abstract concepts and in problem-solving (Malik and Agarwal). Video and film in particular have been shown to assist in empathy-development in learning and facilitating deep thinking (Miller 2016; Stoddard). Online simulations give students the opportunity to learn by doing through high impact practices (Salter; Malik and Agarwal). Even something as simple as effective use of PowerPoint for slide creation or using the Learning Management System (LMS) to its full potential can improve the effectiveness of teaching online. Furthermore, including a variety of multimedia source material has been shown to be especially effective for improving the learning of students who have little foreknowledge of course material (Krippel, et al.). If we want to find ways to best teach our students who most need teaching, dynamic material use through the implementation to multimedia sources may be one of the best strategies we can adopt in online teaching.

Instructors might choose to incorporate regular consumption of professional political science (or related) blogs. Allen (2016) writes that assigning students reading of popular blogs *The Monkey Cage* and *Duck of Minerva* in an introductory level IR survey course resulted in improvements in student scores on multiple choice exams. Students also reported that reading the blogs improved their understanding of course content. Another possibility in an online course is to engage students in the writing of blog or blog-like assignments. This would be especially useful if using a "class blog" where students and the professor regularly updated the blog with current event, research, or related content. Hansen finds that having students complete short, blog-style writing assignments allows for creativity and that students are more likely to use both news sources and professional sources in their writing, a useful skill for the workforce. In an online class, both blog-based approaches could be used, where students are assigned to read and keep up with relevant IR blogs but also required to emulate blog-style writing with either individualized blog-style assignments or through the curation of the "class blog".

Another exciting option is the use of simulations in IR classes. Many of us have used simulations in F2F courses to promote active learning. Indeed, in this volume Cox (Chapter 8) and Rosen and Asal (Chapter 9) discuss in-depth the use of simulations in the IR classroom. Not only can simulations be used in online courses, they are especially effective ways to teach IR online (Malik and Agarwal; Mathews and LaTronica-Herb; Miller; Parmentier) and could be used to simulate a range of IR scenarios, such as United Nations General Assembly meetings, NATO summits, crisis bargaining scenarios, trade talks, etc.

I have tended to use a combination of class blogs, short videos such as Ted Talks or YouTube clips, and podcasts to enhance text-based course materials. Ted.com has many excellent 20 minute or so talks on a range of issues relevant to IR, such as globalization, war and conflict, climate change, human rights, peace and cooperation, and regional issues. Similarly, *Planet Money* is a great resource for podcasts in International Political Economy (IPE) courses, while the BBC's *The World Today* and *Africa Today* provide great international and Africa-specific content, and *The Economist* has a variety of podcast episodes on issues ranging from international business to the United Nations to global pandemics. I use carefully selected audio or video to prompt discussion posts, illustrate abstract concepts with real-world stories, and allow students to visualize the real-world effects of phenomena such as climate change and global development. I have nearly always been pleasantly surprised with the quality of student engagement in these settings, where there is greater need for students to rely on reading materials to complete their posts and all students must participate, rather than hide silently in the back of the classroom.

Teaching Online Contributes to More Inclusive Teaching Practices

Teaching online is a great opportunity to reflect on how we foster inclusivity in the classroom. What is inclusive teaching? Broadly speaking, inclusive teaching refers to the practice of teaching to students of diverse backgrounds, experiences, and learning abilities, including but not limited to students from marginalized racial, ethnic, or cultural groups, students of low socioeconomic status, disabled students, non-traditional students, first generation students, non-native English speakers, etc. (Gannon; Moriarty; Chanock). As higher education has expanded, so too has the range of students who have access to it. But not all students come to the classroom with the same experiences and abilities. Students who have experienced systemic marginalization and exclusion often face significant obstacles to learning that white, middle class, male, traditional students do not face. To teach inclusively is to be aware of the fact that students come into the classroom with a range of experiences, many of which act as overt or subtle messages that tell them they don't belong in a college classroom or a particular field of study, and to actively take steps to counter those messages through the materials we use, the pedagogies we adopt, and the ways in which we make our classes accessible to all students.

Just as online IR courses are ripe for implementing immersive content, so too are online courses great places to start adopting a more inclusive approach to our teaching. In the online course, two important ways to be more inclusive in our teaching are (1) by being mindful of the content we assign and (2) creating content that is accessible to students of a range of abilities. In his recent book *Radical Hope*, historian Kevin Gannon writes of his own realization of the limitations created by not paying attention to inclusive course content. However, once he updated his reading assignments to include books by female authors, he found his teaching "represented a diversity of scholars ... I also concluded that this experiment led me to choose not just different, but *better* materials" (Gannon, 54–55).

The same attention to the material assigned can be given in the IR class-room. In Introduction to International Relations, for example, we can start by making equal space for Feminist Theory and Postcolonialism alongside Realism, Liberalism, and Constructivism. When covering the -isms it can be helpful to leave room to deconstruct the disproportionate influence of white, Anglo-European perspectives on the development and deployment of these theories. Two recent pieces in *Foreign Policy*, "Why is Mainstream International Relations Blind to Racism?" (Bhambra et al.) and "Why Race Matters in International Relations" (Zvobgo and Loken), are excellent commentaries on the racist influences in IR theory and are great for starting conversations in the classroom. Among the works of the -isms, we can assign more readings by female and minority scholars. We can do the same when we move into studying conflict or in other specialized topics or courses. Assigning work by any number of the highly regarded women in the Women in Conflict Studies (WICS) Association is a great place to start for those who are unsure. The Women Also Know Stuff and People of Color Also Know Stuff websites are great resources for finding women and People of Color (POC) scholars working on any number of topics in political science, and these pages can be searched by topic or author. Assigning course readings by scholars who are representative of our students sends a strong signal to those students, that no matter who they are or what their background is, they too can be political scientists.

On the topic of accessibility, creating an inclusive classroom that is mindful of accessibility is always important, but it is especially so in the online class-room. Online education has in many ways been a democratizing force in higher education, allowing for more and more non-traditional students to have access to college courses, certificates, and degrees than ever before (Jorgensen). But with that increased access comes the increased need for accessibility. The more students we reach, the more likely we are to encounter students who have physical, mental, learning, or other disabilities (Jorgensen). Creating inclusive classrooms means also creating accessible classrooms. Become familiar with your university's Disabilities Services office. While they may not have staff whose job it is to take course content and make it accessible, they typically have a world of knowledge and advice about how you can do so on your own. Get to know the Accessibility Checker tools in Microsoft or the software of your choice, and familiarize yourself with university, local, state, or national policies and laws that determine what the requirements are for accessible classrooms in your area.

There are Pitfalls to Overcome

Although online teaching and learning unfairly suffers from negative assumptions, it would be disingenuous to claim that there are not also some common pitfalls that contribute to this. Three of the most likely issues faculty face in online instruction are that it requires significant work (especially at the start) for faculty to adjust to online teaching, students may fall behind more easily than in F2F classes, and both faculty and students at times have to deal with lapses of motivation.

On the first point, in order to construct an effective online course, effort is required (Hardy; Jorgensen). Some universities (but not all) require advanced training for faculty who teach online. Budgeting time to complete any required training is something to take into account when planning to teach online. Plan to familiarize yourself extensively with the ins and outs of your university's LMS, as you will likely need to utilize this tool to a much higher degree than previously. There are also any number of other applications and programs that one might want to learn. We are nearly all familiar with Zoom, but learning how to effectively organize breakout rooms is beneficial for synchronous group work, simulations, or meetings within a larger class session. If you've used and enjoyed iClickers in large F2F classrooms in the past, learning Kahoot might be a good option for instantaneous student feedback polling. Perusall is a great application for assigning students reading and annotating activities for group discussions or projects, such as simulations. The various apps in the Google suite are worth becoming familiar with, especially as more students make the switch from more expensive word processing tools like Microsoft Word or Apple's Pages to the free and user-friendly Google Docs.

In addition to the time needed to become trained in appropriate technologies, you'll also need to take more time developing course materials. You may need to pre-record lectures or other videos, which can take significant advance time, but it is not necessary to have all content of an online class posted and available to students from day one, unless required. Instead, choose to roll out content on a weekly or unit basis to allow more time throughout the semester to plan and prep and to prevent students from being overwhelmed by too much material all at once. Plan to spend time within your LMS developing a well-organized course layout, where readings, assignments, lectures, quizzes, exams, etc., are all easy to find for students. In short, teaching online requires considerable planning and forethought, though this effort is greatest when teaching a class for the first time and/or at the beginning of the term. Once you have taught a class online, it becomes significantly easier to replicate the course for the next term.

The second pitfall is that students may fall behind or drop out at higher rates than in a F2F class (Glazier; Jorgensen). But there are steps faculty can take to reduce these risks. The first is to construct a student-centered, asynchronous course. Student disengagement, lack of community, and few personal interactions often contribute to poor retention. Courses which rely upon a collaborative pedagogy where students engage actively both with one another and with their instructor tend to lead to higher levels of student-reported motivation (Glazier). Creating assignments and projects within an online course that require group work (Zoom breakout rooms, assigning team-style simulations rather than individual role playing, creating group research paper assignments, and group presentations in the form of video or audio recordings) are all strategies that can combat problems of disengagement and create social accountability in online courses. Also, be conscious of issues of access. While it may often be safe to assume that students enrolling in online courses have reliable Internet and computer access, in fact this may not always be the case. Holding students accountable for such things is necessary on a basic level of course, but so too is keeping in mind that students who take online courses are more likely to come from non-traditional backgrounds than students in traditional settings and may not have constant Internet or device access. Being mindful of these realities of postsecondary education in the twenty-first century (and especially in the wake of COVID-19) can help us to take measures to enable the success of all of our students. Keep in mind issues of bandwidth, paywalls, and file sizes when creating course content. Rather than constructing self-paced courses where students have no regular deadlines but must simply complete all requirements by the end of the term, make sure to have predictable, weekly deadlines for completion of some work—a reading quiz due each Thursday, for example—but also remember to be flexible and to make allowances where appropriate. Adopting an inclusive pedagogy requires us to keep in mind issues of equity, and this is especially true in online teaching.

The third pitfall is related heavily to the first two—at times in an online course both we and our students are likely to suffer periodic lapses in motivation. Creating online courses often requires significant work ahead of the semester during valuable "break" time to be ready for the new term. We may have to learn new technology and adopt new (to us) pedagogies to create effective classes. If teaching exclusively online, we may at times feel detached from our students, especially if we have become accustomed to the social interactions of the traditional classroom. Adjusting to a new reality can be difficult. If students in our classes do become disengaged, we may allow ourselves to get sucked into a vicious circle, where poor performances from students create poor performances by us, and vice versa. Students also have to adjust their expectations and find ways to engage and motivate themselves that are different from what they may be used to. However, the good news is that focusing time and attention on many of the issues already discussed can help

Becoming an effective online teacher

us to combat these issues for ourselves and for our students. Thus, this leads us to the final key consideration.

Becoming a Better Online Instructor Can Make Us Better Teachers in the Classroom

As is the case with many things in life, we get out of online teaching what we put into it, and our mindset at the beginning affects our experience. If we as faculty dedicate ourselves to constructing, or reconstructing, our classes and pedagogies, we may find that lapses of motivation in online courses may be just as temporary as those in traditional settings, that we can address student retention, and that the time we spend before teaching a new online class not only improves that class, but can be used to improve our F2F classes, too. Teaching online affords us an opportunity to dust off stale syllabi, improve our teaching fundamentals, and correct bad habits that time and inertia helped us to succumb to. If we embrace these opportunities and if we engage critically with our course material and interactions with our students, we can just as easily be energized and find renewed motivation for teaching!

Online teaching both requires and gives us permission to explore new approaches to the classroom and the material we use. For example, Krain, Kille, and Lantis discuss the importance of teaching cross-nationally in the IR classroom, especially during the era of globalization: "cross-national approaches can yield greater cross-cultural understanding" (143) and cross-national teaching's benefits include better understanding of global content and development of empathy, civic engagement and efficacy, and problem-solving skills, all of which are important for today's students of IR. Such cross-national teaching is particularly fruitful in an online setting where social media can be used to connect students cross-nationally (Shaw). In this volume, Akbaba and Başkan describe their own cross-national project linking students in an IR course in the United States with students in a similar course in Turkey. Such a project could just as easily be done in an online course as in a F2F course.

IR courses that teach quantitative methods or heavily use empirics can also be taught online in a way that harnesses the Internet to create, collect, and analyze data. Bachner and O'Byrne discuss many creative approaches to teaching research methods online, all of which could be easily adapted to the IR classroom. Some of the approaches they suggest include using social media and textual analysis tools to create and collect data, using Mechanical Turk and Qualtrics to create and collect survey data, and using Zoom for teaching data analysis directly to students. All of these could be tailored to focus on IR topics. For example, students could create a survey asking respondents questions about foreign policy attitudes, affinity towards International Governmental Organizations (IGOs), whether they would support a hypothetical conflict, etc., the results of which could be used to perform a rudimentary test of theoretical concepts. Instead of asking students to create their own data, they could be assigned to collect data from Peace Research Institute Oslo's (PRIO) armed conflict data, Freedom House, the World Bank's World Development Indicators, etc., to collaborate on data collection assignments with their peers using Google Sheets. Faculty who begin using such assignments in an online class could then easily continue such activities in a F2F course as well, thus creating active learning components in both settings, and improving student learning in the process.

As we learn to teach online, we may become more comfortable with teaching hybrid courses or with creating "flipped classrooms" (Whitman Cobb). Flipped classrooms, which have become highly buzzed about along with the rise of active learning pedagogies, are essentially a form of hybrid course, which is the most effective type of class for promoting student learning (Bernard et al.; US Department of Education). As faculty become better educated in technologies and strategies for teaching online courses, they can use that knowledge to transform their existing F2F courses into hybrid or flipped courses as well! Once we know how to create an effective video lecture, how to harness the Internet for dynamic material use, and how to use the LMS to create student interactions through discussion posts, blogs, etc., we can then use these same tools in our F2F classes and improve the quality of our teaching and courses there as well. Indeed, one of the most surprising (and welcome) bits of feedback I received from a student after the end of the Spring 2020 semester in which I had to rapidly transform a F2F course into an online one was that I should use many of the online components the next time I taught the class in person. This student loved the use of short videos and podcast episodes to prompt discussion and writing assignments and found them to be highly engaging. Having to condense my lectures down to short, asynchronous video lectures meant I had to focus on delivering the main points and big picture takeaways, and it meant that students could easily return back to those mini-lectures whenever they needed to. It also meant that instead of me telling my students everything they needed to know, now they had been granted the independence to start with my guidance but then go out into the online world to use and apply that knowledge. Robert Beck's excellent article on transforming an International Law class into a hybrid course reflects a similar awakening. He writes,

> I revisited materials that I had not considered for years. I sought out photographs, diagrams, and maps to enliven the case exposition ... Another benefit of my blended course was largely personal: I thoroughly and consistently enjoyed the face-to-face class meetings of my International Law Course. I could feel confident that the more foundational "nuts and bolts" material had already been systematically delivered in my online mini-lectures, and that virtually all my students had already identified

> their primary areas of difficulty with that material. Accordingly, I could focus my face-to-face energies on those areas of greatest student difficulty ... I could concentrate on the more dynamic, interactive, and therefore exciting aspects of case method teaching ... . (Beck, 283–284)

Finally, as we work to build rapport online, we may improve our F2F habits as well. Rapport is crucial to improving student engagement and success in any classroom, but it is especially true for online courses, whereas, as we have already discussed, students can suffer from structural and motivational obstacles to success. Glazier suggests taking special care to create multiple opportunities to interact individually with students. Creating lecture and video content that not only delivers information but also humanizes the professor is important. One particularly interesting suggestion is to use technology to provide students with handwritten feedback electronically using Adobe and a stylus pen is a simple way to convey to students that we as faculty are not so distant. Reaching out to students individually via email at regular intervals to provide them with one-on-one connections is another method. While the online class clearly creates challenges for faculty to create connections with students, becoming more conscious of how we connect with our students in the online class can lead us to also reflect on how we build rapport in our F2F classes, and become more effective there as well.

CONCLUDING THOUGHTS

With the growing and substantial percentage of college and university students enrolling in online courses even before the era of COVID-19, it is clear that more and more faculty will likely teach online in the future. While online teaching and learning suffers from a host of negative stereotypes, some of which were exacerbated by the frantic, crisis-driven approach of 2020, the fact is that the quality of pedagogically informed online courses can be equal to the quality of in-person courses. And teaching these courses can be equally rewarding if faculty approach online course design and execution with the same respect and attention they give to their traditional courses. It is true that online teaching involves a considerable amount of work especially before a course officially begins, but this is true of any high-quality course we might teach, no matter the medium. What's more, IR courses are some of the best suited to online instruction. Faculty can make use of things such as current events, simulations, digital subscriptions to news media, and downloadable and interactive data sources to illustrate key IR concepts such as war, peace, globalization, and human rights. Further, flexible asynchronous course designs that maximize student–student and student–faculty interactions and deliver active learning and high impact practices into our courses enable us to improve student learning and performance in engaging and rewarding ways. Far from being an inferior, impersonal method of instruction, good online teaching in IR courses can help us improve our teaching both online and in F2F classes in ways that enliven and energize ourselves and our students.

15. Collaborative learning in the IR classroom

Heather A. Smith

It's common for collaborative learning to be defined, or implied to be, teaching practices that focus on student collaboration in the virtual or face-to-face classroom characterized by some sort of peer-to-peer interaction (Cusimano; Boyer 2000; Cornell University Center for Teaching Innovation; Bates). Angela Wolfe, for example, adopts the following definition: "Collaborative and cooperative learning – based on the premise of active learning where students become engaged in and responsible for the learning process – use small groups to increase student knowledge and to enhance higher order thinking skills" (Wolfe, 421). Pierre Dillenbourg, in an extensive review of collaborative learning literature shows us that activities that get labelled "collaborative learning" are diverse and vary in terms of the size of the group doing the learning, the assumptions of what constitutes learning and the types of interactions we expect or hope for during the activity that we label "collaborative learning" (Dillenbourg, 1–2).

In International Relations classrooms we can find examples of student collaboration between classrooms across national borders (Krain et al.) and examples of collaboration with community partners and/or variations of service learning (Garcia and Longo; Kyoto University of Foreign Studies). There is also literature that highlights student collaboration in simulations (Boyer 2000) and student collaboration through crowdsourcing (Wilson 2018). Peer-to-peer work, in whatever form it takes, tends to the focus of the literature.

However, these forms of collaborative learning are not the focus of this chapter. I want to ensure that faculty members are part of our discussion of collaborative learning, not as experts or professors, but as learners. Our classrooms must be spaces where we all learn and where we all practice our commitment to collaborative learning. We learn together – students and faculty. I want us to think about the values that inform our understanding of collaborative learning and encourage you to think, "who am I in this process?" I will also share with you some practices for fostering a space of mutual teaching and learning. As Kevin Gannon notes, "a pedagogical philosophy must be more than sloganeering; it has to pervade our decisions and actions as well"

189

(25). Faculty–student collaborative learning starts with the values we adopt in the creation of our class and is manifest in the practices and processes we adopt during our teaching.

In the next section of the chapter, I introduce myself. I do this in part to give you a sense of who I am, but where I teach, what country I teach in, my role and rank and the demographics of my students all matter to how and what I teach. I then turn to a discussion of the values that inform my teaching and highlight the influence of critical and feminist international relations, critical pedagogy and the students-as-partners approach. Consistent with the view that we need to put our values into practice, I also share some of my practices related to syllabus design, formative feedback activities and the application of the values of the students-as-partners model. Ultimately, my hope is that faculty take the opportunity to reflect on how we too are collaborators in teaching and learning.

WHO AM I?

I want to begin by introducing myself because context matters. Who I am, where I am located and the classes I teach all matter to the way in which I approach teaching. And while the insights I share below are designed to be broadly applicable, introducing myself to you will help you to both connect with this work, and have an understanding of where I'm coming from – both literally and figuratively. I do also acknowledge that writing in this form and using my own voice is also a political and theoretical statement (hooks, 70) given that I am not presenting myself "as absent, as distant, and as indifferent to the writing and ideas" (Inayatullah, 5). And so ...

My name is Heather Smith. I'm a Professor of Global and International Studies at the University of Northern British Columbia (UNBC), which is located in Prince George, British Columbia, Canada. UNBC is located on the traditional territory of the Lheidli T'enneh. My university is a small, primarily undergraduate university and "17% of the students self-identify as Indigenous" (UNBC, 5). I've been at UNBC since 1994. I teach both undergraduate and graduate courses in a range of areas and for the fall of 2020 I'll be teaching fully online. My primary areas of research are Canadian foreign policy and the scholarship of teaching and learning. I consider myself a critical feminist. It's also worth noting that I'm middle aged (one might have guessed that given how long I've been at UNBC), a cisgender woman and white. All of these components matter in terms of my approach to teaching and my interpretation of collaborative learning in the International Relations classroom.

WHAT VALUES DO YOU BRING TO YOUR TEACHING?

We need to ask ourselves: what are the values I bring to my teaching? This question is important because reflection on the values we bring to our teaching helps us in our teaching practices. The values that inform my teaching are informed by three different bodies of literature: feminist and critical international relations, critical pedagogy and the students-as-partners approach.

As I have articulated elsewhere (H. A. Smith; Kehler et al.) feminist and critical International Relations scholarship has informed both my research and my teaching. Core insights from the feminist literature can translate directly into our teaching. For example, feminist scholars encourage us to adopt a "feminist curiosity" (Enloe 2004, 3), to investigate "sites of everyday life" (Enloe 2004, 5), to challenge disciplinary practices that seek to shape who and how we study (Doty 2001; Parpart and Parashar) and to regard "theorising as a way of life, a form of life, something we all do, every day, all the time" (Zalewski, 346). If we pose these questions in the context of our teaching, we are reminded that our classrooms, regardless of modality, are political and politicized sites of everyday life.

When we regard our teaching as a site of the everyday, a place and space of politics, we can then ask questions arising from feminist and critical international relations that help us reflect on our teaching practices. For example, Robert Cox's well-known phrase that "theory is always for someone and for some purpose" (207) translates directly to our teaching if we assume that teaching is always for someone and for some purpose. We need to ask for whom is our teaching? Feminist and critical scholars also invite us to ask, where are the silences and margins (Enloe 2004; Parpart and Parashar)? Whose voices do we hear (Doty 2014)? And when we ask questions about voices, margins and silences, we need to pose them in ways that are intersectional. International relations has a long history of "a willful amnesia on the question of race" (Krishna, 401; Zvobgo and Loken), a disregard for questions of gender, and a marginalization of Queer and LBGTQIA+ (lesbian, gay, bisexual, transgender, queer, [or questioning], intersex, and asexual [or allies]) questions (Weber 2014; Richter-Montpetit). These silences and absences can be replicated in our teaching or we can challenge the silences through how and what we teach in our classes.

The second body of literature that has shaped the values that inform my teaching, is critical pedagogy. The work of Henry Giroux reminds me that our institutions generally promote a "the culture of positivism" (20) in which knowledge is treated as objective, impersonal, bounded, measurable, universal and ahistorical (Giroux, 20–21). Teaching practices are about domination, not emancipation, and are informed by "principles of order, control and certainty" (Giroux, 25). Paolo Freire (72–77) calls our attention to "banking education" which discourages critical inquiry, grants authority to teachers as mediators and speakers of knowledge, separates teacher and students, and treats students as mere empty receptors of the knowledge of the teacher. Ira Shor challenges assumptions of students as deficits and reminds us that our classroom practices model our values. Reading bell hooks requires that I reflect on my whiteness because teaching is embodied (hooks, 137). Jessie Stommel's work on ungrading challenges me to think about the meaning and use of grading and options for alternative assessment. In Stommel's words: "Grades are a morass education has fallen into that frustrates our ability to focus on student learning" (np). Kevin Gannon's work, *Radical Hope*, gives me hope – and like all the authors included here – understands that teaching can be a space of radical potential – a space of transformation (hooks). Taken together the work of critical pedagogy scholars reinforces the view that teaching is not neutral. For me, critical pedagogy also compliments the critical and feminist approaches to international relations as insofar as critical pedagogy reminds us that our classrooms, and the way we design our courses, are potential site of silences.

The third body of literature that informs the values I bring to my teaching is the students-as-partners literature. As my collaborators and I have noted elsewhere (H. A. Smith et al.) the literature on students-as-partners is vast (Acai et al.; Ahmad et al.; Bovill et al. 2016; Felten et al.; Healey et al. 2014; Marquis et al.; Seale; Seale et al.). Central to this literature is the assumption that "partnership is a way of doing things, rather than an outcome itself" (Healey et al. 2016, 9). Moreover, partnership is values based. For Healey et al. (2014, 14–15) the values which inform the students-as-partners process are: authenticity, inclusivity, reciprocity, empowerment, trust, challenge, community and responsibility. In the 2016 update of Healey et al. trust, courage, plurality, responsibility, authenticity, honesty, inclusivity, reciprocity and empowerment are identified as the values that inform students-as-partners (Healey et al. 2016, 2).

Partnerships can occur in research, teaching and course design, university governance, university programming, and scholarship of teaching and learning. Partnership is not "add student and stir" and it is not simply about bringing a student into faculty research or governance and claiming that you are engaging in students-as-partners. Partnership is different from student involvement or student participation (Healey et al. 2014, 16). The literature on partnership highlights the "need for students to play not only central roles, but increasingly equitable roles" (Werder et al., 5) and provides for co-creation. Partnership is not easy, and it requires that all participants (students, faculty and administrators) commit to the partnership in ways that will disrupt traditional hierarchies and which emphasize the student voice (Kehler et al.; Bovill). It is essential to note that "partnership may not be possible, or indeed appropriate, in all learning and teaching contexts" (Healey et al. 2016, 15) and that designing and implementing partnerships is also always context specific.

To me, the students-as-partners framework is appealing for a variety of reasons. First, many of the values that inform the student-as-partners framework are consistent with those articulated above. As argued by many students-as-partners advocates, the model has the potential to disrupt hierarchical and non-democratic practices in higher education (Center for Engaged Learning; Peters and Mathias; Mihans et al.). Second, the framework foregrounds the student voice, challenges views of "student as client" (Center for Engaged Learning) and requires all of us to work collaboratively to challenge spaces and processes that can undermine authentic engagement by all partners. Third, while I do believe there are tendencies for the model to be overly self-congratulatory at times and there is often an underestimation of sites of power in our teaching practices (Kehler et al.), there is scholarship that engages with those limitations (Seale et al.; Matthews; Peters and Mathias; Martens et al.) and provides insights into the way in which we can reflect on power in partnerships (Verwoord and Smith).

PUTTING VALUES INTO PRACTICE

If we're going to move beyond the rhetoric of how much we value collaboration, and if we are going to challenge constructions of "us" versus "them", we need to be mindful of the myriad ways in which we express our values. Below you will find a set of suggestions of how to put critical feminist and critical pedagogy values into practice as an instructor, thus facilitating a collaborative space between you and your students.

An essential starting point for our reflections on the creation of collaborative learning spaces is the creation of our course syllabus. Not only does a syllabus construct our discipline for our students, it tells a story of who the instructor is – intentionally or not. As Ira Shor notes: "the syllabus deployed by the teacher gives students a prolonged encounter with structured knowledge and social authority" (14). Our syllabus is often the first impression our students will have of us. In face-to-face classes students have the experience of the tone of our voices, our physical presence as well as the expression of who we are in a course outline. If somehow the impression we give in the course outline is inconsistent with how we engage face-to-face, we can address that gap in person. Online, especially if there is no synchronous component, well … those course outlines are significant representations of who we are.

So, if someone read your syllabus, without knowing you, what impressions might they have? Do you use the "academic" third person? What is the tone? Do you tell the students a bit about yourself and if so, what do you say? Is your self-description full of articles you've written or are there more personal touches? How do you present your assignments, due dates and late penalties? Where are we in our syllabi? As Kevin Gannon writes: "If we create syllabi that are simply information dumps or policy sheets, it's hard for us to stand before our students and talk about things like active learning, engagement and collaboration" (98). Moreover, when we review our syllabi, it's worth asking if they read like a projection of professorial "unilateral authority" (Shor, 19) and create a space where "education is experienced by students as something done to them, not something they do" (Shor, 20).

If we want to foster collaboration with our students, it starts with our syllabus. We need to step away from language that is too distant and detached. We need to inject ourselves into the syllabi and invite students into the process. Our syllabus needs to be welcoming, while also informative and well organized. For some, there are limits in terms of how they might do this given commonly adopted syllabus templates or other curriculum design requirements, but it's worth a try … and maybe it's worth a try to get those requirements changed! Nonetheless, if you have the flexibility to make that change, find yourself a teaching buddy who can give you honest feedback on your syllabus. "Consider having a colleague from well outside your discipline read your syllabus and offer feedback on its clarity, organization and content" (Gannon, 107) and review it from a student perspective. What tone are you setting? What does your syllabus say about the way you hold space and share space with your students? Is it your space or our space?

Content also matters. The readings we assign and the authors we include all matter. If we adopt a textbook in an Introduction to International Relations course, for example, that is dominated by the perspectives of white, Western, male, cis, scholars we are sending a signal to our students about who and what matters in our field. "Textbooks bestow upon students ready-made lenses through which to see international relations, which inevitably constrains the ability to think creatively about potential alternatives" (Smith and Tickner, 2). In addition, we effectively build in structural obstacles to students who may not otherwise see themselves in the constructed "we" of the field. Our content is never neutral. Our content always sends messages about the discipline. If we do not have diverse content in our courses we also send signals about our openness, as instructors, to diverse and complex views of the world. How do you foster collaborative learning spaces between students and the faculty if you don't signal openness to diverse perspectives in your content? Our students need to see themselves in our course.

One final comment related to content is that we should also try, where possible, to adopt or even create, open educational resources (OER) in our classroom. OER "are teaching resources that have an open-copyright license (such as one from Creative Commons), or they are part of the public domain and have no copyright. Depending on the license used, OER can be freely accessed, used, re-mixed, improved, and shared" (BCCampus). This may seem to be a strange suggestion in a chapter on collaborative learning, but the use of OER, where possible, recognizes the structural obstacles to students affording textbooks. If we want to foster collaborative learning, surely we want to ensure the students can access the tools to be part of the learning process? There is significant evidence that the use of OER reduces course costs for students (Dimeo). For those teaching international relations, the E-International Relations, has a wide variety of excellent options, including textbooks (E-International Relations). And OER isn't just textbooks, we also know that by using alternatives or different resources can help with encouraging student engagement. We could also use podcasts and blogs.

Another key way that faculty can build a collaborative ethos in the class and foster collaborative learning between themselves and the students is through the use of formative feedback mechanisms. Formative feedback activities, according to the Tufts University teaching and learning website, are: "activities are typically ungraded or low-stakes opportunities to promote and measure student knowledge and skills" (Tufts University, n.p.). For faculty, formative assessments help us to understand what the students are experiencing in our classes, as we become what Stephen Brookfield calls a "phenomenological detective" (96). These kinds of assessments also help us to identify areas of miscommunication (Brookfield, 108), and helps us to assess if the values we espouse are being experienced by the students (Brookfield, 112). In terms of student learning outcomes, formative assessment supports students in "self-regulation" (Nicol and Dick) which is understood to be "active monitoring and regulation of a number of different learning processes" (Nicol and Dick, 199). For students, the key for me is that through the use of formative assessment, we can support them to become reflective learners (Brookfield; Nicol and Dick).

For me, formative feedback activities signal to the students that, in our classrooms, we are all teachers and we are all learners. If we are to have a collaborative learning space, we must all be willing to learn. As faculty members, we must be willing to meet our students where they are at and we must seek authentic feedback, acknowledge the feedback and adapt. It is also essential to me that formative feedback activities be designed to place the "emphasis on learning rather than on performance" (Bain, 155). These principles have informed the way I design formative feedback activities.

One of the activities I've regularly included in my classes over the years are learning journals. When students engage with them, I find them to be amazing windows into student learning and very helpful to me in terms of supporting the learning of students. In the learning journals, dispersed throughout the semester, I ask students to identify their learning goals or to tell me about what is working for them in the class or to identify what is confusing. For these journals I try to encourage students to unpack how they understand their own learning. For the last learning journal, I ask them to reflect on the evolution of their learning throughout the semester.

I have made the error in the past of giving "points" for completed learning journal entries, thus undermining my own efforts to focus on learning rather than performance. Once you add the "points", for weekly submissions the focus becomes the "points". This year I've adopted an "ungrading" approach as articulated by Jessie Stommel (n.p). Students will be provided with guidance and feedback on their learning journals throughout the semester. Drawing on a suggestion by Darby and Lang (112) my feedback will focus on emphasizing what was done well in the particular learning journal submission and what students should do next time to more fully articulate their learning.

Another feedback mechanism I use regularly in my classes is a mid-semester check in. I typically use "Stop, Start, and Continue" (Humber College). The "Stop, Start, and Continue" feedback process essentially asks students to reflect on what they need to stop, start and continue to do to foster their own learning success and to provide feedback to the instructor on what the instructor can stop, start or continue to do to support student success. This feedback is done anonymously. It could be facilitated by a neutral third party such as someone from a teaching and learning center or could be done using an anonymous survey. You could have students write their responses on paper and submit them, although some students may worry that their handwriting is recognizable and this option privileges students who are able to provide something handwritten, thus potentially marginalizing some students in your class. However, you choose to collect this information anonymity and access must be considered. And remember, that when we are given feedback, we need to address it. We cannot ask students to take responsibility for their own learning if we are unwilling to take responsibility for our learning.

The students-as-partners literature provides us with a host of examples of collaborative learning between faculty, staff and students both within and outside of the classroom (Healey et al. 2016; Bovill, Cook-Sather and Felten). Students-as-partners can be applied to research practices, where the student is more than a research assistant: they are an actual partner and they are a named author. Students-as-partners has also been applied to programs where students act as pedagogic consultants on faculty teaching or course design. Governance and university programming is another area where you can work with student partners. There are numerous possibilities for the adoption of the framework. And while the outcomes for faculty and student will vary according to the way the partnership is designed, the literature highlights a host of possible outcomes. Roisin Curran, drawing from the wide body of students-as-partners literature highlights the following student outcomes: "development of the learner leading to better citizens, ... enhances motivation and learning, ... improves teaching and classroom experience ... improves learning in terms of employability skills" (Curran, 2–3). Engagement outcomes for staff (faculty) include: "transformed thinking about and practice of teaching; changed understandings of learning and teaching through experiencing different viewpoints; reconceptualization of learning and teaching as collaborative processes" (Healey et al. 2014, 20). Below I share a few examples from my experience.

I was an administrator for many years and tried to adopt the students-as-partners model in institutional programming. One instance, which is discussed in detail in a forthcoming piece by myself and Yahlnaaw (Smith and Yahlnaaw), related to designing an "Indigenizing the Curriculum" speaker series. Yahlnaaw is a Haida woman and was a student employee. By working with her, and ultimately having her lead the series, programming that would have otherwise been designed through a process imbued with colonial assumptions, became a series that was designed by an Indigenous woman and designed with Indigenous practices and ways of knowing at the fore. In this instance, the learning for me was extremely powerful and required me to reflect on how my Western, white, everyday administrative practices could ask to silence and marginalize. The student partner became the leader and teacher. If we are actually willing to engage in authentic learning with students our institutional spaces can change to be more inclusive and culturally sensitive spaces.

Within our classrooms there is a variety of activities we could adopt to build in elements of the students-as-partners model. Given the structural power of the faculty member within the classroom that creates hierarchy and the fact that they are grading students it is hard to claim "partnership" in the classroom, as much as we might wish to make that claim. Students are acutely aware of the power structures and will not always buy into claims of partnership (Martens et al.; H. A. Smith et al.). Nonetheless, we can build collaborative spaces that provide opportunities for student ownership and student innovation.

One way to build in collaborative spaces is to use various types of crowdsourcing in our classes. For example, across the range of undergraduate course levels, from first year to fourth year, I regularly leave weeks where the students can select the topic and in some instances they select the topic and the readings for the week. The selection of the topic can be done through some sort of polling mechanism. The selection of the readings could also be done by polling with the instructor providing some guidance, or in smaller classes, you could encourage students to do some research to identify and suggest readings for the week. This latter approach, of having students do some research to identify readings takes a bit of set up in the beginning of the class and could be associated with some sort of class activity, or class engagement, grade.

I've also used crowdsourcing to have the students participate in the creation of exams. I've asked the students to work together to create multiple-choice questions and I've had them work together to create essay style questions. This process provides the instructor amazing insights into what the students think are the key concepts, themes, and debates in a class and so it functions as a feedback mechanism. The process provides the students with an opportunity to review their learning to that point and have a hand in the creation of the exams. The students are also required to provide the answers to the multiple-choice questions. For the essay style questions they create, they are also asked to consider how they would go about answering those questions. We also take some time to work together – students and faculty – on both the wording of the questions and the possible responses. We would together create the final product. This does take time away from content delivery in the course, but the process provides for learning on the part of both faculty and students – it provides for collaborative learning. I will also note that the students regularly create questions that are more difficult than the ones I would create. The value of crowdsourcing for our students is that it "makes students active participants in shaping the learning content and encourages the use of shared resources to support critical thinking" (Wilson, 401).

The opportunities for partnership with students inside and outside the classroom are only limited by our imaginations. The examples I gave, related to inside the classroom, are still rooted in a high degree of instructor control and there are ways in which my courses could be opened up further. Nonetheless, the practices and processes are underpinned by a commitment to my collaborative learning that means we all learn – students and faculty.

CONCLUDING REFLECTIONS

As a far too avid a consumer of teaching and learning posts on Twitter, I'm often struck by posts by faculty members who insist on using some sort of online exam surveillance technology or who insist that students must have their cameras on while in a Zoom classroom. I note this because these examples epitomize the public articulation of values in complete opposition to the values and approaches advocated here. Online exam surveillance speaks of a lack of trust in our students and an inability or unwillingness to think about innovative assessment. Demands for cameras on reflect a lack of sensitivity to the conditions in which the students may be living. These public statements may seem inconsequential to some, but these same faculty members will then wonder why their students are not engaging. The students are not engaging because students have been sent signals that they are untrustworthy and we don't care what about their living conditions and/or privacy. As faculty, we set the tone for collaboration and engagement through our teaching materials, practices and processes.

Collaborative learning in our classrooms is not just about how we create groups. Collaborative learning must include an understanding that both students and faculty learn. Faculty learn from students. Students learn from faculty. For faculty members, taking this position can be risky. I've seen quite politically radical faculty members be quite conservative teachers. They want to inspire learning, but they are risk averse in terms of their own learning. We need to be learners. We need to take the risks and in doing so our teaching and learning spaces become more open and collaborative for all.

PART III

ASSESSMENT AND EFFECTIVENESS

16. Assessment and effectiveness of active teaching and learning in IR

Matthew Krain and Kent J. Kille

As the editors emphasized in the introduction to this volume, international relations instructors are well served by the use of active teaching and learning in their classrooms. Active learning should better connect students to the learning process and encourage stronger educational development. But how do we translate such a "philosophy of student engagement and active learning" into effective practice? Carefully designed and applied assessment of active teaching and learning is central to answering this question. This involves ensuring that instructors are reaching their students as intended through their active teaching, including building assessment in a manner which acknowledges and incorporates different student viewpoints and pedagogical focus. In other words, assessment allows us to make sure that we are meeting the needs of all students through careful feedback and reflection.

The chapter begins by setting the groundwork for effective active teaching and learning in the international relations classroom. Carefully scaffolding the assessment of active teaching and learning, beginning with clear educational objectives before establishing the best applications and procedures for meeting those objectives, is essential. Assessment and reflection then acts to support the active learning cycle. The chapter continues by considering how assessment can be used both to identify whether educational objectives are being met and to help students enhance their learning and achieve those objectives. Next, the chapter provides an overview of general types of assessment measures and tools, followed by specific discussion of a few methods of assessment that are effective for both accountability and improvement. The chapter concludes with a brief discussion of how such thorough use of assessment can support the publication of strong pedagogical research on teaching international relations.[1]

WHAT MAKES ACTIVE TEACHING AND LEARNING EFFECTIVE?

Effective active teaching and learning is pedagogy that yields greater student engagement and deep and enduring learning. Paying careful attention to four central components – educational objectives; examples and range of applications; procedures; and assessment and debriefing – enhances the effectiveness of international relations active teaching and learning (Lantis, Kille, and Krain). As the first step, instructors should ensure that they are focused on the specific educational objectives to be met, which could be of the class, department, program, or broader institutional curriculum. The key point is to ask: "What should the students be learning?" This foundation allows instructors to build up the related exercises, procedures, and assessment of whether this worked. Thus, the specific teaching applications employed, such as those detailed in Part II of this volume, need to be justified relative to the desired educational outcomes. Once an instructor has established the educational outcomes (why) and applications (what), they can turn to the specific procedures (how) for a particular exercise.

The use of active teaching and learning is incomplete without the essential fourth step: assessment. At this stage, students and instructors revisit the educational objectives to ask: did the approach work? Were the objectives met? It is through such reflection that learning truly occurs. Assessment is often viewed as mandated from above, as in the situation with a full program or curricular review. Within the classroom, assessment is often linked solely to summative assessment where student learning is evaluated at the end of instruction. However, when seeking to assess active teaching and learning, it is important to undertake assessment that occurs during the learning process through student feedback. Such assessment guides improvement and closes the assessment loop.

Assessment across the stages of learning provides useful information to both the students and the instructor. Students receive feedback on how well they have learned the concepts, information, and skills for that class. Instructors get feedback that allows them to evaluate how well they are achieving their educational objectives. By prioritizing and linking educational objectives to careful assessment, the focus is on the learning process and the desired learning outcomes, not content delivery. Instructors can better view and review the multiple possible ways to achieve desired outcomes, which allows them to flexibly pivot and adjust as needed. Overall, core class material remains delivered by the instructor, but the learning process becomes more student-centered.

HOW ASSESSMENT FACILITATES LEARNING

Careful, regularized assessment of educational objectives helps us to promote learning. Instructors receive much needed feedback to improve their subsequent teaching, or to identify what ideas need to be clarified. Students also receive important feedback, giving them a clearer sense of whether they are meeting a course's educational objectives. The questions asked to generate that feedback also shape student thinking and learning. They can be more than tools that yield *assessment for accountability*; they can be used as *assessment for improvement* (Angelo 1995; Wehlburg).

This is particularly true for assessing active teaching and learning approaches. Studies show that learning frequently occurs after, rather than during, active learning experiences (Boyer and Smith; Williams and Smith). In large part, this is due to the process of reflection stimulating more critical thinking about educational experiences. Active and experiential learning occurs in four mutually reinforcing stages of a cycle – experience, reflection, analysis, and application – none of which are sufficient on their own (Kolb). During active learning exercises, students are focused on what they are doing or undergoing and are not likely to be reflecting upon the meaning of the exercise. Given the opportunity to reflect afterwards, students can think about what they did and how to understand the significance of that experience. Such reflection leads to a better grasp of the concepts, processes, relationships, and outcomes of the lesson. Students engage in a deeper analysis of what was learned and are better able to apply that knowledge to subsequent situations.

What students are asked to think about as they reflect, and how the reflection questions are posed, shape student learning. Consider, for example, a student who has just completed a simulation of international diplomacy, such as a Model United Nations. A student asked to recall facts about the rules of debate, the position of the country that they represented, or the details of the resolution debated will likely focus on factual knowledge as important takeaways from the experience and will recall these facts later (Powner and Allendoerfer; Kollars and Rosen). A student asked to engage in higher order thinking about the process of diplomacy or the likelihood of international cooperation will be more likely to focus on theoretical or analytical lessons of the simulation, be able to recall the lesson outcomes, and then apply these to other situations (Kille; Obendorf and Randerson). In addition, students asked about their perceptions of how their own knowledge and skills have developed will engage in metacognition (Pettenger, West, and Young; Coticchia, Calossi, and Cicchi). Thus, a careful alignment of educational goals and assessment can be used to push students to more closely engage with and reflect upon the underlying theoretical arguments, concepts, and core knowledge to be derived. For this to be a valuable experience for both the student and instructor, instructors must explicitly guide students toward clear educational goals, connect student thinking to the lesson at hand, and then ensure that they reflect upon teaching successes and challenges (Wehlburg; Grussendorf and Rogol).

GENERAL TYPES OF ASSESSMENT MEASURES

Student learning can be assessed directly or indirectly. Instructors want to know whether students have actually mastered the material or can transfer that knowledge to new contexts. In those cases, *direct assessment* of what students have actually learned is appropriate. In other instances, instructors may be interested in other educational outcomes related the learning process. These may include student engagement with the material, enjoyment of the learning process, or metacognitive issues such as what students perceive they have learned, how confident they feel about their knowledge and their ability to deploy this understanding, or how they are processing the information. In such circumstances, *indirect assessment* – examining students' perceptions of their own thinking and learning process – can be a valuable approach (Angelo 1999; Walvoord and Anderson).

Qualitative measures focus on data collected as descriptive information or observations. Examples include qualitative performance assessment of student participation in an exercise (Obendorf and Randerson), analyses of themes that emerge from class discussions or debriefings (Kille; Krain and Lantis), student reflective journals, essays, or other structured reflection opportunities (Engel, Pallas, and Lambert; Hosman and Jacobs), project portfolios (Obendorf and Randerson), oral presentations (Biswas and Haufler), analysis of open-ended survey questions or minute papers (Smith and Boyer; Robinson and Goodridge; Rooney-Varga et al.), evaluation by peers (Burcu), student overall self-assessment (Pettenger, West, and Young; González-Betancor, Bolívar-Cruz, and Verano-Tacoronte), and even focus groups (Rooney-Varga et al.) or semi-structured interviews with students (Oberle, Leunig, and Ivens).

Quantitative measures focus on data collected as definite numerical or "quantifiable" amounts. This can include direct measures such as scores on quizzes or pre- and post-test questionnaires (Luna and Winters; Rooney-Varga et al.), rubric-based assessment of written assignments or oral presentations (Biswas and Haufler; Brown, James, and Soroka), frequency counts of key words or phrases used in student reflective essays (Simon), and performance assessment of student activity such as scores on a game, number of tasks completed, or effective arguments made during a debate (Eukel et al.). They can also be used to develop indirect assessment measures such as polling students for their opinions on a topic, feeling thermometers, self-assessment of activity performance, or questions measuring perceptions of understanding and/or engagement (Pettenger, West, and Young; Berdahl et al.). Qualitative feedback can also be quantified for further systematic evaluation (Rittinger).

In choosing among these types of measures, instructors must consider which assessment tools will best capture their intended educational outcome(s).

Instructors should also consider using multiple measures of assessment – direct and indirect, qualitative and quantitative – as they may capture different outcomes. For example, using direct quantitative measures of assessment Krain and Lantis found that simulations led to knowledge gains, but did not yield better student performance on fact-based pre- and post-test quizzes than a typical lecture and discussion approach. However, their indirect quantitative (Likert scale self-evaluations of level of understanding) and qualitative (analyses of open-ended survey questions and class debriefing discussions) assessment showed that simulations did lead students to obtain deeper and more nuanced understanding of the relevant concepts, processes, and moral dilemmas. In a recent study, Oberle, Leunig, and Ivens also demonstrate the benefits of a mixed-method approach, uncovering the effects of simulations that were not obvious in their accompanying large N quantitative analysis by also using interviews, content analysis, and qualitative comparative analysis.

METHODS OF ASSESSMENT FOR BOTH ACCOUNTABILITY AND IMPROVEMENT

Some of the most common and effective assessment techniques employed include: pre-test/post-test surveys or quizzes (Rooney-Varga et al.; Berdahl et al.), analysis of student writing and/or oral presentations (Grussendorf and Rogol; Biswas and Haufler; Brown, James, and Soroka), open-ended questions in written and/or oral debriefings (Rittinger), and student self- and peer evaluation (Pettenger, West, and Young; Burcu). All of these tools are effective ways of assessing whether students have learned concepts, theories, or processes to provide *assessment for accountability*. Examples abound of when and how they are used to measure the attainment of other educational objectives. The rest of this chapter surveys just a few of the wide array of assessment techniques available to instructors in the active teaching and learning international studies classroom that are also effective at enhancing student learning, i.e. *assessment for improvement*.

Using Rubrics for Assessment

A rubric is an assessment tool that "lists the criteria for a piece of work … and articulates gradations of quality for each criterion" (Andrade, 27). Rubrics are effective ways for instructors to reduce the amount of time grading, identify levels of proficiency in student achievement, and reduce bias (and perception of bias) in, and improve the reliability of, the evaluation of student work (Brualdi Timmons; Brown, James, and Soroka). *Holistic rubrics* provide evaluative guidelines for the entire student work output. They are useful in assessing whether the student was able to achieve a level of overall proficiency, when limited feedback is required, or when the purpose is summative assessment. *Analytic rubrics*, such as the one developed by Fung to assess learning objectives of a simulation of nuclear and humanitarian talks regarding a fictional Korean peninsula crisis, assess both individual skills or elements evidenced in the student work and also provide an overall assessment. Such rubrics provide more focused guidance and feedback on a variety of skills or tasks but are harder to construct and slower to use (Mertler). Either can be used to both assess learning and guide student learning, although analytic rubrics provide more fine-grained guidance for both tasks.

Many teachers use these tools as *grading rubrics* after an assignment, exam, or classroom exercise is complete to score student work and assess learning (Fung; Grussendorf and Rogol). However, they can also be used to facilitate the learning process. These *instructional rubrics* – such as those developed by Biswas and Haufler to guide students in developing employment-related soft skills in international relations classes – help students think about educational objectives *before* completing an exercise, thereby providing them guidelines on how to meet those objectives. Both types help instructors clarify their own educational objectives, clearly lay out clear expectations, and focus their assessment (and the students' intellectual work) on mastering a specific set of skills or ideas. Instructional rubrics in particular also allow students and instructors to focus on the key educational objectives of any assignment or exercise, learn specific skills, and engage in more analytical thinking and metacognition, thereby facilitating learning while doing (Andrade; Rublee; Brown, James, and Soroka).

Rubrics do have limits, however, as tools both to guide and to evaluate learning. For instance, Brown, James, and Soroka show that, while the use of rubrics leads to some improvement in student performance, the enhancement was small and not statistically significant. They argue that repeated use of rubrics over the course of a semester could create cumulative learning improvements, though their findings suggest that a one-time use has no such effect. A recent study by González-Betancor, Bolívar-Cruz, and Verano-Tacoronte demonstrates that rubrics are not as accurate when used for student self-assessment when compared to use by faculty members to assess student achievement of educational objectives. Self-assessment results are also often gendered. Despite clear rubric guidelines, men are more likely to give themselves higher scores than women. Students who later received lower scores on faculty-scored rubrics were also less likely to accurately assess their own performance using the same rubric than students who were later scored higher by their professors. Taken together, these studies suggest that rubrics are most effective as a tool to enhance learning when used repeatedly and cumulatively over time as part of instruction, and as an evaluative tool when used by the instructor rather than by the student.

The Minute Paper: Theme and Variations

Another assessment tool that is very effective at stimulating student reflection and metacognition, and also at providing instructors with targeted feedback, is the "minute" paper (Chizmar and Ostrosky). Students are asked to pause at some point during a class session (often two minutes before the end of class), given note cards, and asked to write down the answer to a simple but summative question, such as: "What is the most important thing that you learned today?" The goal is to get students to pause, process the class material, think about the "big picture" takeaway from class, and reflect on what they have just learned. The feedback instructors get from these cards helps them to determine whether students took away the intended points or made the expected connections. However, the tool is also effective for helping students process what they have just learned or experienced as well as deepening their understanding (Light; Angelo and Cross).

A variation on this is the "muddiest point" paper – where students are asked to write in reaction to this question: "What is the muddiest point still remaining at the conclusion of today's class?" Here the goal is for both faculty members and students to identify not what students comprehend, but what they still do not clearly understand. Instructors can then tailor the next lesson to these muddy points, or follow up individually with students (Orr; Lucas), and students can reflect on what else they need to focus on in order to better learn the material (Chizmar and Ostrosky).

Another variation is the "application card", where students are asked to consider and write a brief response regarding how one might apply the concepts or material from that class session to a real-world situation (Angelo and Cross; Kas and Sheppard). The goal here is to see whether students understand how to apply the material and to enable the transfer of that knowledge to new contexts (Norman and Schmidt). There are many other types of minute papers, as well as other very short (but longer than one minute) writing prompts that can stimulate reflection and give instructors "instant assessment" (Orr, 108) – a window into student understanding of class material, quickly and easily (Pernecky; McMillan).

Open-Ended Debriefing Questions

Structured reflection at the end of an exercise or lesson provides necessary closure to any active learning experience. Best practices often have individual students answer a debriefing survey with open-ended questions that allow for reflection, and then engage in a larger sharing of ideas and responses in a guided class debriefing discussion led by the instructor. The opportunity to reflect upon and discuss individual and group experiences is particularly important because experiential learning frequently occurs after, rather than during, an exercise (Kolb; Lantis). Without reflection, students may see the activity as an isolated event, rather than an opportunity for systematic observation and analysis, which leads to less knowledge retention than active learning exercises followed by debriefing (Levin-Banchik).

With structured reflection, instructors can both assess and facilitate learning. Open-ended debriefing questions are particularly useful in this regard. On the one hand, they allow instructors to see whether students have drawn the expected lessons from the active learning experience by framing the question generally and allowing students to respond with their own insights. They also help structure student reflection, focusing students on a particular element, concept, or dynamic that they may have experienced, and asking them to consider its meaning or implication. For example, asking students what a simulation of international negotiations tells us about the prospects for international cooperation helps instructors identify whether the students understood the barriers to international cooperation, but also allows students to reflect on where those barriers could or could not have been overcome, and to understand why (Krain and Lantis). Open-ended structured reflection on student experiences playing a game to simulate conflict and diplomacy can "[draw] students' attention to both the 'process' of theorization and the actual 'content' of world politics" (Rittinger, 42; see also Raymond and Usherwood).

ONLINE DISCUSSION BOARD POSTS

As the section above indicates, instructors can use structured group discussions as opportunities to assess and enhance student learning. This is true of discussions in non-debriefing settings as well, whether in class or online (Hativa; Bender). Online discussions are uniquely suited to both assessment of understanding and assessment for learning. Instructors have the opportunity to examine student posts and discussions about class materials without the students feeling put on the spot (Orr). They also allow a sneak peek inside numerous student-to-student conversations that would otherwise be happening simultaneously in a class setting, which would thus be hard to observe. Online group discussions have been shown to promote dialogue, self-assessment, reflection, critical thinking, and deeper understanding (Wilson, Pollock, and Hamann; Williams and Lahman). They also create opportunities where "students were able to ask questions or present ideas that they may not have within the larger class or in another format ... and formed learning relationships that provided affective support that further aided their learning and development" (Kayler and Weller, 145). Thus, this approach serves the purpose of both allowing instructors to observe student learning and providing students with the opportunity to use these discussions to reflect, discuss, test out their ideas, and enhance their understanding – and to do so *before* class has begun.

For example, one of the chapter's authors has used pre-class online discussions of class readings as a method of assessment for a Theories of International Relations course. Students are required to post at least one discussion question in reaction to the class readings, and to respond to at least one other student's discussion question prior to class. This generates both initial student analyses of the readings (a short reaction paper, of sorts) as well as initial small group discussion about them before in-class engagement. This also guarantees that students have done the reading, an issue with which many instructors struggle. The instructor can then see, prior to class, whether and how deeply students have read and understood the material, what questions remain in students' minds, and what direction class discussion is likely to take. The instructor can then use that feedback to help guide a more productive in-class discussion session, building on student insights and addressing questions and misconceptions. The result, anecdotally, is a richer in-class discussion and students that learn the material more deeply than they might otherwise.

SKETCHING IDEAS AS ASSESSMENT: CONCEPT MAPPING AND CARTOONING

The preceding sections discussed assessment tools that are fairly familiar in the international relations scholarship on teaching and learning. In this section we introduce two other assessment tools (*concept maps* and *cartooning*) borrowed from other fields, that require students to think creatively and visually depict ideas. As with the tools discussed in the prior section, these push students to engage in reflection and metacognition, and help instructors "see" and therefore assess the learning process and outcomes. Each can be used either for *assessment for accountability* or *assessment for improvement*, depending on the needs of the instructor. As such, these approaches could be useful additions to the international relations pedagogue's assessment toolbox.

Concept Maps

Concept maps are visual representations of concepts and the relationships between them. Students can map their understandings in a graphic organizer of interconnected ideas arranged hierarchically. They can utilize words, arrow lines, and shapes. This enables students to engage in metacognition, and for instructors to identify students' understandings of conceptual and process relationships, temporal ordering, and easily identify gaps in knowledge, misunderstandings, and misconceptions (Novak; Calderón-Steck).

Studies in other social science fields have shown concept mapping's utility as a way to assess changes in students' course-related knowledge, and to help students correct misperceptions, and more accurately understand complex relationships between concepts (Amundsen, Gryspeerdt, and Moxness; Jacobs-Lawson and Hershey). Concept mapping has recently been applied innovatively to both pedagogy (James 2018) and research in international relations (James 2019). Yet, it has not yet been adopted within the field as an assessment tool. Nevertheless, concept maps can be effective showing the level of a student's understanding of complex political theories, phenomena, processes, or even the research process itself.

For example, Figure 16.1 depicts concept maps of a positivist research process from two international relations students in a research methods and design class taught by one of the authors. By comparing the two concept maps, the instructor can see that the second student (map on the right) has a better understanding of how hypotheses are informed by the relevant literature and theories than the first student (map on the left), and can therefore circle back and reinforce that understanding. Moreover, the students, by constructing their maps and sharing them in pairs or in groups, clearly articulate their own assumptions and (mis)understandings, and can more effectively examine them.

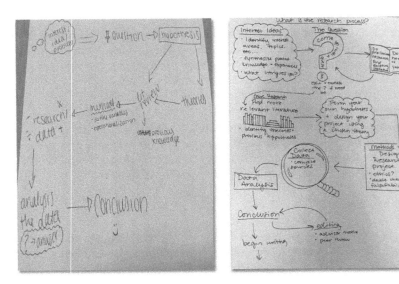

Figure 16.1   Two concept maps from a research methods and design course

Thus, the assessment helps the instructor know if the student understands the material, while simultaneously helping the student to learn.

Cartooning

Cartooning is "a process of conceptualizing, drawing, and writing that results in a work which incorporates image and language" (Cho, Osborne, and Sanders, 45). Cartooning in the classroom has been found to support active learning, enable critical thinking, and to be valuable for the assessment of student understanding of concepts, processes, and complexity (Birisci, Metin, and Karakas; Fradkin). For instance, Cho, Osborne, and Sanders found that cartooning was a useful way to assess students' mathematical understanding and their ability to pose problems and apply mathematical concepts to the real world. Social science teacher–scholars have routinely used cartoons in the classroom to teach difficult concepts and issues (Dougherty; K. Owens et al.). However, few have followed the lead of education, psychology, and the natural sciences in using cartooning as a teaching and assessment tool in the classroom despite the fact that cartooning can be effective at making clear a student's understanding of complex political theories, phenomena, processes, or methodologies.

Figure 16.2   Cartooning an article's research design

For example, Figure 16.2 depicts a cartoon done by a team of three students working together to depict the research design of an experiment in an article assigned in the same research methods and design class referenced for the concept map examples. Teams were instructed to draw a detailed cartoon of the two-paragraph description in the article that laid out the experimental methodology used, and to include all relevant methodological choices or elements. By examining the cartoon (and those of the other teams) the instructor can see whether the team of students understood not just the variables tested and methods used, but also the logic of control and the elements of the experiment used to impose control. This then sparks an all-class conversation about what elements were missing from some drawings and why those might be important to the design of the study. Similar exercises could be developed to depict foreign policy decision-making frameworks (such as two-level games), exploitative core-periphery relationships, and other complex theoretical concepts and processes in international relations.

CONCLUSION

There are numerous assessment tools available for use in the international relations classroom, including ones that can be borrowed from other fields. The key to selecting the appropriate assessment tool lies in clearly identifying one's educational objectives and deciding whether the goal is assessment for accountability, assessment for improvement, or both. Moreover, assessment tools need not be used in isolation. Indeed, one can assess whether educational objectives are being met using multiple methods where appropriate.

Not surprisingly, the systematic effort to assess classroom exercises also supports publishable pedagogical research. The scholarship of teaching and learning within international relations has proliferated in both quality and quantity, which seems to be connected to the recent interest in, and greater experience with, the use of assessment in pedagogy. When instructors assess their pedagogy, they start by designing classroom exercises, then develop a methodology to gather and record student learning or reactions, then analyze the impact of exercise, and then use the findings to improve teaching and learning. This progression mirrors the research process to improve our understanding, where scholars conceptualize and design theories and hypotheses, develop a methodology to gather and record data, analyze that information to draw a conclusion, and write up the findings for publication. Careful systematic assessment makes for good pedagogy, but also for good scholarship of teaching and learning. The use of assessment should be embraced for both – to support student learning and to enhance the learning about good pedagogical practice in our field.

NOTE

1. The authors would like to thank the organizers of, and participants in, the 2018 and 2019 International Studies Association Innovative Pedagogy Conferences, where material used for this chapter was originally presented, as well as student research assistants Elisabeth Kille, Matt Mayes, and Emmy Todd for their help in gathering additional reference material.

17. The vital role of assessment in active teaching and learning

Kerstin Hamann

Successful teaching of international relations (IR) in today's college and university classrooms requires regularized assessment. A growing body of research has documented that active learning is overall more effective than "passive" learning; that is, students may be learning better when they engage with the material in more ways than primarily listening to information related by the professor through lectures while taking notes and reading assigned materials. While much of the literature lauds active approaches as advantageous to teaching and learning, a pedagogy structured around active learning can take many different approaches, as the chapters in this volume attest. Active learning pedagogies can certainly help make instruction more student-centered and provides engagement activities that facilitate student success, but not all active learning innovations result in the same improved learning outcomes, better retention, or an equal distribution of learning benefits for all student groups. Thus, it is important that student learning is assessed early and often to understand the effectiveness of active learning approaches and the attainment of overall learning outcomes in departments and programs.

Assessment informs instructors' understanding of what students have learned or are able to do in classes and in programs, how effective their active learning approaches are, and how to improve their teaching. It also helps programs identify strengths and weaknesses, and it may guide instructors to choose specific active learning strategies that support program goals. While faculty members are often skeptical about the usefulness and desirability of assessment, a shift in our thinking can render assessment a useful tool in implementing active learning in IR classrooms and programs. The core question underlying assessment is "How do we know that what we do in our classrooms and programs 'works,' in other words, is effective in teaching students what we want them to learn and be able to do?" After all, only when we understand better what our students learn, and what the most effective methods are to teach them, can we improve our programs and classes. Thus, assessment offers opportunities to inform our teaching as we guide students through our classes and programs.

This chapter provides an overview of assessment, summarizes the benefits of active learning approaches identified in the assessment literature, and provides some illustrative examples of assessment in IR classes that point to specific learning gains related to the active learning approach. The chapter concludes by evaluating the role of assessment in active learning.

THE ROLE OF ASSESSMENT

Assessment plays a vital role in evaluating what students learn in individual classes and in their programs. Faculty generally use direct assessments like grades to determine whether a student's work is outstanding, very good, good, acceptable, or poor. Yet, grades do not necessarily tell the whole story. For example, depending on the grading criteria, a student who scored a B grade on a research paper may have excelled in grammar, spelling, writing, and structure, but perhaps did less well in constructing an argument and citing the relevant literature. Another student who scored the same grade may have had a superior argument and a good grasp of the literature, but poor writing skills. The same is true for course grades. A student with a B grade as their final course grade may have performed very well in the first part of the course but mastered the second portion of the material at an average level; another student may have excelled in the second half but done just okay in the first half. To extend this logic, when students graduate, we generally only know that they did well enough across their courses to satisfy graduation requirements. Their grade point average (GPA) provides some additional information, but it tells us little about the specific knowledge and skills students have acquired by the time they graduate, and, consequently, we know little about what "worked" in our courses and how we can improve our instruction, including active learning.

The American Association of Higher Education (AAHE) refers to assessment as "a systematic process of gathering, interpreting and using information about student learning" not just for individual courses, but also at the level of a program or institution; the purpose of assessment is to assist with improving education (Astin et al. 1; see also Angelo 11; Lancey and Bhati). Assessment helps us understand what students are learning by collecting empirical data in a process that compares learning against clearly set standards. The results are then used to review curricula and improve instruction, what is often referred to as "closing the loop." Therefore, assessment can be a useful tool for professors to improve their own teaching, as it provides insights into student learning.

Many departments have initiated program assessment in response to external pressures and demands – from university administrators, accreditation agencies, state legislatures, parents, employers, or students. Charged with demonstrating what their students have learned, faculty are sometimes fearful that assessment could potentially harm individual faculty and programs when learning outcomes fall below program goals. This can fuel resentment of assessment because it adds to the faculty workload and may not be effective in improving their courses and programs. Not surprisingly, almost 60% of faculty members think that assessment efforts "seem primarily focused on satisfying outside groups such as accreditors or politicians" instead of being focused on students (Lederman 2019b).[1] Nevertheless, despite broad criticism, all US regional accreditation agencies now require regular program evaluations and assessment. The question for many programs has moved from "how can we avoid assessment" to "how can we make assessment useful and practical." Proponents contend that assessment can be a meaningful and valuable exercise that could, and should, stimulate faculty discussion about program goals, learning outcomes, and curriculum structure (see Fletcher et al.; Deardorff, Hamann, and Ishiyama; Smoller).

The field of IR, and political science in general, are relative latecomers to the assessment movement (McClellan). Consequently, disciplinary resources to support assessment of any kind were late to develop although more general resources on assessment have been widely available for several decades. Roadmaps and guides to meaningful assessment have become more accessible even within the discipline (e.g. AAHE; Banta, Jones, and Black; Hamann; Huba and Freed; Kelly and Klunk; Kuh et al. 2010; Lancey and Bhati; Suskie 2009; Young). Research in the field of Scholarship of Assessment[2] is still less common, including in political science and IR (see Deardorff, Hamann, and Ishiyama 2009a; Rust). That is, many disciplinary studies analyze the pedagogical effects of teaching practices and innovations, while fewer studies analyze the assessment process itself and how assessment succeeds in improving student learning.

Parallel to the growing presence of program assessment, professors have also started to systematically assess learning outcomes in their own classes, often in relation to a specific pedagogy.[3] Assessment at the classroom level is potentially linked to program assessment, for what students learn in the classroom informs program assessment. Furthermore, program assessment sometimes builds on specific learner outcomes demonstrated in classrooms, so that classroom assessment exercises can be a direct source of data and information for program assessment. Increasingly, professors interested in classroom assessment engage in the Scholarship of Teaching and Learning and share the findings of their studies publicly through conference papers and publications in academic journals, including in a growing number of disciplinary journals, such as *International Studies Perspectives*, *PS: Political Science & Politics*, *Journal of Political Science Education*, and the UK journal *Politics*, among others.

Understanding how a teaching method affects student learning may be of particular interest when a professor is implementing a new pedagogical approach, perhaps moving a class or part of a class online, or substituting lectures with active learning components, or using a flipped classroom. While we may be quite confident (rightly or wrongly) about student learning in "traditional" pedagogical settings, we are perhaps less sure about learning gains or advantages of using new pedagogies when we delve into new instructional methods, such as active learning. How do we know that our teaching innovations focused on active learning "work," that is, that students learn in this context, and perhaps learn better than in the way previously taught? Assessment assists us in identifying the effectiveness of our teaching approaches, including active learning. As Miller states cogently, "Faculty members need to know the strengths and weaknesses of student performance in their courses, along with their own skills in fostering student learning" (95).

ACTIVE LEARNING AND ASSESSMENT

Connecting assessment with active learning allows us to confront several questions: Why do we engage in active learning strategies? What are the objectives we attempt to reach with active learning? Furthermore, how do we select specific active learning strategies, and how do these strategies support the broader mission and goals of the program? Some of the potential benefits of active learning are suggested by its very definition, indicating that this approach lends itself to student engagement, analysis, and application of knowledge:

> Active learning is any approach to instruction in which students are asked to engage in the learning process. Active learning stands in contrast to "traditional" modes of instruction in which students are passive recipients of knowledge, generally delivered in lecture format by a subject matter expert – the professor ... Commonly, students will engage in small or large activities centered around writing, talking, problem solving, or reflecting. (Center for Educational Innovation)

Existing studies recognize a broad range of potential benefits of active learning (e.g. Freeman et al.). These include improved retention of knowledge; heightened student engagement in the class as well as engagement with the material; emotional connections to the material, which in turn supports learning; and enhanced higher-order learning such as critical thinking, and improvement in teamwork and collaborative skills if team-based activities are included, while other benefits may include enhanced interest and a higher motivation for students to prepare for class (Cavenagh; D. Owens et al.; Prince). In the field of IR and peace and conflict studies, Sjöstedt finds that an overall active learning approach combining multiple strategies for student engagement and active learning in first-semester introductory IR courses yielded considerably better student performance than when the same course was taught based primarily on lectures.

Active learning has also been connected to student success in their educational career more generally. This is of increasing relevance in US higher education, as state legislatures, accreditors, parents, and students are focused on student retention and graduation rates, and performance-based funding by state legislatures is frequently tied to overall student success rather than specific learning outcomes (Gándara and Rutherford; Polatajko and Monaghan). As a consequence, universities are increasingly embracing High Impact Practices (HIPs), which are tied to initiatives and experiences falling under the active learning umbrella. These HIP engagement opportunities including active and collaborative learning have positive effects on student success and particularly so for students from demographics that have historically been underrepresented in higher education (see Kuh, O'Donell, and Schneider). The Association of American Colleges & Universities (AACU n.d.a) lists 11 different High Impact Educational Practices, most of which could fall under the active learning umbrella (First-Year Seminars and Experiences, Common Intellectual Experiences, Learning Communities, Writing-Intensive Courses, Collaborative Assignments and Projects, Undergraduate Research, Diversity/Global Learning, ePortfolios, Service Learning/Community-Based Learning, Internships, Capstone Courses and Projects). Several of these measures have positive outcomes on students' college career and success. For example, first-year seminars are associated with retention and lifelong learning; writing-intensive courses are connected to better learning and academic success; group work may provide academic benefits; undergraduate research promotes learning; and service learning has been credited with improved classroom learning and personal development, which are linked to college success (Johnson and Stage).

How do these general insights on the benefits of active learning apply to the IR classroom? Professors have shared their active learning components from IR classes – including games, discussions, presentations, writing assignments, experiential learning, service learning, problem-based learning, simulations, role playing, flipped classrooms, group work, and so on – at conferences, in academic journals, blogs,[4] and in newsletters. As others may be interested in adopting such engagement opportunities, perhaps with some modifications, it is useful to know whether these specific activities actually improve and facilitate student learning. Furthermore, as college students are increasingly diverse, it is important to understand whether some students benefit more from these approaches than others. For example, do students learn better in small group discussions or in discussions including all students in a class (see Hamann, Pollock, and Wilson)? Do students who tend to score lower grades benefit from some of those strategies, such as one-minute papers, or does that strategy not assist their mastery of the course material? Does it matter whether simulations are conducted in the classroom, or do virtual simulations provide comparable or perhaps superior learning outcomes? What do students learn in experiential environments, such as the Model UN[5] program, in internships, or through service learning, that they do not learn in traditional classroom settings? Do active learning approaches have different outcomes in lower-level introductory courses, or in upper-level courses? Meaningful classroom assessment can elucidate these questions and thereby assist professors in intentionally selecting active approaches to teaching and learning.

As various active learning strategies may yield different learner outcomes, the choice of active learning tools should be carefully thought out. They should be appropriate for the course goals, student population, and course settings, and linked to student learning outcomes in the course, or the program, or both. Such an approach provides the basis for defining how we know that the active learning tool "works." For example, if a course on diplomacy utilizes a simulation as an active learning strategy, the desired outcomes could be multiple: in-depth understanding of a complex situation with historical details; the role of different agents and agencies involved in the scenario; the actions of specific leaders; presentation skills; team building and team work; analytical thinking; handling conflict; writing briefs; increased interest in IR; retention in the course; a better course grade; retention in the program; and so on. Small group discussions in a large lecture class are likely to yield different outcomes than an online simulation conducted over several weeks; problem-based learning activities are likely to result in different outcomes than writing a book review.

Furthermore, different student demographics may have differential gains from different types of active learning strategies. For example, an internship may affect a student who has never held a job differently than a student who is full-time or part-time employed and has workplace experience, even if it is in a different setting. Similarly, Henning et al. find that students' hidden identities, including sexual orientation, political leanings, religion, or whether they commute to campus as opposed to being a residential student, also influence their perceptions of active learning environments. Students who are politically conservative, religious, commute to campus, and identify as queer feel less included in active learning situations and group work. Thus, while students overall may perform better in an active learning environment, the benefits of specific innovations may not be spread evenly across all student demographics and may in some ways make the classroom less rather than more inclusive.

Assessment of active learning is thus most useful when the motivations for the specified strategy are explicit, and when the assessment of the effectiveness of the active learning innovation is tailored to the desired learning outcomes. Furthermore, studies have shown that students do not universally embrace active learning strategies because they expect to be "taught" by the professor rather than having "to teach themselves," and they sometimes voice their frustration with active learning experiences in classrooms when evaluating courses and professors at the end of the semester (D. Owens et al.). Thus, it is not just important that the activity is well thought out and linked to a course learning objective, but also that students understand why and how they are supposed to engage in an activity in order to decrease resistance to active learning.

WHAT HAVE WE LEARNED FROM ASSESSMENT OF ACTIVE TEACHING IN IR CLASSES?

Classroom assessment can provide unique insights into active learning in IR classes. To illustrate, simulations are a frequently used tool in IR classrooms. Numerous studies have described specific simulation exercises and assessed their effects on student learning. A sizable literature on games and simulations in IR concludes that this particular type of active learning results in varies types of beneficial student learning. Here, I present some illustrative examples of insight gained from assessing active learning in IR courses:

Alves et al. find that using the Challenge Game as an active learning tool in their IR classroom had the potential to increase students' motivation for learning and interest in the subject matter while also providing a useful foil for discussing theoretical concepts. Asking students to evaluate the usefulness of an IR simulation on terrorism and global issues, Shellman and Turan (30) find that "the simulation enhances both substantive knowledge and critical and analytical thinking skills." Similarly, Wunische compares the effectiveness of lectures and simulations. While the results show that lectures are more effective teaching tools for short-term learning, long-term retention was higher when the topic was taught as a simulation rather than a lecture. Also focusing on long-term knowledge retention, Levin-Banchik utilizes variations of using the "Iranian Plane" simulation on decision making in crisis situations and finds that combining the simulation with a debriefing exercise outperformed a simulation without debriefing for knowledge retention, and both were superior to teaching the material without a simulation.

Assessment of active learning in IR courses extends to behavioral, attitudinal, and affective objectives. In Hendrickson's study, an American Foreign Policy and National Security course utilized a range of active learning techniques, including simulations, a debate, and counterfactual analysis. Students were then assessed about their attitudes and feelings regarding the course, such as excitement about the course, interest in the substantive material, and expectations of succeeding in the course resulting from the each of the components of the course design. Students' self-assessments on these questions reflected that the students responded to the active learning components with heightened excitement, interest, and self-efficacy, all of which could potentially boost student learning gains.

Active learning exercises can also promote affective learning, conceptualized as "emotional growth or maturation of students" benefits from simulations as students engage in role play and develop increased self-awareness (Jones, 406). Jones focuses on affective learning and changes in patterns of student interactions as a learning goal for the EuroSim, a cross-continent simulation aimed at improving students' understanding of the European Union, improving transatlantic relations by bringing students from Europe and the United States together, and building relationships among students (Jones, 409). This also assesses how students' interactions change as a result of participating in a simulation, and how it contributes to students' ability to judge their own performance. Thus, in contrast to studies that focus on cognitive gains of active learning, Jones understands affective learning and changes in student interactions as core goals of the simulation rather than a side effect. The study's findings suggest that, overall, the simulation improved students' affective learning as well student interaction; however, not all students benefited equally. One key difference was between students from the United States and those from Europe; for example, US students demonstrated higher learning gains in the area of affective learning.

Similarly, other studies have focused on assessment of deep learning and cognition. West and Halvorson assess a range of learner objectives for their simulation of a United Nations Security Council Debate in a large introductory IR class. They conclude that the simulation successfully engaged and motivated students while also promoting deeper cognitive understanding and metacognitive reflection. Other studies confirm the effectiveness of simulations to improve desired learner objectives including factual, conceptual, procedural, and metacognitive knowledge (e.g. see Pettenger, West, and Young). Other assessment of Model UN experiences also show that this simulation promotes deep learning, especially conceptual learning regarding IR theories, and metacognitive skills, which improved students' professional skills development (Engel, Pallas, and Lambert). At the same time, learning and skill gains from simulations such as Model UN are not necessarily equally distributed across different student demographics. To wit, Coughlin finds that male and female students' experience of participating in a Model UN simulation differs significantly, with male students reporting higher participation level, likely mirroring gender stereotypes in society and in the political realm in particular. In all these studies, assessment of active learning components was driven by clearly articulated learning goals that included cognitive, affective, and behavioral dimensions.

CONCLUSION

Program assessment establishes the goals and objectives for teaching students, helping to align instruction in both specific classes and in department or program missions. Active learning can be an integral part of pursuing these objectives. Thinking about active learning as contributing towards program assessment can assist professors in making informed choices about the types of active learning strategies to pursue and how to evaluate their effectiveness. However, it is also important to approach this carefully and systematically. If classroom assessment of active learning is to inform program goals, it is necessary that the two processes are integrated and clearly articulated. Consider that in a 2018 national survey of faculty, 38% of respondents disagreed that their campus assessment process has "Improved the quality of teaching and learning" while just one quarter (25%) agreed; similarly, 36% disagreed that assessment "helped increase degree completion rates" compared to 27% who agreed (Lederman 2019b). Over half of the respondents (52%) reported that they do not regularly receive assessment data, twice the rate of the those that do (26%). It is certainly challenging to link classroom assessment with program assessment if these processes are not linked. At the same time, a third of respondents (34%) reported that they have used assessment data to improve their own teaching (Lederman 2019b).

In order to be most useful, assessment needs to be done thoughtfully and needs to get at the questions we really want answers to as educators (McConnell). We might not ask the same questions over time. Our goals for our students may shift. Some questions may relate to students' overall development, skill development, or success in finding employment, while others might focus on understanding of subject matter. We might have different questions for students in our classes than department chairs and university administrators, or accreditation bodies. As Baranowski and Weir point out in their meta-study of political simulations, when the effectiveness of simulations is not assessed rigorously, we are not in a strong position to judge their value as teaching tools.

Standardized assessment is vital to help guide us as we strive to improve our own teaching, and in informing us what our students learned and can do, whether what we do in our courses supports program and university goals, and whether we equip students to be successful in their life after college – as critical thinkers, lifelong learners, or specialists in a field of study. This is best done when faculty are empowered to contribute to setting program goals and identifying appropriate ways to assess the extent to which students have reached those, while being able to implement strategies in their courses that support the course goals as well as the program goals. Active learning is an important pedagogical strategy to embrace as we support student learning and success, and assessment can help us in making active learning an important part of an integrated curriculum.

NOTES

1. Faculty have been critical of assessment as a concept that has purpose and meaning in higher education in and of itself; of the way assessment has been implemented at their institutions or departments; of the way assessment data are assembled and used; of the political intent behind legislatures and accreditation agencies' requirements to conduct assessment; of the idea that broader goals in higher education can be measured and quantified through the assessment process; and so on. See, for example, Deardorff and Folger; Lederman (2018); Worthen (2018). Criticism of current assessment practices and suggestions for revisions also exist within the assessment community (Lederman 2019b; Price et al.).

2. Banta and Associates (x) define the Scholarship of Assessment as "systematic inquiry designed to deepen and extend the foundation of knowledge underlying assessment. It involves basing studies on relevant theory and/or practice, gathering evidence, developing a summary of findings, and sharing those findings with the growing community of assessment scholars and practitioners."

3. There are many useful guides for classroom assessment techniques, e.g. Angelo and Cross (1993).

4. See, for example, the Active Learning in Political Science blog (http://activelearningps.com/ [accessed April 18, 2021]), which contains a great number of active learning strategies in political science and international relations.

5. Numerous programs similar to Model UN exist that focus on other organizations such as Model European Union, Model NATO, Model African Union, Model Arab League, Model Organization of American States, and others.

References

AAC&U. VALUE Rubric Development Project. n.d.b. https://www.aacu.org/value/rubrics (accessed April 20, 2021).

AAC&U. *What Liberal Education Looks Like: What It Is, Who It's For, & Where It Happens.* Association of American Colleges and Universities, 2020.

AAC&U. "The Rise of Active Learning: Findings from the HERI Survey on Teaching Strategies of Undergraduate Faculty." December, 2014. https://www.aacu.org/aacu-news/newsletter/rise-active-learning-findings-heri-survey-teaching-strategies-undergraduate (accessed May 31, 2020).

AAHE. "Nine Principles of Good Practice for Assessing Student Learning." 1996. http://www.academicprograms.calpoly.edu/pdfs/assess/nine_principles_good_practice.pdf (accessed April 20, 2021).

Abboud, Samer. "Teaching the Arab World and the West ... As an Arab in the West." *Journal of Political Science Education*, vol. 11, 2015, pp. 233–244.

Acai, Anita, et al. "Success in Student Faculty/Staff SoTL Partnerships: Motivations, Challenges, Power, and Definitions." *Canadian Journal for the Scholarship of Teaching and Learning*, vol. 8, no. 2, June 2017, pp. 1–17. DOI: https://doi.org/10.5206/cjsotl-rcacea.2017.2.8.

Acharya, Amitav. "Teaching Global International Relations." *International Studies Perspectives*, vol. 25, September, 2020. https://doi.org/10.1093/isp/ekaa009 (accessed April 15, 2021).

Acharya, Amitav. "Global International Relations (IR) and Regional Worlds: A New Agenda for International Studies." *International Studies Quarterly*, vol. 58, no.4, 2014, pp. 647–659.

Acharya, Amitav and Barry Buzan (eds). *Non-Western International Relations Theory: Perspectives On and Beyond Asia.* Routledge, 2010.

Ahmad, Arshad, et al. "Partnership in Practice: Implementing Healey's Conceptual Model." *International Journal for Students as Partners*, vol. 1, no. 2, 2017, pp. 1–10. DOI: 10.15173/ijsap.v1i2.3197.

Akbaba, Yasemin and Filiz Başkan. "How to Merge Courses via Skype™? Lessons from an International Blended Learning Project" *Research in Learning Technology*, vol. 25, 2017. Open Access Journal. https://journal.alt.ac.uk/index.php/rlt/article/view/1915 (accessed April 20, 2021).

Alexander, Amanda. "Engaging a Developmentally Disabled Community through Arts-based Service-learning." *Journal of Higher Education Outreach and Engagement*, vol. 189, no. 4, pp.183–206.

Allen, Deborah E., Richard S. Donham and Stephanie A. Bernhardt. "Problem-Based Learning." *New Directions for Teaching and Learning*, vol. 128, no. 1, 2011, pp. 21–29.

Allen, Michael A. "Blog Consumption and International Relations." *Journal of Political Science Education*, vol. 12, no. 2, 2016, pp. 169–185.

Allen, Michael A. and Justin S. Vaughn (eds). *Poli Sci Fi: An Introduction to Political Science Through Science Fiction.* Routledge, 2016.

References

Allin, Linda. "Collaboration Between Staff and Students in the Scholarship of Teaching and Learning: The Potential and the Problems." *Teaching and Learning Inquiry*, vol. 2, no. 1, 2014, pp. 95–102. DOI: https://doi.org/10.2979/teachlearninqu.2.1.95.

Allison, Graham T. *Essence of Decision: Explaining the Cuban Missile Crisis.* HarperCollins, 1971.

Alves, Cia, Elia Elisa, Ana Paula Maielo Silva and Gabriela Gonçalves Barbosa. 2019. "A Framework for Active Learning in International Relations: The Case of the Challenge Game." *Journal of Political Science Education.* DOI: 10.1080/15512169.2019.1612755.

Ambrose, Susan A., Michael W. Bridges, Michele DiPietro, Marsha C. Lovett and Marie K. Norman. *How Learning Works: Seven Research-Based Principles for Smart Learning.* 2010. Jossey-Bass.

American Political Science Association. *2018 Diversity and Inclusion Report*, https://www.apsanet.org/DIVERSITY/Diversity-and-Inclusion-Programs (accessed April 20, 2021).

Amstutz, Mark R. *International Ethics: Concepts, Theories, and Cases in Global Politics*, 5th ed. 2018. Rowman & Littlefield.

Amundsen, Cheryl, Danielle Gryspeerdt and Katherine Moxness. "Practice-Centred Inquiry: Developing More Effective Teaching." *The Review of Higher Education*, vol. 16, no. 3, 1993, pp. 329–353.

Andersen, Espen and Bill Schiano. *Teaching with Cases: A Practical Guide.* Harvard Business Review Press, 2014.

Anderson, Bret, et al. "Think Globally, Teach Locally: Experiencing the Foreign Aid Debate Through Service Learning." *Forum for Social Economics*, vol. 48, no. 4, Routledge, Oct. 2019, pp. 334–53. DOI:10.1080/07360932.2016.1222946.

Anderson, Lorin W., David R. Krathwohl, Peter W. Airasian, Kathleen A. Cruikshank, Richard E. Mayer, Paul R. Pintrich, James Raths and Merlin C. Wittrock. *A Taxonomy for Learning, Teaching and Assessing: A Revision of Bloom's Taxonomy of Educational Objectives.* 2001. Pearson.

Anderson, Philip H., et al. "Short-Term Study Abroad and Intercultural Sensitivity: A Pilot Study." *International Journal of Intercultural Relations*, vol. 30, no. 4, 2006, pp. 457–69. DOI: 10.1016/j.ijintrel.2005.10.004.

Anderson, William L., Steven M. Mitchell, and Marcy P. Osgood. "Comparison of Student Performance in Cooperative Learning and Traditional Lecture-based Biochemistry Classes." *Biochemistry and Molecular Biology Education*, vol. 33, no. 6, 2005, pp. 387–393.

Andrade, Heidi Goodrich. "Teaching With Rubrics: The Good, the Bad, and the Ugly." *College Teaching*, vol. 53, no. 1, 2005, pp. 27–30.

Angelo, Thomas A. "Doing Assessment as if Learning Matters Most." *AAHE Bulletin*, vol. 51, no. 9, 1999, pp. 3–6.

Angelo, Thomas A. "Reassessing Assessment: Embracing Contraries, Bridging Gaps, and Resetting the Agenda." *AAHE Bulletin*, vol. 47, no. 8, 1995, pp. 10–14.

Angelo, Thomas A. and K. Patricia Cross. *Classroom Assessment Techniques: A Handbook for College Teachers*, 2nd ed. Jossey-Bass, 1993.

Arnold, Richard. "Where's the Diplomacy in Diplomacy: Using a Classic Board Game in 'Introduction to International Relations.'" *PS: Political Science & Politics* vol. 48, no. 1, 2015, pp. 162–166.

Asal, Victor. "Playing Games with International Relations." *International Studies Perspectives* vol. 6, no. 3, 2005, pp. 359–373.

Asal, Victor, and Lewis Griffith. "A Terrible Beauty is Born: Teaching about Identity Salience and Conflict." *Dynamics of Asymmetric Conflict*, vol. 10, no. 1, 2017, pp. 3–13.

Asal, Victor, and Marcus Schulzke. "A Shot Not Taken: Teaching About the Ethics of Political Violence." *International Studies Perspectives*, vol. 13. no. 4, 2012, pp. 408–422.

Asal, Victor, Lewis Griffith, and Marcus Schulzke. "The Dalig and Vadan Exercise: Teaching Students about Strategy and the Challenges of Friction and Fog." *International Studies Perspectives*, vol. 15, no. 4, 2014, pp. 477–490.

Asal, Victor, Steve Sin, Nolan Fahrenkopf, and Xiaoye She. "The Comparative Politics Game Show." *International Studies Perspectives*, vol. 15, no. 3, 2014, pp. 347–358.

Asia Society. (n.d.). *Going Global: Preparing Our Students for an Interconnected World.* http://asiasociety.org/files/Going%20Global%20Educator%20Guide.pdf (accessed April 20, 2021).

Astin, Alexander, et al. "Principles of Good Practice for Assessing Student Learning." American Association of Higher Education. 1992. https://www.learningoutcomes assessment.org/wp-content/uploads/2019/08/AAHE-Principles.pdf (accessed April 20, 2021).

Atchison, Amy. "Where Are the Women? An Analysis of Gender Mainstreaming in Introductory Political Science Textbooks." *Journal of Political Science Education*, vol. 13, no. 2, 2017, pp. 185–199.

Ba, Alice D. and Matthew J. Hoffmann. "Making and Remaking the World for IR 101: A Resource for Teaching Social Constructivism in Introductory Classes." *International Studies Perspectives*, vol. 4, no. 1, 2003, pp. 15–33.

Bachner, Jennifer and Sarah O'Byrne. "Teaching Quantitative Skills in Online Courses: Today's Key Areas of Focus and Effective Learning Tools." *Journal of Political Science Education*, 2019, DOI: 10.1080/15512169.2019.1677475.

Bai, Jieru, et al. "Cross-Cultural Pedagogy: Practical Strategies for a Successful Interprofessional Study Abroad Course." *The Journal of Scholarship of Teaching and Learning*, vol. 16, no. 3, 2016, pp. 72–81. DOI: 10.14434/josotl.v16i3.19332.

Bain, Ken. *What The Best College Students Do.* 2012. The Belknap Press of Harvard University Press.

Banta, Trudy and Associates. *Building a Scholarship of Assessment.* 2002. Jossey Bass.

Banta, Trudy, Elizabeth A. Jones and Karen E. Black. *Designing Effective Assessment: Principles and Profiles of Good Practice.* 2009. Jossey Bass.

Baranowski, Michael K. and Kimberly A. Weir. "Political Simulations: What we Know, What We Think We Know, and What We Still Need to Know." *Journal of Political Science Education*, vol. 11, no. 4, 2015, pp. 391–403.

Barasuol, Fernanda and André Reis da. Silva. "International Relations Theory in Brazil: Trends and Challenges in Teaching and Research." *Revista Brasileira De Política Internacional*, vol. 59, no. 2, 2016, pp. 1–20.

Barr, Robert B. and John Tagg. "From Teaching to Learning: A New Paradigm for Undergraduate Education." *Change* (November/December), 1995, pp. 12–23.

Barrows, H.S. "A Taxonomy of Problem-Based Learning Methods." *Medical Education*, vol. 20, no. 6, 1986, pp. 481–486.

Basu, Soumita. "Security as Emancipation: A Feminist Perspective." In *Feminism and International Relations: Conversations about the Past, Present and Future*, ed. J. Ann Tickner and Laura Sjoberg, Routledge, 2011, pp. 98–114.

Bates, A. *Teaching in a Digital Age*, 2nd ed. 2019. https://opentextbc.ca/teachinginad igitalage/chapter/6-5-online-collaborative-learning/ (accessed July 15, 2020).

Bauer, Kelly and Kelly Clancy. "Teaching Race and Social Justice at a Predominantly White Institution." *Journal of Political Science Education*, vol. 14, no. 1, 2018, pp. 72–85.

Baylis, John, Steve Smith, and Patricia Owens, eds. *The Globalization of World Politics: An Introduction to International Relations*, 7th ed. 2017. Oxford University Press.

BCCampus. "What are Open Educational Resources?" 2020. https://open.bccampus.ca/what-is-open-education/what-are-open-educational-resources/ (accessed July 15, 2020).

Bean, John C. *Engaging Ideas: The Professor's Guide to Integrating Writing, Critical Thinking, and Active Learning in the Classroom*, 2nd ed. 2011. Jossey-Bass.

Beavers, Staci L. "Getting Political Science in on the Joke: Using *The Daily Show* and Other Comedy to Teach Politics." *PS: Political Science and Politics*, vol. 44, no. 2, 2011, pp. 415–419.

Beck, Robert J. "Teaching International Law as a Partially Online Course: The Hybrid/ Blended Approach to Pedagogy." *International Studies Perspectives*, vol. 11, no. 3, 2010, pp. 273–290.

Becker, Lawrence. "Wristwatches, Learning and My Own (Imperfect) Adaptation to Digital Students." *Newsletter of the Western Political Science Association*, vol. 3, no. 1, 2011, pp. 8–28.

Beckham, M. and N. Hensel. "Making Explicit the Implicit: Defining Undergraduate Research." *Council for Undergraduate Research Quarterly*, vol. 29, no. 4, pp. 40–44.

Behera, Navnita Chadka. "Knowledge Production". *International Studies Review*, vol. 18, no. 1, 2016, pp. 153–155. DOI: 10.1093/Isr/Viv024.

Bell, Heather L., et al. "Transformational Learning through Study Abroad: US Students' Reflections on Learning About Sustainability in the South Pacific." *Leisure Studies*, vol. 35, no. 4, 2016, pp. 389–405, DOI: 10.1080/02614367.2014.962585.

Below, Amy. "Reflections on the OUS Cuba Programme: Internationalisation Via a 'Double Hybrid Model.'" *European Political Science*, vol. 15, no. 1, 2016, pp. 49–60, DOI: 10.1057/eps.2015.42.

Bender, Tisha. *Discussion-Based Online Teaching to Enhance Student Learning: Theory, Practice, and Assessment*. 2003. Stylus Publishing.

Berdahl, Loleen, et al. "Teaching Critical Thinking in Political Science: A Case Study." *Journal of Political Science Education*, 2020. DOI:10.1080/15512169.2020.1744158.

Bergmann, Jonathan and Aaron Sams. *Flip your Classroom: Reach Every Student in Every Class Every Day*. 2012. ISTE.

Bernard, Robert, et al. "How Does Distance Education Compare With Classroom Instruction? A Meta-Analysis of Empirical Literature." *Review of Educational Research*, vol. 74, no. 3, 2004, pp. 379–439.

Bertrand, Julia Lau and Ji-Young Lee. "Teaching International Relations to a Multicultural Classroom." *International Journal of Teaching and Learning in Higher Education*, vol. 24, no. 1, 2012, pp. 128–133.

Bhambra, Gurminder K., et al. "Why Is Mainstream International Relations Blind to Racism?" *Foreign Policy*, July 3, 2020. https://foreignpolicy.com/2020/07/03/why-is-mainstream-international-relations-ir-blind-to-racism-colonialism/ (accessed July 10, 2020).

Birisci, Salih, Mustafa Metin, and Mehmet Karaks. "Pre-Service Elementary Teachers' Views on Concept Cartoons: A Sample from Turkey." *Middle East Journal of Scientific Research*, vol. 5, no. 2, 2010, pp. 91–97.

Biswas, Bidisha, and Virginia Haufler. "What Can I Do with This Class? Building Employment-Related Skills in International Relations Courses." *Journal of Political Science Education*, vol. 16, no. 1, 2020, pp. 67–78.

Blackmore, Paul and G. Cousin. "Linking Teaching and Research through Research-Based Learning." *Educational Developments*, vol. 4, no. 4, 2003, pp. 24–27.

Blakemore, Sarah-Jayne and Uta Frith. *The Learning Brain: Lessons for Education*. 2005. Blackwell Publishing.

Blaney, David L. and Arlene B. Tickner. "Worlding, Ontological Politics and The Possibility of a Decolonial IR". *Millennium*, 45(3), 2017a, pp. 293–311.

Blaney, David L. and Arlene B. Tickner. "International Relations in The Prison of Colonial Modernity." *International Relations*, vol. 31, no. 1, 2017b, pp. 71–75.

Blaney, David L. "Global Education, Disempowerment, and Curricula for a World Politics." *Journal of Studies in International Education*, vol. 6, no. 3, 2002, pp. 268–282.

Blanton, Shannon L. and Charles W. Kegley. *World Politics: Trend and Transformation*, 17th ed. 2021. Cengage.

Bloom, Benjamin, S. *Taxonomy of Educational Objectives: The Classification of Educational Goals*. 1956. Longman.

Bloom, Benjamin S. (ed.), M.D. Englhart, E.J. Furst, W.H. Hill, and D.R. Krathwohl. *Taxonomy of Educational Objectives: Handbook I: Cognitive Domain*. 1956. David McKay Publishers.

Boehrer, John and Marty Linsky. "Teaching with Cases: Learning to Question." In *The Changing Face of College Teaching*, ed. Marilla D. Svinicki. 1990. Jossey-Bass, pp. 41–57.

Bonwell, C.C. and J.A. Eison. *Active Learning: Creative Excitement in the Classroom*. 1991. The George Washington University, School of Education and Development.

Boos, Eric and Karene M. Boos. "Losing Ground: How the Lack of Opportunity for Women to Own Land Impales the Tanzanian Economy." In *Feminist Conversations: Women, Trauma, and Empowerment in Post-Transitional Societies*, ed. Dovilė Budrytė, Lisa M. Vaughn and Natalya T. Riegg. 2009. University Press of America, pp. 73–80.

Booth, Ken. "Security and Emancipation." *Review of International Studies*, vol. 17, 1991, pp. 313–26. https://www.jstor.org/stable/20097269 (accessed April 20, 2021).

Bovill, Catherine. "An Investigation of Co-Created Curricula Within Higher Education in the UK, Ireland and the USA." *Innovations in Education and Teaching International* vol. 51, no. 1, 2014, pp.15–25. http://dx.doi.org/10.1080/14703297.2013.770264 (accessed April 20, 2021).

Bovill, Catherine, et al. "Addressing Potential Challenges in Co-creating Learning and Teaching: Overcoming Resistance, Navigating Institutional Norms, and Ensuring Inclusivity in Student Staff Partnerships." *Higher Education*, vol. 71, no. 2, 2016, pp. 195–208. https://doi.org/10.1007/s10734-015-9896-4 (accessed April 20, 2021).

Bovill, Catherine, P. Cook Sather and P. Felten. "Changing Participants in Pedagogical Planning: Students as Co-creators of Teaching Approaches, Course Design, And Curricula." *International Journal for Academic Development*, vol. 16, no. 2, 2011, pp. 133–145.

Boyd, Mary K. and Jodi L. Wesemann, eds. *Broadening Participation in Undergraduate Research: Fostering Excellence and Enhancing the Impact*. 2009. Council on Undergraduate Research.

Boyer, Mark A. "Coalitions, Motives and Payoffs: A Simulation of Mixed-Motive Negotiations." In *The New International Studies Classroom: Active Teaching, Active*

Learning, ed. Jeffrey S. Lantis, Lynn M. Kuzma and John Boehrer. 2000. Lynne Rienner, pp. 95–110.

Boyer, Mark, Natalie F. Hudson and Michael J. Butler. *Global Politics.* 2019. Oxford University Press.

Boyer, Mark A., and Elizabeth T. Smith. "Developing Your Own In-Class Simulation: Design Advice and a 'Commons' Simulation Example." In *Handbook on Teaching and Learning in Political Science and International Relations,* ed. John Ishiyama, William J. Miller and Ezster Simon. 2015. Edward Elgar Publishing, pp. 315–326.

Braskamp, Larry A. "Internationalization in Higher Education: Four Issues to Consider." *Journal of College and Character,* vol. 10, no. 6, 2009, pp. 1–7.

Brew, A. "Teaching and Research: New Relationships and their Implications for Inquiry-Based Teaching and Learning in Higher Education." *Higher Education Research & Development,* vol. 22, no. 1, 2003, pp. 3–18.

Bridge, Dave, and Simon Radford. "Teaching Diplomacy by Other Means: Using an Outside-of-Class Simulation to Teach International Relations Theory." *International Studies Perspectives,* vol. 15, no. 4, 2014, pp. 423–437.

Brock, Kathy L., and Beverly J. Cameron. "Enlivening Political Science Courses with Kolb's Learning Preference Model." *PS: Political Science & Politics,* vol. 25, no. 3, 1999, pp. 251–256.

Brookhart, S. *How to Assess Higher-Order Thinking Skills in Your Classroom.* 2010. ASCD.

Brookfield, Stephen D. *Becoming a Critically Reflective Teacher.* 1995. Jossey-Bass.

Brooks, Jacqueline Grennon and Martin G. Brooks. *In Search of Understanding: The Case for Constructivist Classrooms.* 1993. ASCD.

Brown, Colin M., Sarah E. James, George Soroka. "Explicit Content: Two Experiments on Bringing Writing Instruction into the Political Science Classroom." *Journal of Political Science Education,* 2020. DOI: 10.1080/15512169.2020.1716239.

Brown, Joseph M. "Efficient, Adaptable Simulations: A Case Study of a Climate Negotiation Game." *Journal of Political Science Education,* vol. 14, no. 4, 2018, pp. 511–522.

Brualdi Timmins, Amy C. "Implementing Performance Assessment in the Classroom." *Practical Assessment, Research, and Evaluation,* vol. 6, no. 2, 1998. https://doi.org/10.7275/kgwx-6q70 (accessed April 20, 2021).

Brynen, Rex, and Gary Milante. "Peacebuilding with Games and Simulations." *Simulation & Gaming,* vol. 44, no. 1, 2013, pp. 27–35.

Budesheim, Thomas L. and Arlene R. Lundquist. "Consider the Opposite: Opening Minds Through In-class Debates on Course-related Controversies." *Teaching of Psychology,* vol. 26, 1999, pp. 106–110.

Burch, Kurt. "A Primer on Problem-Based Learning for International Relations Courses." *International Studies Perspectives,* vol. 1, no. 1, 2000, pp. 31–44.

Burcu, Oana. "Refocusing Group Work on Collaborative Learning and Diversifying Assessments in Political Science Departments." *European Political Science,* vol. 19, no. 1, 2020, pp. 140–57.

Butcher, Charity. "Teaching Foreign Policy Decision Making Processes Using Role-Playing Simulations: The Case of US–Iranian Relations: Teaching Foreign Policy Decision-Making Processes." *International Studies Perspectives,* vol. 13, no. 2, 2012, pp. 176–194.

Buzan, Barry. "Could IR Be Different?" *International Studies Review,* 2016. DOI: 10.1093/Isr/Viv025.

Calderón-Steck, Flora V. "Concept Mapping as a Teaching/Learning Tool about Race Relations." In *Proceedings of the Second International Conference on Concept Mapping, San José, Costa Rica*, ed. A.J. Cañas and J.D. Novak. 2006. Institute for Human and Machine Cognition, University of Malta, pp. 00–00.

Campbell, Coral J.L. and Caroline Walta. "Maximising Intercultural Learning in Short Term International Placements: Findings Associated with Orientation Programs, Guided Reflection and Immersion." *Australian Journal of Teacher Education*, vol. 40, no.10, 2015, pp. 1–15.

Campbell, Joel R. and Gigi Gokcek. *International Relations Through Star Trek and Star Wars*. 2019. Lexington Books.

Carter, Ralph G., ed. *Contemporary Cases in U.S. Foreign Policy: From Terrorism to Trade*, 6th ed. forthcoming 2021. Rowman & Littlefield. 5th ed. 2014. CQ Press.

Carvalho, Gustavo. "Virtual Worlds Can Be Dangerous: Using Ready-Made Computer Simulations for Teaching International Relations." *International Studies Perspectives*, vol. 15, no. 4, 2014, pp. 538–557.

Cashman, Greg. *What Causes War? An Introduction to Theories of International Conflict*. 2013. Rowman & Littlefield.

Cavdar, Gamze, Yavuz Yasar, and Jonathan Fisk. "Student Biases About the Middle East: Lessons from an Experiment." *Journal of Political Science Education*, vol. 15, no. 3, 2019, pp. 299–317.

Cavenagh, Sarah Rose. *The Spark of Learning: Energizing the College Classroom with the Science of Emotion*. 2016. West Virginia Press.

Centellas, Miguel. "Pop Culture in the Classroom: *American Idol*, Karl Marx, and Alexis de Tocqueville." *PS: Political Science and Politics*, vol. 43 no. 3, 2010, pp. 561–565.

Center for Educational Innovation. "Active Learning." n.d. University of Minnesota. https://cei.umn.edu/active-learning (accessed April 20, 2021).

Center for Engaged Learning. "Students as Partners." 2019. Elon University. https://www.centerforengagedlearning.org/doing-engaged-learning/students-aspartners/ (accessed July 25, 2020).

Chambliss, Daniel and Christopher Takacs. *How College Works*. 2014. Harvard University Press.

Chang, H. "Turning an Undergraduate Class into a Professional Research Community." *Teaching in Higher Education*, vol. 10, no. 3, 2005, pp. 387–94.

Chanock, Kate. "Towards Inclusive Teaching and Learning in Humanities: Alternatives to Writing." *Learning and Teaching in Higher Education*, vol. 3, no. 1, 2008, pp. 19–32.

Chasek, Pamela S. "Power Politics, Diplomacy and Role Playing: Simulating the UN Security Council's Response to Terrorism." *International Studies Perspectives*, vol. 6, no. 1, 2005, pp. 1–19.

Chizmar, John F., and Anthony L. Ostrosky. "The One-Minute Paper: Some Empirical Findings." *The Journal of Economic Education*, vol. 29, no. 1, 1998, pp. 3–10.

Cho, Hoyun, Carolyn Osborne, and Tobie Sanders. "Classroom Experience about Cartooning as Assessment in Pre-service Mathematics Content Course." *Journal of Mathematics Education at Teachers College*, vol. 6, no. 1, 2015, pp. 45–53.

Chowdhry, Geeta, and Sheila Nair. "Introduction: Power in a Postcolonial World: Race, Gender and Class in International Relations." In *Power, Postcolonialism and International Relations: Reading Race, Gender and Class*, ed. Geeta Chowdhry and Sheila Nair, Routledge, 2002, pp. 1–32.

Christensen, C. Roland, David A. Garvin and Ann Sweet (eds). *Education for Judgment: The Artistry of Discussion Leadership*. Harvard Business School Press, 1991.

References   231

Clark, Nicholas, et al. "EU Simulations and Engagement: Motivating Greater Interest in European Union Politics." *Journal of Political Science Education*, vol. 13, no. 2, 2017, pp. 152–170.

Clausewitz, Carl Von. *On War*. Translated by Michael Howard and Peter Paret. Reprint. 1984. Princeton University Press.

Combs, James. *Movies and Politics: The Dynamic Relationship*. 1993. Garland Publishing.

Cooley, Valerie, and Andrew Pennock. "Teaching Policy Analysis Through Animated Films: A Mickey Mouse Assignment?" *PS: Political Science & Politics*, vol. 48, no. 4, 2015, pp. 601–606.

Coombs, Norman. *Making Online Teaching Accessible: Inclusive Course Design for Students with Disabilities*. 2010. Jossey-Bass.

Cornell University Center for Teaching Innovation "Collaborative Learning." n.d. https://teaching.cornell.edu/teaching-resources/engaging-students/collaborative -learning. (accessed August 15, 2020).

Corrigan, Timothy. *A Short Guide to Writing about Film*, 9th ed. 2014. Pearson.

Coryell, Joellen E. "The Foreign City as Classroom: Adult Learning in Study Abroad." *Adult Learning*, vol. 22, no. 3, 2011, pp. 4–11, DOI: 10.1177/104515951102200301.

Costello, Matthew J., and Kent Worcester. "The Politics of the Superhero." *PS: Political Science & Politics*, vol. 47, no. 1, 2014, pp. 85–89.

Coticchia, Fabrizio, Enrico Calossi, and Lorenzo Cicchi. "A Reality Check for Students? How Participating to the Model United Nations Influences Skills, IR Perceptions, and Perspectives on Future Career." *Politics*, vol. 40, no. 2, 2020, pp. 245–261.

Coughlin, Richard W. "Gender and Negotiation in Model UN Role-Playing Simulations." *Journal of Political Science Education*, vol. 9, no. 3, 2013, pp. 320–335.

Cox, Eric. "Does Statecraft Improve Student Learning Outcomes? A Controlled Comparison." *Journal of Political Science Education*, 2019. Online First. DOI: 10.1080/15512169.2019.1667812.

Cox, Robert W. "Social Forces, States and World Orders: Beyond International Relations Theory." In *Neorealism and Its Critics*, ed. Robert O. Keohane. 1986. Columbia University Press, pp. 204–254.

Craig, John. "What Have We Been Writing About? Patterns and Trends in the Scholarship of Teaching and Learning." *Journal of Political Science Education*, vol. 10, no. 1, 2014, pp. 23–36.

Crossley-Frolick, Katy A. "Beyond Model UN: Simulating Multi-Level, Multi-Actor Diplomacy using the Millennium Development Goals." *International Studies Perspectives*, vol. 11, no. 2, 2010, pp. 184–201.

Curran, Roisin. "Students As Partners – Good For Students, Good For Staff: A Study On The Impact Of Partnership Working And How This Translates to Improved Student–Staff Engagement." *International Journal for Students as Partners*, vol. 1, no. 2, 2017. https://mulpress.mcmaster.ca/ijsap/article/view/3089/2891 (accessed April 20, 2021).

Cusimano, Maryann. "Case Teaching without Cases." In *The New International Studies Classroom: Active Teaching, Active Learning*, ed. Jeffrey S. Lantis, Lynn M. Kuzma and John Boehrer. 2000. Lynne Rienner, pp. 77–92.

Daalder, I.H. *The Clinton Administration and Multilateral Peace Operations*. Case 462. 1994. Institute for the Study of Diplomacy.

Dahlgren, Madeleine Abrandt, Tara Fenwick, and Nick Hopwood. "Theorising Simulation in Higher Education: Difficulty for Learners as an Emergent Phenomenon." *Teaching in Higher Education*, vol. 21, no. 6, 2016, pp. 613–627.

Danielson, Robert W. and Gale M. Sinatra. "A Relational Reasoning Approach to Text-Graphic Processing." *Educational Psychology Review*, vol. 29, no. 1, 2017, pp. 55–72.

D'Anieri, Paul. *International Politics: Power and Purpose in Global Affairs*, 4th ed. 2016. Cengage.

Darby, Flower and James M. Lang. *Small Teaching Online: Applying Learning Science in Online Classes* (digital edition). 2019. Jossey-Bass.

Davidovitch, Nitza. "Learning-centered Teaching and Backward Course Design from Transferring Knowledge to Teaching Skills." *Journal of International Education Research*, vol. 9, no. 2, 2013, pp. 329–338.

Davidson, Cathy. *The New Education: How to Revolutionize the University to Prepare Students for a World in Flux*. 2017. Basic Books, 2017.

Dawson, Bryan L. "Touchy Subjects: Utilizing Handedness as a Precursor to Discussing Privilege and Diversity in the Classroom." In *Engaging Difference: Teaching Humanities and Social Science in Multicultural Environments*, ed. Dovilė Budrytė and Scott A. Boykin. 2017. Rowman and Littlefield, pp. 67–74.

Deardorff, Darla K. "Assessing Intercultural Competence in Study Abroad Students." In *Living and Studying Abroad: Research and Practice*, ed. Michael Byram and Anwei Feng. 2006. Multilingual Matters, pp. 232–256.

Deardorff, Michelle and Paul Folger. "Making Assessment Matter: Structuring Assessment, Transforming Departments." In *Assessment in Political Science*, ed. Michelle D. Deardorff, Kerstin Hamann and John Ishiyama. 2009. American Political Science Association, pp. 77–95.

Deardorff, Michelle D., Kerstin Hamann and John Ishiyama, eds. *Assessment in Political Science*. 2009a. American Political Science Association.

Deardorff, Michelle D., Kerstin Hamann and John Ishiyama. "Introduction." In *Assessment in Political Science*, ed. Michelle D. Deardorff, Kerstin Hamann, and John Ishiyama. 2009b. American Political Science Association, pp. 3–15.

Deciancio, Melisa. "International Relations from The South: A Regional Research Agenda For Global IR." *International Studies Review*, vol. 18, 2016, pp. 106–119.

Deibel, Terry L. "Teaching Foreign Policy with Memoirs." *International Studies Perspectives*, vol. 3, no. 2, 2002, pp. 128–138.

Desch, Michael. *Cult of the Irrelevant: The Waning Influence of Social Science on National Security*. 2019. Princeton University Press.

de Swielande, Tanguy. S., David Walton, Thomas Wilkins, and Dorothee Vandamme, eds. *Rethinking Middle Powers in the Asian Century: New Theories, New Cases*. Routledge, 2019.

Devereaux. Charan, Robert Z. Lawrence, and Michael D. Watkins. *Case Studies in US Trade Negotiation, Vol. 1: Making the Rules*. 2006a. Institute for International Economics.

Devereaux, Charan, Robert Z. Lawrence, and Michael D. Watkins. *Case Studies in US Trade Negotiation, Vol. 2: Resolving Disputes*. 2006b. Institute for International Economics.

Dewey, John. *Experience and Education*. 1938. Collier Books.

Dewey, John. *Experience and Education*. Reprint Edition. Touchstone, 1997.

de Wit, Hans. "Internationalization of Higher Education: The Need for a More Ethical and Qualitative Approach." *Journal of International Students*, vol. 10, no. 1, 2020, pp. i–iv.

de Wit, Hans. "Changing Rationales for the Internationalization of Higher Education." *International Higher Education*, no. 15, 1999, pp. 2–3.

DiCicco, Jonathan M. "National Security Council: Simulating Decision-Making Dilemmas in Real Time." *International Studies Perspectives*, vol. 15, no. 4, 2014, pp. 438–458.

Dillenbourg, Pierre. "What Do You Mean by Collaborative Learning?" *Collaborative-Learning: Cognitive and Computational Approaches*, ed. P. Dillenbourg. 1999. Elsevier, pp.1–19.

Dimeo, Jean. 2017. "Saving Students Money." *Inside Higher Education*. June 28, 2017. https://www.insidehighered.com/digital-learning/article/2017/06/28/report-saving -students-money-oer (accessed July 15, 2020).

Dochy, Filip, Mien Segers, Piet Van den Bossche and David Gijbels. "Effects of Problem-Based Learning: a Meta-Analysis." *Learning and Instruction*, vol. 13, no. 5, 2003, pp. 533–568.

Doty, Roxanne Lynn. "Desert Tracts: Statecraft in Remote Places." *Alternatives*, vol. 26, no. 4, 2001, pp. 523–543. DOI:10.1177/030437540102600407.

Doty, Roxanne Lynn. "Maladies of Our Souls: Identity And Voice In The Writing Of Academic International Relations." *Cambridge Review of International Affairs*, vol. 1, no. 2, 2004, pp. 377–392. DOI: 10.1080/0955757042000245951.

Dougherty, Beth K. "Comic Relief: Using Political Cartoons in the Classroom." *International Studies Perspectives*, vol. 3, no. 3, 2002, pp. 258–270.

Dreyer, David R. "War, Peace, and Justice in Panem: International Relations and *The Hunger Games* Trilogy." *European Political Science*, vol. 15, 2016, pp. 251–265.

Dubinsky, Janet M., et al. "Contributions of Neuroscience Knowledge to Teachers and Their Practice." *The Neuroscientist*, vol. 25, no. 5, 2019, pp. 394–407.

Duch, Barbara, Susan E. Groh and Deborah E. Allen, eds. *The Power of Problem-Based Learning: A Practical "How-to" for Teaching Undergraduate Courses in Any Discipline.* 2001. Stylus Publishing.

E–International Relations. 2020. https://www.e-ir.info/ (accessed July 1, 2020).

Eckert, James, et al. "Developing Short-Term Study Abroad Programs: Achieving Successful International Student Experiences." *American Journal of Business Education*, vol. 6, no. 4, 2013, pp. 439–458. DOI: 10.19030/ajbe.v6i4.7943.

Edmunds, Julia, and Rebecca Shore. "Study Abroad Participation and University Students' Intercultural Sensitivity." *Journal of Applied Educational and Policy Research*, vol. 5, no. 1, 2020, pp. 51–58.

ENAR (European Network against Racism). "Intersectionality and Policymaking on Discrimination in the European Union." https://www.enar-eu.org/IMG/pdf/2018 _intersectionality_enar_briefing_for_online_final.pdf (accessed July 17, 2020).

Engel, Susan, Josh Pallas and Sarah Lambert. "Model United Nations and Deep Learning: Theoretical and Professional Learning." *Journal of Political Science Education*, vol. 13, no. 2, 2017, pp.171–184.

Engle, Lilli. "The Rewards of Qualitative Assessment Appropriate to Study Abroad." *Frontiers: The Interdisciplinary Journal of Study Abroad*, vol. 22, no. 1, Jan. 2013, pp. 111–126. DOI: 10.36366/frontiers.v22i1.321.

Enloe, Cynthia. *Bananas, Beaches and Bases: Making Feminist Sense of International Politics*, 2nd ed. (ebook). 2014. University of California Press.

Enloe, Cynthia. *The Curious Feminist: Searching for Women in a New Age of Empire.* 2014. University of California Press.

Epley, J. "Learning by Doing: Using an Online Simulation Game in an International Relations Course." *Journal of Interactive Learning Research*, vol. 27, no. 3, 2016, pp. 201–218.

Escobar, Arturo. "Thinking–feeling with the Earth: Territorial Struggles and the Ontological Dimension Of The Epistemologies Of The South." *Revista De Antropología Iberoamericana*. vol. 11, no. 1, 2016, pp. 11–32.

Eukel, Heidi, et al. "Unlocking Student Engagement: Creation, Adaptation, and Application of an Educational Escape Room Across Three Pharmacy Campuses." *Simulation & Gaming*, vol. 51, no. 2, 2020, pp. 167–179.

Evans, Anthony J., Terence Tse and Jeremy Baker. "The Great EU Debt Write-Off: A Classroom Simulation." *Simulation & Gaming*, vol. 47, no. 4 , 2016, pp. 543–556.

Felten, Peter, et al. "Reimagining the Place of Students in Academic Development." *International Journal of Academic Development*, vol. 24, no. 2, 2019, pp. 192–203. DOI: 10.1080/1360144X.2019.1594235.

Ferreira, Marcos Alan S. V. "The Rise of International Relations Programs in the Brazilian Federal Universities: Curriculum Specificities and Current Challenges." *Journal of Political Science Education*, vol. 13, no. 3, 2016, pp. 241–255.

Fletcher, Richard B., Luanna H. Meyer, Helen Anderson, Patricia Johnston and Malcolm Rees. "Faculty and Students Conceptions of Assessment in Higher Education." *Higher Education*, vol. 64, no. 1, 2012, pp. 119–133. https://doi.org/10.1007/s10734 -011-9484-1 (accessed April 20, 2021).

Forbes-Mewett, Helen. "International Education Preparation: Minimising Risk and Furthering Security." *International Journal of Contemporary Sociology*, vol. 48, no.1, 2011, pp. 61–92.

Forest, James J.F. "Teaching Cultural Perspectives to Future Army Officers at West Point." *Journal of Political Science Education*, vol. 1, 2005, pp. 61–82.

Fradkin, Chris. "The Use of Cartoon Illustration for the Assessment of Social Science Concepts." *Visual Communication*, vol. 18, no. 4, 2019, pp. 549–556.

Franklin, Daniel P. *Politics and Film: The Political Culture of Television and Movies*. 2017. Rowman & Littlefield.

Freeman, Scott, et al. "Active Learning Increases Student Performances in Science, Engineering, and Mathematics." *Proceedings of the National Academy of Sciences*, vol. 111, no. 23, 2014, pp. 8410–8415.

Freire, Paulo. *Pedagogy of the Oppressed*, 30th Anniversary ed., Continuum, 2000.

Frueh, Jamie. *Pedagogical Journeys through World Politics*. 2020. Palgrave Macmillan.

Frueh, Jamie and Paul F. Diehl. eds. *The Introductory Course in International Relations: Regional Variations, International Studies Perspectives*, forthcoming.

Frueh, Jamie and Jeremy Youde. "Teaching International Relations Theory in Introductory Global Politics Courses." In *Oxford Research Encyclopedia of International Studies*. 2020. https://doi.org/10.1093/acrefore/9780190846626.013 .578 (accessed April 20, 2021).

Fung, Courtney J. "Negotiating the Nuclear and Humanitarian Crisis on the Korean Peninsula: A Simulation and Teaching Guide." *PS: Political Science & Politics*, vol. 52, no. 1, 2019, pp. 113–16.

Gaia, Celeste A. "Short-Term Faculty-Led Study Abroad Programs Enhance Cultural Exchange and Self-Awareness." *The International Education Journal: Comparative Perspectives*, vol. 14, no. 1, 2015, pp. 21–31.

Gándara, Denisa and Amanda Rutherford. "The Effects of Premiums for Underserved Populations in Performance Funding Policies for Higher Education." *Research in Higher Education*, vol. 59, no. 6, pp. 681–703.

Gannon, Kevin, M. *Radical Hope: A Teaching Manifesto*. 2020. West Virginia University Press.

Garcia, Nuria Alonso and Nicholas V. Longo. "Going Global: Re-Framing Service-Learning in an Interconnected World." *Journal of Higher Education Outreach and Engagement*, vol. 17, no. 2, 2013, pp. 111–135. https://files.eric.ed.gov/fulltext/EJ1005307.pdf (accessed April 20, 2021).

Gerner, Deborah. "Films and the Teaching of Foreign Policy." *Foreign Policy Analysis Notes*, vol. 15, no. 3, 1988, pp. 3–6.

Gibney, Mark. *Watching Human Rights: The 101 Best Films*. 2013. Routledge.

Giedt, Todd, et al. "International Education in the 21st Century: The Importance of Faculty in Developing Study Abroad Research Opportunities." *Frontiers: The Interdisciplinary Journal of Study Abroad*, vol. 26, no. 1, 2015, pp. 167–86. DOI: 10.36366/frontiers.v26i1.365.

Giglio, Ernest D. *Here's Looking at You: Hollywood, Film & Politics*, 4th ed., 2014. Peter Lang.

Gijbels, David, Filip Dochy, Piet Van den Bossche and Mien Segers. "Effects of Problem-Based Learning: A Meta-Analysis from the Angle of Assessment". *Review of Educational Research*, vol. 75, no.1, 2005, pp. 27–61.

Gilbert, Lewis. *The Spy Who Loved Me*. 1977. United Artists.

Giroux, Henry, A. *Pedagogy and The Politics of Hope: Theory, Culture, and School*. 1997. Westview Press.

Giroux, Henry A. "Rethinking Education as the Practice of Freedom: Paulo Freire and the Promise of Critical Pedagogy." *Policy Futures in Education*, vol. 8, no. 6, 2010, pp. 715–721.

Glasgow, Sara M. "Stimulating Learning by Simulating Politics: Teaching Simulation Design in the Undergraduate Context." *International Studies Perspectives*, vol. 15, no. 4, 2014, pp. 525–537.

Glassman, Amanda and Miriam Temin. *Millions Saved: New Cases of Proven Success in Global Health*. Washington, DC: Center for Global Development, 2016.

Glazier, Rebecca A. "Building Rapport to Improve Retention and Success in Online Classes." *Journal of Political Science Education*, vol. 12, no. 4, 2016, pp. 437–456.

Glisczinski, Daniel J. "Lighting Up the Mind: Transforming Learning Through the Applied Scholarship of Cognitive Neuroscience." *International Journal for the Scholarship of Teaching and Learning*, vol. 5, no. 1, 2011. https://doi.org/10.20429/ijsotl.2011.050124 (accessed April 20, 2021).

Glover, Robert W. and Daniel Tagliarina, eds. *Teaching Politics Beyond the Book: Film, Texts, and New Media in the Classroom*. 2013. Bloomsbury.

Golich, Vicki L. "The ABCs of Case Teaching." *International Studies Perspectives* 1, 2000, pp. 11–29.

Golich, Vicki L., Mark Boyer, Patrice Franko, and Steve Lamy. *The ABCs of Case Teaching: Pew Case Studies in International Affairs*. Institute for the Study of Diplomacy, Georgetown University, 2000. http://researchswinger.org/others/case-method-teaching.pdf (accessed February 2020).

Goldstein, Joshua and Jon Pevehouse. *International Relations*, 12th ed. 2020. Pearson.

González-Betancor, Sara M., Alicia Bolívar-Cruz and Domingo Verano-Tacoronte. "Self-Assessment Accuracy in Higher Education: The Influence of Gender and Performance of University Students." *Active Learning in Higher Education*, vol. 20, no. 2, 2019, pp. 101–114.

Gopal, Priyamvada. "Yes, We Must Decolonize: Our Teaching has to Go Beyond Elite White Men." *The Guardian*. October 27, 2017. https://www.theguardian.com/commentisfree/2017/oct/27/decolonise-elit...-men-decolonising-cambridge-university-english-curriculum-literature (accessed April 20, 2021).

Gough, Heidi, et al. "Journaling and Reflection as Education Tools for Engineering Study Abroad." *Journal of Professional Issues in Engineering Education and Practice*, vol. 144, no. 4, 2018, pp. 5018010-1–5018010-11.

Gregg, Robert W. *International Relations on Film*. 1998. Lynne Rienner Publishers.

Gregg, Robert W. "The Ten Best Films About International Relations." *World Policy Journal*, vol. 16, no. 2, 1999, pp. 129–134.

Grussendorf, Jeannie, and Natalie C. Rogol. "Reflections on Critical Thinking: Lessons from a Quasi-Experimental Study." *Journal of Political Science Education*, vol. 14, no. 2, 2018, pp. 151–166.

Gurin, Patricia, Biren (Ratnesh) A. Nagda, and Gretchen E. Lopez. "The Benefits of Diversity in Education for Democratic Citizenship." *Journal of Social Issues*, vol. 60, no. 1, 2004, pp. 17–34.

H-Diplo ROUNDTABLE XXI-39, https://hdiplo.org/to/RT21-39 (accessed July 16, 2020).

Haak, D.C., HilleRisLambers, J., Pitre, E., and Freeman, S. "Increased Structure and Active Learning Reduce the Achievement Gap in Introductory Biology." *Science*, vol. 332, 2011, pp. 1213–1216.

Haber, Jonathan. *Critical Thinking*. 2020. MIT Press.

Hagman, Jonas and Thomas J. Biersteker. "Beyond the Published Discipline: Toward a Critical Pedagogy of International Relations Scholarship." *European Journal of International Relations*, vol. 20, no. 2, 2014, pp. 291–315. DOI: 10.1177/1354066112449879.

Haines, Charles G. "Report on Instruction in Political Science in Colleges and Universities." The American Political Science Review, vol. 8, no. 1, Supplement: Proceedings of the American Political Science Association at Its Tenth Annual Meeting, February, 1914, pp. 249–270.

Halpern, Diane F. and Milton D. Hakel. "Applying the Science of Learning." *Change*, July/August, 2003, pp. 36–41.

Hamann, Kerstin. "Curricular and Program Assessment Techniques in the United States." In *Handbook of Teaching and Learning in Political Science and International Relations*, ed. John Ishiyama, Will Miller, and Eszter Simon. 2015. Edward Elgar Publishing, pp. 74–84.

Hamann, Kerstin; Philip H. Pollock, and Bruce M. Wilson. "Assessing Student Perceptions of the Benefits of Discussions in Small-Group, Large-Class, and Online Learning Contexts." *College Teaching*, vol. 60, no. 2, 2012, pp. 65–75.

Hamati-Ataya, Inanna. "Beyond (post) Positivism: The Missed Promises of Systemic Pragmatism." *International Studies Quarterly*, vol. 56, no. 2, 2012, pp. 291–305.

Hamid, Mohsin. *The Reluctant Fundamentalist*. 2008. Harcourt Books.

Hammersley-Fletcher, Linda and Christopher Hanley. "The Use of Critical Thinking in Higher Education in Relation to the International Student: Shifting Policy and Practice." *British Educational Research Journal*, vol. 42, no. 6, 2016, pp. 978–992.

Haney, Patrick. "Learning About Foreign Policy At the Movies." *The New International Studies Classroom: Active Teaching, Active Learning*, ed. Jeffrey S. Lantis et al. 2000. Lynne Rienner, pp. 239–253.

Hannafin, Michael J., Janette R. Hill and Susan M. Land. "Student-Centered Learning and Interactive Multimedia: Status, Issues, and Implication." *Contemporary Education*, vol. 68, no. 2, 1997, pp. 94–99.

Hansen, Holley E. "The Impact of Blog-Style Writing on Student Learning Outcomes: A Pilot Study." *Journal of Political Science Education*, vol. 12, no. 1, 2016, pp. 85–101.

Hardy, Mat. "Modelling Online Innovation Among IR and Politics Lecturers." *Journal of Political Science Education*, vol. 13, no. 4, 2017, pp. 464–482.

Hastedt, Glenn, Donna L. Lybecker and Vaughan P. Shannon. *Cases in International Relations: Pathways to Conflict and Cooperation*, rev. ed. 2015. CQ Press/Sage.

Hativa, Nira. *Teaching for Effective Learning in Higher Education*. 2000. Springer Netherlands.

Hawn, Heather L. "Utilising Popular Music to Teach Introductory and General Education Political Science Classes." *European Political Science*, vol. 12, no. 4, 2013, pp. 522–534.

Hayden, Craig. "The Procedural Rhetorics of *Mass Effect:* Video Games as Argumentation in International Relations." *International Studies Perspectives*, vol. 18, no. 2, 2017, pp. 175–193.

Haynes, Kyle. "Simulating the Bargaining Model of War." *PS: Political Science & Politics*, vol. 48, no. 4, 2015, pp. 626–629.

Healey, M. and Jenkins, A. *Developing Undergraduate Research and Inquiry*. 2009. The Higher Education Academy.

Healey, Mick, et al. *Engagement Through Partnership: Students as Partners In Learning And Teaching In Higher Education*. 2014. HE Academy.

Healey, Mick et al. "Students as Partners: Reflections on a Conceptual Model." *Teaching & Learning Inquiry*, vol. 4, no. 2, 2016, pp. 8–20.

Henderson, Errol. "Hidden in Plain Sight: Racism in International Relations Theory." *Cambridge Review of International Affairs*, vol. 26, no. 1, 2013, pp. 71–92.

Hendrickson, Petra. "Effect of Active Learning Techniques on Student Excitement, Interest, and Self-Efficacy." *Journal of Political Science Education*, 2019. DOI: 10.1080/15512169.2019.1629946.

Henning, Jeremiah A., Cissy J. Ballen, Sergio A. Molina and Sehoya Cotner. "Hidden Identities Shape Student Perceptions of Active Learning Environments." *Frontiers in Education* 4 (article 129), 2019, pp. 1–13. https://doi.org/10.3389/feduc.2019.00129 (accessed April 20, 2021).

Hildreth, David. "From Professor to Student and Back Again: What a Long Strange Trip and Lessons Learned." *National Teacher Education Journal*, vol. 5, no. 3, 2004.

Hobbes, Thomas. "Of the Natural Condition of Mankind as Concerning their Felicity and Misery." In *Classics of International Relations*, ed. John. Vasquez. 1996. Prentice-Hall.

Hoffman, Stanley. "An American Social Science: International Relations." *Daedalus*, vol. 106, no. 3, 1977, pp. 41–60

Holsti, Ole R. "Case Teaching: Transforming Foreign Policy Courses with Cases." *International Studies Notes*, vol. 19, 1994, pp. 7–13.

Holsti, Ole R. "Reflections on Teaching and Active Learning." In *The New International Studies Classroom: Active Teaching, Active Learning*, ed. Jeffrey S. Lantis, Lynn M. Kuzma, and John Boehrer. 2000. Lynne Rienner.

hooks, bell. *Teaching to Transgress: Education as the Practice of Freedom*. 1984. Routledge.

Hoover, Linda. "Thoughts on Higher Education." *Proteus*, vol. 25, no. 2, 2008, pp. 1–2.

Hosman, Laura, and Ginger Jacobs. "From Active Learning to Taking Action: Incorporating Political Context into Project-Based, Interdisciplinary, International Service Learning Courses." *Journal of Political Science Education*, vol. 14, no. 4, 2018, pp. 473–490.

Houghton, David P. *The Decision Point: Six Cases in U.S. Foreign Policy Decision Making*. Oxford University Press, 2013.

Hovey, R. "Critical Pedagogy and International Studies: Reconstructing Knowledge Through Dialogue with The Subaltern." *International Relations*, vol. 18, no. 2, 2004, pp. 241–254.

Howard, Kimberley and Brian Keller. "Study Tours: Strategies for Serving Business Students." *Journal of International Business Education*, vol. 4, 2009, pp. 135–150.

Hu, Shouping, Scheuch, Kathyrine, Schwartz, Robert, Joy Gaston and Shaoquing Li, eds. "Reinventing Undergraduate Education: Engaging College Students in Research and Creative Activities." *ASHE Higher Education Report*, vol. 33, no. 4, 2008, pp. 1–103.

Huba, M. E. and Freed, J. E. *Learner-Centered Assessment on College Campuses – Shifting the Focus from Teaching to Learning*. 2000. Allyn and Bacon.

Huber, M.T. "Disciplines, Pedagogy, and Inquiry-Based Learning about Teaching." In *Exploring Research-Based Teaching*, ed. C. Kreber. 2006. Jossey-Bass, pp. 69–77.

Hudzik, John K. "Comprehensive Internationalization: From Concept to Action." *NAFSA*, vol. 51, 2011.

Hulstrand, Janet. "Best Practices for Short-Term, Faculty-Led Programs Abroad." *International Educator*, vol. 24, no. 3, May 2015, pp. 58–64.

Humber College. "Centre for Teaching and Learning: Stop, Start and Continue", 2020. https://www.humber.ca/centreforteachingandlearning/instructional-strategies/teaching-methods/classroom-strategies-designing-instruction/activities-and-games/stop-start-continue.html (accessed August 15, 2020).

Hunter, Anne-Barrie, Timothy J. Weston, Sandra L. Laursen and Heather Thiry. "URSSA: Evaluating Student Gains from Undergraduate Research in the Sciences". *CUR Quarterly*, vol. 29, no. 3, 2008, pp. 15–19.

Hutchings, Pat, Mary Taylor Huber and Anthony Ciccone. *The Scholarship of Teaching and Learning Reconsidered: Institutional Integration and Impact*. 2011. Jossey-Bass.

Hutchings, Robert and Jeremi Suri, eds. *Foreign Policy Breakthroughs: Cases in Successful Diplomacy*. 2015. Oxford University Press.

Inayatullah, Naeem. "Falling and Flying: An Introduction." In *Autobiographical International Relations: I, IR*, ed. Naeem Inayatullah. 2011. Routledge, pp. 2–12.

Inoue, Cristina Yumie Aoki. "Worlding the Study of Global Environmental Politics in the Anthropocene: Indigenous Voices from the Amazon." *Global Environmental Politics*, vol. 18, 2018, p. 25–42.

Inoue, Cristina Yumie Aoki and Matthew Krain. "One World, Two Classrooms, Thirteen Days: Film as an Active-Teaching and Learning Tool in Cross-National Perspective." *Journal of Political Science Education*, vol. 10, no. 4, 2014, pp. 424–442.

Inoue, Cristina Yumie Aoki and Paula Franco Moreira. "Many Worlds, Many Nature(s), One Planet: Indigenous Knowledge in the Anthropocene." *Revista Brasileira de Política Internacional* (online), vol. 49, 2017, p. 119.

Inoue, Cristina Yumie Aoki, Thais L. Ribeiro and Ítalo S.A Resende. "Worlding Global Sustainability Governance." In *Routledge Handbook of Global Sustainability Governance*, ed. Agni Kalfagianni, Doris Fuchs and Anders Hayden, 1st ed. 2020. Routledge, pp. 59–71.

International Studies Association, "ISA 2020 Call for Proposals: Multiple Identities and Scholarship in a Global IR", https://www.isanet.org/Conferences/Honolulu-2020/Call (accessed April 20, 2021).

Ishiyama, John, et al. "A Century of Continuity and (Little) Change in the Undergraduate Political Science Curriculum." *American Political Science Review*, vol. 100, no. 4, 2006, pp. 659–665.

Ishiyama, J. "Frequently used active learning techniques and their impact: A critical review of existing journal literature in the United States." *European Political Science*, vol. 12, no. 1, 2013, pp. 116–126.

Jacobs-Lawson, Joy M., and Douglas A. Hershey. "Concept Maps as an Assessment Tool in Psychology Courses." *Teaching of Psychology*, vol. 29, no. 1, 2002, pp. 25–29.

Jahn, Beate. *The Cultural Construction of International Relations: The Invention of the State of Nature.* 2000. Palgrave.

James, Patrick. "What Do We Know About Crisis, Escalation and War? A Visual Assessment of the International Crisis Behavior Project." *Conflict Management and Peace Science*, vol. 36, no. 1, 2019, pp. 3–19.

James, Patrick. "Teaching for the Tenure and Beyond: How Classroom Innovation Can Promote Professional Advancement (and Fulfillment)." Presented at the International Studies Association Innovative Pedagogy Conference, St. Louis, November 15, 2018.

Jensen, Eric. *Teaching with the Brain in Mind.* 1998. Association for Supervision and Curriculum Development.

Jimenez, Luis F. "The Dictatorship Game: Simulating a Transition to Democracy." *PS: Politics & Political Science*, vol. 48, no. 2, 2015, pp. 353–357.

John, Vaughn M. "Teaching Peace Education at a South African University." *Peace Review*, vol. 30, no. 1, 2018, pp. 53–61.

Johnson, David W., Roger T. Johnson and Karl A. Smith. "Cooperative Learning Returns to College: What Evidence Is There That It Works?" *Change*, July/August, 1998, pp. 27–35.

Johnson, David W., Roger T. Johnson and Karl A. Smith. *Cooperative Learning: Increasing College Faculty Instructional Productivity.* ASHE-ERIC Higher Education Report no. 4. 1991. School of Education and Human Development, George Washington University.

Johnson, Sarah Randall and Frances King Stage. "Academic Engagement and Student Success: Do High-Impact Practices Mean Higher Graduation Rates?" *The Journal of Higher Education*, vol. 89, no. 5, 2018, pp. 753–781. DOI: 10.1080/00221546.2018.1441107.

Johnston, Alastair Iain. "Treating International Institutions as Social Environments." *International Studies Quarterly*, vol. 45, no. 4, 2001, pp. 487–515.

Jonassen, D. H. and Hung, W. "All Problems are Not Equal: Implications for Problem-Based Learning." *Interdisciplinary Journal of Problem-Based Learning*, vol. 2, no. 2, 2008, pp. 6–28.

Jones, Rebecca. "Evaluating a Cross-Continent EU Simulation." *Journal of Political Science Education*, vol. 4, no. 4, 2008, pp. 404–434. DOI: 10.1080/15512160802413790.

Jorgensen, Daphne. "The Challenges and Benefits of Asynchronous Learning Networks." In *The Reference Librarian.* 2002. Haworth Information Press, pp. 3–17.

Juneau, Thomas and Mira Sucharov. "Narratives in Pencil: Using Graphic Novels to TeachIsraeli-Palestinian Relations." *International Studies Perspectives*, vol. 11, no. 2, 2010, pp. 172–183.

Kalpakian, Jack. "Teaching IR in Morocco." *International Studies Perspectives*, forthcoming.

Kas, Kinga, and Elizabeth Sheppard. "Best Practices in Undergraduate Lecturing: How to Make Large Classes Work." In *Handbook on Teaching and Learning in Political Science and International Relations*, ed. John Ishiyama, William J. Miller and Ezster Simon, Edward Elgar Publishing, 2015, pp. 422–433.

Kayler, Mary and Karen Weller. "Pedagogy, Self-Assessment, and Online Discussion Groups." *Journal of Educational Technology & Society*, vol. 10, no. 1, 2007, pp. 136–147.

Kehl, Jenny. "Indicators of the Increase of Political Science Scholarship on Teaching and Learning in Political Science." *PS: Political Science & Politics*, vol. 35, no. 2, 2002, pp. 229–232.

Kehler, Angela, et al. "We Are the Process: Reflections on the Underestimation of Power in Students as Partners in Practice." *International Journal for Students as Partners*, vol. 1, no. 1, 2017, pp. 1–15, DOI: 10.15173/ijsap.v1i1.3176.

Keller, Jonathan W. "Misusing Virtual Worlds can be Dangerous: A Response to Carvalho." *International Studies Perspectives*, vol. 15, no. 4, 2014, pp. 558–563.

Kelly, Marisa and Brian E. Klunk. 2003. "Learning Assessment in Political Science Departments: Survey Results." *PS: Political Science & Politics*, vol. 36, no. 3, pp. 451–455.

Kember, David and Doris Y.P. Leung. "The Influence of Active Learning Experiences on the Development of Graduate Capabilities." *Studies in Higher Education*, vol. 30, no. 2, 2005, pp. 155–170.

Kiehl, William P., ed. *The Last Three Feet: Case Studies in Public Diplomacy*. 2014. Public Diplomacy Council.

Kille, Kent J., Matthew Krain and Jeffrey S. Lantis. "Active Teaching and Learning: The State of the Literature." In *Oxford Research Encyclopedia of International Studies*, ed. Nukhet Sandal. 2019. Oxford University Press. https://oxfordre.com/internationalstudies/view/10.1093/acrefore/9780190846626.001.0001/acrefore-9780190846626-e-427 (accessed April 20, 2021).

Kille, Kent J. "Simulating the Creation of a New International Human Rights Treaty: ActiveLearning in the International Studies Classroom." *International Studies Perspectives*, vol. 3, no. 3, 2002, pp. 271–90.

Killick, David. *Internationalisation and Diversity in Higher Education: Implications for Teaching, Learning and Assessment*. 2017. Palgrave.

Knight, J. "Internationalization: Management Strategies and Issues." *International Education Magazine*, vol. 9, 1993, pp. 6, 21–22.

Knight, Sarah Cleeland. "Even Today, a Western and Gendered Social Science: Persistent Geographic and Gender Biases in Undergraduate IR Teaching." *International Studies Perspectives*, vol. 20, no. 2, 2019, pp. 203–225.

Knowlton, Dave S. "A Theoretical Framework for the Online Classroom: A Defense and Delineation of a Student-Centered Pedagogy." *New Directions for Teaching and Learning*, vol. 84, 2000, pp. 5–14.

Kolb, David A. *Experiential Learning: Experience as the Source of Learning and Development*. 1984. Prentice-Hall.

Kollars, Nina A., and Amanda M. Rosen. "Simulations as Active Assessment?: Typologizing by Purpose and Source." *Journal of Political Science Education*, vol. 9, no. 2, 2013, pp. 144–156.

Kopenawa, Davi And Bruce Albert. *The Falling Sky. Words of A Yanomami Shaman*. Kindle Edition. 2013. The Belknap Press of Harvard University Press.

Kollars, Nina and Amanda Rosen. "Bootstrapping and Portability in Simulation Design." *International Studies Perspectives*, vol. 17, no. 2, 2016, pp. 202–213.

Koomen, Jonneke. "International Relations/Black Internationalism: Reimagining Teaching and Learning about Global Politics." *International Studies Perspectives*, vol. 20, 2019, pp. 390–411.

Krain, Matthew, and Anne Nurse. "Teaching Human Rights Through Service Learning." *Human Rights Quarterly*, vol. 26, no. 1, 2004, pp. 189–207.

Krain, Matthew, and Jeffrey S. Lantis. "Building Knowledge? Evaluating the Effectiveness of the Global Problems Summit Simulation." *International Studies Perspectives*, vol. 7, no. 4, 2006, pp. 395–407.

Krain, Matthew. "The Effects of Different Types of Case Learning on Student Engagement." *International Studies Perspectives*, vol. 11, no. 3, 2010, pp. 291–308.

Krain, Matthew, Kent J. Kille and Jeffrey S. Lantis. "Active Teaching and Learning in Cross-National Perspective." *International Studies Perspectives*, vol. 16, no. 2, 2015, pp. 142–155.

Kreber, C., ed. *Exploring Research-Based Teaching*. 2006. Jossey-Bass.

Krippel, Gregory, A. James McKee and Janette Moody. "Multimedia Use in Higher Education: Promises and Pitfalls." *Journal of Instructional Pedagogies*, vol. 2, no. 1, 2012, pp. 1–8.

Krishna, Sankaran. "Race, Amnesia, and the Education of International Relations." *Alternatives: Global, Local, Political*, vol. 26, no. 4, 2001, pp. 401–424.

Kuh, George, Ken O'Donnell and Carol Geary Schneider. "HIPs at Ten." *Change: The Magazine of Higher Education*, vol. 49, no. 5, 2017, pp. 8–16.

Kuh, George D., Stanley O. Ikenberry, Natasha A. Jankowski, Timothy Reese Cain, Peter T. Ewell, Pat Hutchings, and Jillian Kinzie. *Using Evidence of Student Learning to Improve Higher Education*. Jossey Bass, 2015.

Kuh, G. D., Kinzie, J., Schuh, J. H., & Whitt, E. J. *Student Success in College: Creating Conditions that Matter*. Jossey-Bass, 2010.

Kuzma, Lynn M. and Patrick J. Haney. "And … Action! Using Films to Learn about Foreign Policy." *International Studies Perspectives*, vol. 2, no. 1, 2001, pp. 33–50.

Kyoto University of Foreign Studies. "Community Engagement." 2020. https://www .kufs.ac.jp/en/faculties/ge/community_engagement.html (accessed August 20, 2020).

Laffey, Mark, and Jutta Weldes. "Decolonizing the Cuban Missile Crisis." *International Studies Quarterly*, vol. 52, no. 3, 2008, pp. 555–77. https://www.jstor.org/stable/29734251 (accessed April 20, 2021).

Lamy, Steven, John Masker, John Baylis, Steve Smith, and Patricia Owens. *Introduction to Global Politics*, 5th ed. 2018. Oxford University Press.

Lancey, Patricia and Divya Bhati. *Program and Administrative Unit Assessment Overview*. n.d. University of Central Florida, OEAS. https://oeas.ucf.edu/doc/Program_and_Administrative_Unit_Assessment_Overview.pdf (accessed April 20, 2021).

Lang Jr., Anthony F. and James M. Lang. "Between Theory and History: *The Remains of The Day* in the International Relations Classroom." *PS: Political Science & Politics*, vol. 31, no. 2, 1998, pp. 209–215.

Lantis, Jeffrey S. "Simulations and Experiential Learning in the International Relations Classroom." *International Negotiation*, vol. 3, no. 1, 1998, pp. 39–57.

Lantis, Jeffery S. and Jessica DuPlaga. *The Global Classroom: An Essential Guide to Study Abroad*. 2010. Paradigm Publishers.

Lantis, Jeffrey S., Kent J. Kille and Matthew Krain. "Active Teaching and Learning: The State of the Literature." In *Oxford Research Encyclopedia of International Studies*, ed. Renée Marlin-Bennett. 2019. Oxford University Press. DOI: 10.1093/acrefore/9780190846626.013.427.

Lantis, Jeffrey S., Lynn M. Kuzma and John Boehrer. "Active Teaching and Learning at a Critical Crossroads." In *The New International Studies Classroom: Active*

Teaching, Active Learning, ed. Jeffrey S. Lantis, Lynn M. Kuzma and John Boehrer. 2000a. Lynne Rienner, pp. 1–18.

Lantis, Jeffrey S., Lynn M. Kuzma and John Boehrer, eds. *The New International Studies Classroom: Active Teaching, Active Learning*. 2000b. Lynne Rienner.

Lawler, Andrew. "Civilization's Double-Edged Sword." *Science*, May 18, 2012, pp. 832–833.

Lawrence, Christopher N., and Julie A. Lester. "Evaluating the Effectiveness of Adopting Open Educational Resources in an Introductory American Government Course." *Journal of Political Science Education*, 14, pp. 555–566.

Laws, P., Rosborough P. and Poodry, F. "Women's Responses to an Activity-Based Introductory Physics Program." *American Journal of Physics*, vol. 67, 1999, pp. S32–S37.

Lederman, Doug. "Online Enrollments Grown, But Pace Slows." *Inside Higher-Ed*, December 11, 2019a. https://www.insidehighered.com/digital-learning/article/2019/12/11/more-students-study-online-rate-growth-slowed-2018 (accessed May 31, 2020).

Lederman, Doug. "Harsh Take on Assessment … From Assessment Pros." *Inside Higher Ed*, April 17, 2019b. https://www.insidehighered.com/news/2019/04/17/advocates-student-learning-assessment-say-its-time-different-approach (accessed April 20, 2021).

Lederman, Doug. "Conflicted Views of Technology: A Survey of Faculty Attitudes." *Inside HigherEd*, October 31, 2018. https://www.insidehighered.com/news/survey/conflicted-views-technology-survey-faculty-attitudes (accessed April 20, 2021).

Leonard, Eric K., ed. *Building Your IR Theory Toolbox: An Introduction to Understanding World Politics*. 2018. Rowman & Littlefield Publishers.

Levin-Banchik, Luba. "Assessing Knowledge Retention, With and Without Simulations." *Journal of Political Science Education*, vol. 14, no. 3, 2018, pp. 341–359.

Levy, Denise L. and Daniel C. Byrd. "Why Can't We Be Friends? Using Music to Teach Social Justice." *Journal of the Scholarship of Teaching and Learning*, vol. 11, no. 2, 2011, pp. 64–75.

Lichbach, Mark Irving, and Alan S. Zuckerman. *Comparative Politics: Rationality, Culture, and Structure*. 2009. Cambridge University Press.

Light, Richard J. *The Harvard Assessment Seminars: Explorations with Students and Faculty about Teaching, Learning and Student Life*. 1990. Harvard Graduate School of Education and Kennedy School of Government.

Lightfoot, Simon. "Promoting Employability and Job Skills Via the Political Science Curriculum." In *Handbook on Teaching and Learning in Political Science and International Relations*, ed. John Ishiyama, William J. Miller and Eszter Simo. 2015. Edward Elgar Publishing, pp. 144–154.

Linantud, John, and Joanna Kaftan. "The Statecraft Effect: Assessment, Attitudes, and Academic Honesty." *Journal of Political Science Education*, vol. 15, no. 1, 2019, pp. 64–81.

Liu, T. T. T. "Teaching IR to the Global South: Some Reflections and Insights." *Revista Brasileira De Política Internacional*, 59(2), 2016, pp. 1–20.

Lobasz, Jennifer K., and Brandon Valeriano. "Teaching International Relations with Film and Literature: Using Non-Traditional Texts in the Classroom." In *Handbook on Teaching and Learning in Political Science and International Relations*, ed. John Ishiyama, William J. Miller, and Eszter Simon. 2015. Edward Elgar Publishing, pp. 399–409.

Longview Foundation, The. *Teacher Preparation for the Global Age: The Imperative for Change*. 2008. The Longview Foundation. http://www.longviewfdn.org/programs/internationalizing- teacher-prep (accessed May 24, 2020).

Lopatto, D. "The Essential Features of Undergraduate Research." *CUR Quarterly*, vol. 24, 2003, pp. 139–42.

Lorenzo, M., Crouch, C.H., Mazur, E. "Reducing the Gender Gap in the Physics Classroom." *American Journal of Physics*, vol. 74, 2006, pp. 118–122.

Lucas, Gale M. "Initiating Student–Teacher Contact Via Personalized Responses to One-Minute Papers." *College Teaching*, vol. 58, no. 2, 2010, pp. 39–42.

Luckett, Kathy. "Curriculum Contestation in A Post-colonial Context: A View from The South." *Teaching in Higher Education*, 21, no. 4, 2016, pp. 415–428.

Luna, Yvonne M., and Stephanie A. Winters. "'Why Did You Blend My Learning?' A Comparison of Student Success in Lecture and Blended Learning Introduction to Sociology Courses." *Teaching Sociology*, vol. 45, no. 2, 2017, pp. 116–130.

Lynn, Laurence E. *Teaching & Learning with Cases: A Guidebook*. 1999. Chatham House Publishers/Seven Bridges Press.

MacLabhrainn, Iain. *Higher Education and Civic Engagement: International Perspectives*, ed. Lorraine McIlrath. 2007. Ashgate Publishing.

Madden, Timothy M., et al. "This Is Not a Vacation: The Shadow Side of Study Abroad Programs for Faculty." *Journal of Management Education*, vol. 43, no. 2, 2018, pp. 185–99, DOI: 10.1177/1052562918815212.

Majeski, Robin and Merrily Stover. "Interdisciplinary Problem-Based Learning in Gerontology: A Plan of Action." *Educational Gerontology*, vol. 31, no. 10, 2005, pp. 733–743.

Malachowski, M. "The Importance of Placing Students First in Designing Research Programs at Predominately Undergraduate Institutions." *CUR Quarterly*, vol. 24, 2004, pp. 106–108.

Malewski, Erik, and Joann Pillion. "Making Room in the Curriculum: The Raced, Classed, and Gendered Nature of Preservice Teachers' Experiences Studying Abroad." *Journal of Curriculum Theorizing*, vol. 25, no. 3, 2009, pp. 48–67.

Malik, S. and A. Agarwal. "Multimedia as a new Educational Technology Tool – A Study." *International Journal of Information and Education Technology*, vol. 2, no. 5, 2018, pp. 468–471.

Maliniak, Daniel, Ryan Powers, and Barbara F. Walter. "The Gender Citation Gap in International Relations." *International Organization*, vol. 67, no. 4, 2013, pp. 889–922.

Marine, Susan Sonchik. "Designing a Study Abroad Course in Chemistry: Information from Three Different Courses to Europe." *Journal of Chemical Education*, vol. 90, no. 2, 2013, pp. 178–82, DOI: 10.1021/ed200690p.

Martens, Samantha E., et al., "A Students' Take on Student–Staff Partnerships: Experiences and Preferences." *Assessment & Evaluation in Higher Education*, vol. 44, no. 6, 2019, pp. 910–919. DOI: 10.1080/02602938.2018.1546374.

Marquis, Elizabeth et al. "Navigating the Threshold of Student–Staff Partnerships: A Case Study From an Ontario Teaching and Learning Institute." *International Journal for Academic Development*, vol. 21, no. 1, pp. 4–15, 2016, DOI: 10.1080/1360144X.2015.1113538

Mathews, A. Lanethea and Alexandra Latronica-Herb. "Using Blackboard to Increase Student Learning and Assessment Outcomes in a Congressional Simulation." *Journal of Political Science Education*, vol. 9, 2013, pp. 168–183.

Matlin, Stephen and Ilona Kickbusch, eds. *Pathways to Global Health: Case Studies in Global Health Diplomacy*, Vol. 2. Singapore: World Scientific Publishing, 2017.

Matos Ala, Jacqueline de. "Introducing International Relations to Students in a South African Context." *International Studies Perspectives*, forthcoming.

Matos Ala, Jacqueline de. "Making the Invisible, Visible: Challenging the Knowledge Structures Inherent in International Relations Theory In Order To Create Knowledge Plural Curricula." *Revista Brasileira De Política Internacional* 60, no. 1, 2017

Matthews, Kelly. "Five Propositions for Genuine Students As Partners Practice". *International Journal for Students As Partners*, vol. 1, no. 2, 2017, pp. 1–9. DOI: 10.15173/ijsap.v1i2.3315.

Mattlin, Mikael. "Adapting the Diplomacy Board Game Concept for 21st Century International Relations Teaching." *Simulation & Gaming*, vol. 49, no. 6, 2018, pp. 735–750.

Matzner, Nils, and Robert Herrenbrück. "Simulating a Climate Engineering Crisis: Climate Politics Simulated by Students in Model United Nations." *Simulations & Gaming*, vol.48, no.2, 2017, pp. 268–290.

Mazur, Amber D., Barbara Brown, and Michele Jacobsen. "Learning Designs Using Flipped Instruction." *Canadian Journal of Learning and Technology*, vol. 41, no. 2, 2015, pp. 1–26.

McCall, Leslie. "The Complexity of Intersectionality." In *Intersectionality and Beyond: Law, Power and the Politics of Location*, ed. Emily Grabham, Davina Cooper, Jane Krishnadas and Didi Herman. 2009. Routledge-Cavendish, pp. 49–75.

McCarthy, J.P. and L. Anderson. "Active Learning Techniques Versus Traditional Teaching Styles: Two Experiments form History and Political Science." *Innovative Higher Education*, vol. 24, no. 4, 2000, pp. 279–294.

McClellan, Fletcher. "An Overview of the Assessment Movement." In *Assessment in Political Science*, ed. Michelle D. Deardorff, Kerstin Hamann and John Ishiyama. 2009. American Political Science Association, pp. 39–58.

McConnell, Kate Drezek. "What Assessment is Really About." *Inside HigherEd*, March 1, 2018. https://www.insidehighered.com/views/2018/03/01/assessment-isnt-about-bureaucracy-about-teaching-and-learning-opinion (accessed April 20, 2021).

McIlrath, Lorraine, and Iain MacLabhrainn, editors. *Higher Education and Civic Engagement: International Perspectives*. 2007. Ashgate Publishing.

McLaren, Constance H. "A Comparison of Student Persistence and Performance in Online and Classroom Business Statistics Experiences." *Decision Sciences Journal of Innovative Education*, vol. 2, no. 1, 2004, pp. 1–10.

McMillan, Samuel Lucas. "Bravo for Brevity: Using Short Paper Assignments in International Relations Classes." *International Studies Perspectives*, vol. 15, no. 1, 2014, pp. 109–120.

McNair, Malcolm P., ed.. *The Case Method at the Harvard Business School: Papers by Present and Past Members of the Faculty and Staff.* 1954. McGraw-Hill.

Means, Barbara, Yukie Toyama, Robert Murphy, and Marianne Baki. "The Effectiveness of Online and Blended Learning: A Meta-Analysis of the Empirical Literature." *Teachers College Record*, vol. 115, 2013, pp. 1–47.

Meibauer, Gustav, and Andreas Aagaard Nøhr. "Teaching Experience: How to Make and Use PowerPoint-Based Interactive Simulations for Undergraduate IR Teaching." *Journal of Political Science Education*, vol. 14, no.1, 2018, pp. 42–62.

Mertler, Craig A. "Designing Scoring Rubrics for Your Classroom." *Practical Assessment, Research, and Evaluation*, vol. 7, no. 25, 2000. DOI: 10.7275/gcy8-0w24.

Metz, T., and J. B. R. Gaie. "The African Ethic of Ubuntu/Botho: Implications for Research on Morality." *Journal of Moral Education*, vol. 39, no. 3, 2010, pp. 273–290.

Meyers, Steven A. "Using Transformative Pedagogy When Teaching Online." *College Teaching*, vol. 56, no. 4, 2008, pp. 219–224.

Mihans, Richard J. II, et al. "Power and Expertise: Student-Faculty Collaboration in Course Design and the Scholarship of Teaching and Learning." *International Journal for the Scholarship of Teaching and Learning*, vol. 2, no. 2, 2008, pp. 1–9. https://doi .org/10.20429/ijsotl.2008.020216 (accessed April 20, 2021).

Miller, Michelle D. *Minds Online: Teaching Effectively with Technology.* 2016. Harvard University Press.

Miller, William J. "Course-based Assessment and Student Feedback." In *Handbook of Teaching and Learning in Political Science and International Relations*, ed. John Ishiyama, Will Miller, and Eszter Simon. Edward Elgar Publishing, 2015, pp. 95–110.

Mills, LaVelle H., et al. "Short-Term Study Abroad Programs: A Diversity of Options." *The Journal of Human Resource and Adult Learning*, vol. 6, no. 2, 2010, pp. 1–13.

Mingst, Karen A. and Katsuhiko Mori, eds. *Teaching International Affairs with Cases: Cross-National Perspectives.* 1997. Westview Press.

Mingst, Karen, Heather Elko McKibben and Ivan Arreguin-Toft. *Essentials of International Relations*, 8th ed. 2019. W.W. Norton.

Miri, B., B. David and Z. Uri. "Purposely Teaching for the Promotion of Higher-order Thinking Skills: A Case of Critical Thinking." *Research in Science Education*, vol. 37, 2007, pp. 353–369.

Mislan, David B. and Philip Streich. *Weird IR: Deviant Cases in International Relations.* 2019. Palgrave Macmillan.

Mitchell, Donald, and Ashley Maloff. "Racial Positionalities, Professional Development, and a Master's Study Abroad Experience in Jamaica for Preparing Student Affairs Professionals." *The College Student Affairs Journal*, vol. 34, no. 2, 2016, pp. 3–15. DOI: 10.1353/csj.2016.0010.

Mitchell, Sara McLaughlin, Samantha Lange, and Holly Brus. "Gendered Citation Patterns in International Relations Journals." *International Studies Perspectives*, vol. 14, no. 4, 2013, pp. 485–492.

Morgan, April L. "The Poisonwood Bible: An Antidote for What Ails International Relations?" *International Political Science Review*, vol. 27, no. 4, 2006, pp. 379–403.

Moriarty, Mary A. "Inclusive Pedagogy: Teaching Methodologies to Reach Diverse Learners in Science Instruction." *Equity and Excellence in Education*, vol. 43, no. 3, 2007, pp. 252–265.

Mueller, Pam A. and Daniel M. Oppenheimer. "The Pen Is Mightier Than the Keyboard: Advantages of Longhand Over Laptop Note Taking." *Psychological Science*, vol. 25, no. 6, 2014, pp. 1159–1168.

Mulcare, Daniel M., and Allan Shwedel. "Transforming Bloom's Taxonomy into Classroom Practice: A Practical Yet Comprehensive Approach to Promote Critical Reading and Student Participation." *Journal of Political Science Education*, vol. 13, no. 2, 2017, pp. 121–137.

Mule, Lucy, et al. "Short-Term, Faculty-Led Study Abroad and Global Citizenship Identification: Insights from a Global Engagement Program." *Frontiers: The Interdisciplinary Journal of Study Abroad*, vol. 30, no. 3, 2018, pp. 20–37. DOI: 10.36366/frontiers.v30i3.425.

Nayak, Meghana and Eric Selbin. *Decentering International Relations*. Bloomsbury, 2010.

Neuhauser, Charlotte. "Learning Style and Effectiveness of Online and Face-to-Face Instruction." *The American Journal of Distance Education*. vol. 16, no. 2, 2002, pp. 99–113.

Nguyen, Tuan. "The Effectiveness of Online Learning: Beyond No Significant Difference and Future Horizons." *Journal of Online Learning and Teaching*, vol. 11, no. 2, 2015, pp. 309–319.

Nicol, David J. and Debra Macfarlane-Dick. "Formative Assessment and Self-Regulated Learning: A Model and Seven Principles of Good Feedback Practice." *Studies in Higher Education*, vol. 31, no. 2, 2006, pp. 199–218. DOI: 10.1080/03075070600572090.

Nilson, Linda B. and Ludwika A. Goodson. *Online Teaching at its Best*. 2018. Jossey-Bass.

Nilson, L. B. *Teaching at its Best: A Research-Based Resource for College Instructors*, 3rd ed. 2010. Jossey-Bass.

Nishikawa, Katsuo A. and Joseph Jaeger. "A Computer Simulation Comparing the Incentive Structures of Dictatorships and Democracies." *Journal of Political Science Education*, vol. 7, no. 2, 2011, pp. 135–142.

Norman, Geoffrey R., and Henk G. Schmidt. "The Psychological Basis of Problem-Based Learning: A Review of the Evidence." *Academic Medicine*, vol. 67, no. 9, 1992, pp. 557–565.

Novak, Joseph D. "Concept Maps and Vee Diagrams: Two Metacognitive Tools to Facilitate Meaningful Learning." *Instructional Science*, vol. 19, no. 1, 1990, pp. 29–52.

Nussbaum, Martha. *Not for Profit: Why Democracy Needs the Humanities*. Princeton, NJ: Princeton University Press, 2016.

Obendorf, Simon, and Claire Randerson. "Evaluating the Model United Nations: Diplomatic Simulation as Assessed Undergraduate Coursework." *European Political Science*, vol. 12, no. 3, 2013, pp. 350–364.

Oberle, Monika, Johanna Leunig, and Sven Ivens. "What Do Students Learn from Political Simulation Games? A Mixed-Method Approach Exploring the Relation between Conceptual and Attitudinal Changes." *European Political Science*, 2020. DOI: 10.1057/s41304-020-00261-2.

Oblinger, Diana, and James Oblinger. "Is It Age or IT: First Steps Toward Understanding the Net Generation." *CSLA Journal*, vol. 29, no. 2, 2006, pp. 8–16.

Odoom, Isaac and Nathan Andrews. "What/Who Is Still Missing in International Relations Scholarship? Situating Africa as an Agent in IR Theorising." *Third World Quarterly*, 2016, pp. 1–19.

Ogg, Frederic A. "Political Science as a Profession: From the Standpoint of Teaching." *The Journal of Politics*, vol. 3, no. 4, 1941, pp. 509–518.

Olivo, Christiane. "Bringing Women In: Gender and American Government and Politics Textbooks." *Journal of Political Science Education*, vol. 8, 2012, pp. 131–146.

Olson, Christa L., Rhodri Evans and Robert F. Shoenberg. *At Home in the World: Bridging The gap between Internationalization and Multicultural Education*. June, 2007. American Council on Education. Available at https://www.acenet.edu/Documents/at-home-in-the-world.pdf (accessed July 13, 2020).

Omelicheva, Mariya Y. and Olga Avdeyeva. "Teaching with Lecture or Debate? Testing the Effectiveness of Traditional versus Active Learning Methods of Instruction." *PS: Political Science and Politics*, 2008, vol. 41, no. 3, pp. 603–607.

Orr, John C. "Instant Assessment: Using One-Minute Papers in Lower-Level Classes." *Pedagogy*, vol. 5, no. 1, 2005, pp. 108–11.

Otten, Matthias. "Intercultural Learning and Diversity in Higher Education." *Journal of Studies in International Education*, vol. 7, no. 1, Spring 2003, pp. 12–26.

Owens, David C., Troy D. Sadler, Angela T. Barlow and Cindy Smith-Walters. "Student Motivation from and Resistance to Active Learning Rooted in Essential Science Practices." *Research in Science Education*, vol. 50, no. 2, 2020, pp. 253–277. https://doi.org/10.1007/s11165–017–9688–1 (accessed April 20, 2021).

Owens, Katharine A., et al. "Comic-Con: Can Comics of the Constitution Enable Meaningful Learning in Political Science?" *PS: Political Science & Politics*, vol. 53, no. 1, 2020, pp. 161–66.

Packard, Josh. "The Impact of Racial Diversity in the Classroom: Activating the Sociological Imagination." *Teaching Sociology*, vol. 41, no. 2, 2011, pp. 144–158.

Palloff, Rena M. and Keith Pratt. *Building Learning Communities in Cyberspace: Effective Strategies for the Online Classroom*. 1999. Jossey-Bass.

Paras, Andrea, et al. "Understanding How Program Factors Influence Intercultural Learning in Study Abroad: The Benefits of Mixed-Method Analysis." *Frontiers: The Interdisciplinary Journal of Study Abroad*, vol. 31, no. 1, 2019, pp. 22–45. DOI: 10.36366/frontiers.v31i1.441.

Parker, Jenni, Dorit Maor and Jan Herington. "Authentic Online Learning: Aligning Learner Needs, Pedagogy and Technology." *Issues in Educational Research*, vol. 23, no. 2, 2013, pp. 227–241.

Parmentier, Mary Jane C. "Simulating in Cyberspace: Designing and Assessing Simple Role Playing Activities for Online Regional Studies Courses." *International Studies Perspectives*, vol. 14, no. 2, 2013, pp. 121–133.

Parmentier, Mary Jane C. and Sharlissa Moore. "'The Camels Are Unsustainable': Using Study Abroad as a Pedagogical Tool for Teaching Ethics and Sustainable Development." *Teaching Ethics*, vol. 16, no. 2, 2016, pp. 207–21. DOI: 10.5840/tej2016113038.

Parpart, Jane L and Swati Parashar, eds. *Rethinking Silence, Voice and Agency in Contested Gendered Terrains*. 2019. Routledge.

Pashler, Harold, Mark McDaniel, Doug Rohrer and Robert Bjork. 2009. "Learning Styles: Concepts and Evidence." *Psychological Science in the Public Interest*, vol. 9, pp. 105–119.

Pelz, Bill. "(My) Three Principles of Effective Online Pedagogy." *Journal of Asynchronous Learning Networks*, vol. 14, no. 1, 2003, pp. 103–116.

Pernecky, Mark. "Reaction Papers Enrich Economics Discussions." *College Teaching*, vol. 41, no. 3, 1993, pp. 89–91.

Perry, Edward H. and Michelle L. Pilati. "Online Learning." *New Directions for Teaching and Learning*, no. 128, 2011, pp. 95–104.

Peters, John and Leoarna Mathias. "Enacting Student Partnership As Though We Really Mean It: Some Freirean Principles for a Pedagogy of Partnership". *International Journal for Students As Partners*, vol. 2, no. 2, 2018, pp. 53–70. DOI: 10.15173/ijsap.v2i2.3509.

Peterson, Spike V. "Gendered Identities, Ideologies, and Practices in the Context of War and Militarism." In *Gender, War, and Militarism: Feminist Perspectives*, ed, Laura Sjoberg and Sandra Via. 2010. Praeger, pp. 17–29.

Pettman, Jan Jindy. *Worldling Women: A Feminist International Politics*. 1996. Routledge.

Pettenger, Mary, Douglas West, and Niki Young. "Assessing the Impact of Role Play Simulations on Learning in Canadian and US Classrooms." *International Studies Perspectives*, vol. 15, no. 4, 2014, pp. 491–508.

Phillips, Janet M. "Strategies for Active Learning in Online Education." *The Journal of Continuing Education in Nursing*, vol. 36, no. 2, 2005, pp. 77–83.

Pini, Andre Mendes. "A Predominância Tácita do Tradicionalismo nas Relações Internacionais: O Panorama Brasileiro." *RARI - Revista Acadêmica de Relações Internacionais* , vol. 1, 2013, pp. 13–21.

Pintrich, Paul R. "A Conceptual Framework for Assessing Motivation and Self-Regulated Learning in College Students." *Education Psychology Review*, vol. 16, no. 4, 2004, pp. 385–407.

Pipitone, Jennifer M. "Place as Pedagogy: Toward Study Abroad for Social Change." *The Journal of Experiential Education*, vol. 41, no. 1, 2018, pp. 54–74. DOI: 10.1177/1053825917751509.

Polatajko, Mark M. and Catherine H. Monaghan. "Performance Funding of United States' Public Higher Education: Impact on Graduation and Retention Rates." In *Handbook of Research on Administration, Policy, and Leadership in Higher Education*, ed. S. Mukerji and P. Tripathi. 2017. IGI Global, pp. 496–517.

Poole, Dawn M. "Student Participation in a Discussion Oriented Online Course: A Case Study." *Journal of Research on Computing in Education*, vol. 33, no. 2, 2000, pp. 162–177.

Powel, Brieg. "Blinkered Learning, Blinkered Theory: How Histories In Textbooks Parochialize IR". *International Studies Review*, vol. 22, no. 4, 2019, pp. 957–982.

Powner, Leanne C., and Michelle G. Allendoerfer. "Evaluating Hypotheses about Active Learning." *International Studies Perspectives*, vol. 9, no. 1, 2008, pp. 75–89.

Praeg, Leonhard. *A Report on Ubuntu*. 2014. University of KwaZulu Natal Press.

Price, Margaret, Jude Carroll, Berry O'Donovan and Chris Rust. "If I was Going there I Wouldn't Start from Here: A Critical Commentary on Current Assessment Practice." *Assessment & Evaluation in Higher Education*, vol. 26, no.4, 2011, pp. 479–492. https://doi.org/10.1080/02602930903512883 (accessed April 20, 2021).

Prince, Michael. "Does Active Learning Work? A Review of the Research." *Journal of Engineering Education*, vol. 93, no. 3, 2004, pp.223–231. https://doi.org/10.1002/j .2168–9830.2004.tb00809.x (accessed April 20, 2021).

Querejazu, Amaya. "Encountering the Pluriverse: Looking For Alternatives In Other Worlds." *Revista Brasileira De Política Internacional*, vol. 59, no. 2, 2016. https:// doi.org/10.1590/0034-7329201600207 (accessed April 20, 2021.

Qiang, Zha. "Internationalization of Higher Education: towards a conceptual framework." *Policy Futures in Education*, vol. 1, no. 2, 2003.

Rafshoon, Ellen G. "Making Strangers of Ourselves: Role-Playing the Immigrant Experience in a College Classroom." In *Engaging Difference: Teaching Humanities and Social Science in Multicultural Environments*, ed. Dovilė Budrytė and Scott A. Boykin. 2017. Rowman and Littlefield, pp. 83–93.

Ramsey, James D. and Linda A. Kiltz, eds. *Critical Issues in Homeland Security: A Casebook*. 2018. Routledge.

Rasmussen, Amy Cabrera. "Toward an Intersectional Political Science Pedagogy." *Journal of Political Science Education*, vol. 10, 2014, pp. 102–116.

Raymond, Chad. "Can't Get No (Dis)Satisfaction: The Statecraft Simulation's Effect on Student Decision Making." *Journal of Political Science Education*, vol. 10, no. 3, 2014, pp. 302–314.

Raymond, Chad and Simon Usherwood. "Assessment in Simulations." *Journal of Political Science Education*, vol. 9, no. 2, 2013, pp. 157–167.

Raymond, Chad, et al. "Using Experimental Research to Test Instructional Effectiveness: A Case Study." *Journal of Political Science Education*, vol. 14, no. 2, 2018, pp. 167–176.

RBPI. "Many worlds, many theories? – A Special Issue of RBPI." https://networks.h -net.org/node/20292/discussions/60217/many-worlds-many-theories--special-issue -rbpi (accessed April 15, 2021).

Redlich, Josef. *The Common Law and the Case Method in American University Law Schools: A Report to the Carnegie Foundation for the Advancement of Teaching.* 2009, original printing 1914. University of Michigan Library.

Reed, Alfred Zantzinger. *Training for the Public Profession of the Law*, vol. 15. 2017, original printing 1921. Forgotten Books.

Rexeisen, Richard J. "Study Abroad and the Boomerang Effect: The End Is Only the Beginning." *Frontiers: The Interdisciplinary Journal of Study Abroad*, vol. 22, no. 1, 2013, pp. 166–81. DOI: 10.36366/frontiers.v22i1.325.

Rhodes, Carolyn. *Pivotal Decisions: Selected Cases in Twentieth-Century International Politics.* 2000. Harcourt Brace.

Richter-Montpetit, Melanie. "Everything You Always Wanted to Know about Sex (in IR) But were Afraid to Ask: The 'Queer Turn' in International Relations." *Millennium* vol. 46 no. 2, 2017, pp. 220–240.

Riegg, Natalya T. "Intersectionality and Popular Empowerment in International Relations." In *Engaging Difference: Teaching Humanities and Social Science in Multicultural Environments*, ed. Dovilė Budrytė and Scott A. Boykin. 2017. Rowman and Littlefield, pp. 1–10.

Rittinger, Eric R. "Inspiring Students to Think Theoretically About International Relations Through the Game of Diplomacy." *Journal of Political Science Education*, vol. 16, no. 1, 2020, pp. 41–56.

Robinson, Tony. "Service-learning as Justice Advocacy: Can Political Scientists Do Politics?" *PS: Political Science and Politics*, vol. 33, no. 3, 2000, pp. 605–612.

Robinson, Andrew M., and Michelle Goodridge. "Objective Assessment of Pedagogical Effectiveness and the Human Rights Foreign Policy Simulation Game." *Journal of Political Science Education*, 2019. DOI: 10.1080/15512169.2019.1623048.

Rooney-Varga, Juliette N., et al. "The Climate Action Simulation." *Simulation & Gaming*, vol. 51, no. 2, 2020, pp. 114–140.

Rösch, Felix. "The Power of Dance: Teaching International Relations Through Contact Improvisation." *International Studies Perspectives*, vol. 19, no. 1, 2018, pp. 67–82.

Rose, Gideon, ed. *American Foreign Policy: Cases and Choices.* 2003. Council on Foreign Relations.

Rosen, Amanda M. "The Value of Games and Simulations in the Social Sciences." In *Learning from Each Other: Refining the Practice of Teaching in Higher Education*, ed. Michele Lee Kozimor and Jeffrey Chin. 2018. University of California Press.

Rosskam, Ellen and Ilona Kickbusch, eds. *Negotiating and Navigating Global Health: Case Studies in Global Health Diplomacy.* 2012. World Scientific Publishing.

Roy, D., Kustra, E. and Borin, P. What is Unique about Inquiry Courses? 2003. http:// cll.mcmaster.ca/resources/misc/whats_unique_about_inquiry.html (accessed July 1, 2020).

Ruane, Abigail E., and Patrick James. *The International Relations of Middle-earth: Learning from the Lord of the Rings.* 2012. University of Michigan Press.

Ruane, Abigail E., and Patrick James. "The International Relations of Middle Earth: Learning from *The Lord of the Rings.*" *International Studies Perspectives*, vol. 9, no. 4, 2008, pp. 377–394.

Rubin, Jeffrey Z., Dean G. Pruitt, and Sung Hee Kim. *Social Conflict: Escalation, Stalemate, and Settlement.* 1994. McGraw-Hill.

Rublee, Maria Rost. "Rubrics in the Political Science Classroom: Packing a Serious Analytical Punch." *PS: Political Science & Politics*, vol. 47, no. 1, 2014, pp. 199–203.

Runyan, Anne Sisson, and V. Spike Peterson. *Global Gender Issues in the New Millennium: Dilemmas in World Politics*, 4th ed. (ebook). 2014. Routledge.

Rust, Chris. "Towards a Scholarship of Assessment." *Assessment & Evaluation in Higher Education*, vol. 32 no. 2, 2007, pp. 229–237. DOI: 10.1080/02602930600805192.

Sachleben, Mark. *World Politics on Screen: Understanding International Relations Through Popular Culture.* 2014. The University Press of Kentucky.

Saiya, Nilay. "How Dangerous are Virtual Worlds Really? A Research Note on the Statecraft Simulation Debate." *Social Science Computer Review*, vol. 35, no. 2, 2017, pp. 287–296.

Saiya, Nilay. "The Statecraft Simulation and Foreign Policy Attitudes Among Undergraduate Students." *Journal of Political Science Education*, vol. 12, no. 1, 2016, pp. 58–71.

Salter, Mark B. "Crowdsourcing: Student-Driven Learning Using Web 2.0 Technologies in an Introduction to Globalization Course." *Journal of Political Science Education*, vol. 9, no. 4, 2013, pp. 362–365.

Santos, B.S. "Beyond Abyssal Thinking: From Global Lines to Ecologies of Knowledges." *Review (Fernand Braudel Center)*, vol. 30, no. 1, 2007, pp. 45–89.

Savery, John R. "Overview of Problem-Based Learning: Definitions and Distinctions." *Interdisciplinary Journal of Problem-Based Learning*, vol. 1, no. 1, 2006, pp. 9–20.

Scott, James M. "Developing Student Scholars: Best Practices in Promoting Undergraduate Research." In *Handbook of Teaching and Learning in Political Science and International Relations*, ed. J. Ishiyama, W. Miller, and E. Simon. 2015. Edward Elgar Publishing, pp. 384–398.

Scott, James M., Ralph G. Carter, and A. Cooper Drury. *IR: Seeking Security, Prosperity, and Quality of Life in a Changing World*, 4th ed. 2022. CQ Press.

Scott, James M., Ralph G. Carter, and A. Cooper Drury. *IR: International, Economic, and Human Security in a Changing World*, 3rd ed. 2019. Sage/CQ Press.

Seale, Jane. "Doing Student Voice Work in Higher Education: An Exploration of the Value of Participatory Methods." *British Educational Research Journal*, vol. 36, no. 6, 2010, pp. 995–1015. DOI: 10.1080/01411920903342038.

Seale, Jane, et al. "Power and Resistance: Reflections on The Rhetoric and Reality of Using Participatory Methods to Promote Student Voice and Engagement in Higher Education." *Journal of Further and Higher Education*, vol. 39, no. 4, 2015, pp. 534–552. DOI: 10.1080/0309877X.2014.938264

Sears, Nathan Alexander. "War and Peace in International Relations Theory: A Classroom Simulation." *Journal of Political Science Education*, vol. 14, no. 2, 2018, pp. 222–239.

Shaklee, Beverly D. and Supriya Baily, eds. *Internationalizing Teacher Education in the United States.* 2012. Rowman and Littlefield.

Shannon, Vaughn Parnell. "Role-Play Simulations and Changing Perceptions of the Other: Model UN, Model Arab League, and Student Views of the Muslim World." *International Studies Perspectives*, vol. 21, no. 3, 2020, pp. 219–239.

Shaw, Carolyn M. "Connecting Students Cross-Nationally Through Facebook." *Journal of Political Science Education*, vol. 12, no. 3, 2016, pp. 353–368.

Shaw, Carolyn M. "Using Role-Play Scenarios in the IR Classroom: An Examination of Exercises on Peacekeeping Operations and Foreign Policy Decision Making." *International Studies Perspectives*, vol. 5, no.1, 2004, pp. 1–22.

Shaw, Carolyn, and Amanda M. Rosen. "Designing and Using Simulations and Games." In *Oxford Research Encyclopedia of International Studies*, forthcoming.

Shaw, Carolyn M., and Bob Switky. "Designing and Using Simulations in the International Relations Classroom." *Journal of Political Science Education*, vol. 14, no. 4, 2018, pp. 523–534.

Shellman, Stephen M. and Kürşad Turan. "Do Simulations Enhance Student Learning? An Empirical Evaluation of an IR Simulation." *Journal of Political Science Education*, vol. 2, no. 1, 2006, pp. 19–32.

Shifrinson, Joshua R. *Rising Titans, Falling Giants: How Great Powers Exploit Power Shifts*. Cornell University Press.

Shimko, Keith. *International Relations: Perspectives, Controversies and Readings*, 5th ed. 2015. Cengage.

Shinko, Rosemary E. "Thinking, Doing, and Writing International Relations Theory." *International Studies Perspectives*, vol. 7, no. 1, 2006, pp. 43–50.

Shiraev, Eric and Vladislav Zubok. *International Relations*, 3rd ed. 2019. Oxford University Press.

Shor, Ira. *Empowering Education: Critical Teaching for Social Change*. 1992. University of Chicago Press.

Shostya, Anna, and Joseph C. Morreale. "Fostering Undergraduate Research Through a Faculty-Led Study Abroad Experience." *International Journal of Teaching and Learning in Higher Education*, vol. 29, no. 2, 2017, pp. 300–308.

Shulman, Judith H. *Case Methods in Teacher Education*. 1992. Teachers College Press.

Shulman, Lee S. "Professing the Liberal Arts." In *Education and Democracy: Reimagining Liberal Learning in America*, ed. R. Orril. 1997. The College Board, pp. 151–173.

Siegel, David A. and Joseph K. Young. "Simulating Terrorism: Credible Commitment, Costly Signaling, and Strategic Behavior." *PS: Politics & Political Science*, vol. 42, no. 4, 2009, pp. 765–771.

Silver, Susan L. and Lisa T. Nickel. "Are Online Tutorials Effective? A Comparison of Online and Classroom Library Instruction Methods." *Research Strategies*, vol. 20, no. 4, 2005, pp. 389–396.

Sil, Rudra, and Peter J. Katzenstein. *Beyond Paradigms: Analytic Eclecticism in the Study of World Politics*. 2010. Palgrave Macmillan.

Simon, Agnes. "Teaching and Learning about Foreign Policy Decision-Making via Board-Gaming and Reflections." *European Political Science*, vol. 19, no. 1, 2020, pp. 9–28.

Simpson, Archie W., and Bernd Kaussler. "IR Teaching Reloaded: Using Films and Simulations in the Teaching of International Relations." *International Studies Perspectives*, vol. 10, no. 4, 2009, pp. 413–27.

Singh, Raghu and David Hurley. "The Effectiveness of Teaching–Learning Process in Online Education as Perceived by University Faculty and Instructional Technology Professionals." *Journal of Teaching and Learning with Technology*, vol. 6, no.1, 2017, pp. 65–75.

Sjoberg, Laura. "Seeing Sex, Gender, and Sexuality in International Security." *International Journal: Canada's Journal of Global Policy Analysis*, vol. 70, no. 3, 2015, pp. 434–453.

Sjoberg, Laura, and Caron E. Gentry. *Mothers, Monsters, Whores: Women's Violence in Global Politics*, Zed Books, 2007.

Sjoberg, Laura, and J. Ann Tickner. "Introduction: International Relations through Feminist Lenses." In *Feminism and International Relations: Conversations about the Past, Present and Future*, ed. J. Ann Tickner and Laura Sjoberg, Routledge, 2011, pp. 1–21.

Sjöstedt, Roxanna. "Assessing a Broad Teaching Approach: The Impact of Combining Active Learning Methods on Student Performance in Undergraduate Peace and Conflict Studies." *Journal of Political Science Education*, vol. 11, no. 2, 2015, pp. 204–220.

Slavin, R. E. *Co-operative Learning: Theory, Research and Practice*. 1990. Prentice Hall.

Smith, Daryl. *Diversity's Promise for Higher Education. Making It Work*. 2009. Johns Hopkins University Press.

Smith, Elizabeth T. and Mark A. Boyer. "Designing In-Class Simulations." *PS: Political Science and Politics*, vol. 29, no. 4, 1996, pp. 690–94.

Smith, Hayden and Niall Michelsen. "Pursuing Ideology with Statecraft." *Journal of Political Science Education*, vol. 13, no. 3, 2017, pp. 317–332.

Smith, Heather A. "Unlearning: A Messy and Complex Journey with Canadian Foreign Policy." *International Journal*, vol. 72, no. 2, 2017, pp. 203–216. DOI: 10.1177/0020702017711702.

Smith, Heather A. and Yahlnaaw. "Disruption as Reconciliation: Lessons Learned When Students as Partners Become Students as Teachers." In *Teaching International Relations in the Age of Disruption* ed. Heather A. Smith and David J. Hornsby, under review with Palgrave Macmillan.

Smith, Heather A., et al. "Unpacking Power Hierarchies in Students as Partners Practices" Research Report Submitted to BCcampus, September 2019. https://bccampus.ca/wp-content/uploads/2019/10/BCCampus-Research-Report-Unpacking-Power-Hierarchies-in-Students-as-Partners-Practices.pdf (accessed August 20, 2020).

Smith, Karen and Arlene B. Tickner, "Introduction: International Relations from the Global South." In *International Relations from The Global South. Worlds of Difference*, ed. Arlene B. Tickner and Karen Smith. 2020. Routledge, pp. 1–14.

Smoller, Fred. "Assessment Is Not a Four-Letter Word." *PS: Political Science & Politics*, vol. 27, no. 6, 2004, pp. 871–874.

Snow, Donald M. *Cases in International Relations: Principles and Applications*, 7th ed. 2018a. Rowman & Littlefield.

Snow, Donald M. *Regional Cases in U.S. Foreign Policy*. 2018b. Rowman & Littlefield.

Soper, Christopher. "Rock and Roll Will Never Die: Using Music to Engage Students in the Study of Political Science." *PS: Political Science & Politics*, vol. 43, no. 2, 2010, pp. 363–367.

Sorti, Craig. *The Art of Crossing Cultures*. 2007. Intercultural Press.

Sousa Santos, B. *Epistemologies of The South: Justice Against Epistemicide*. 2015. Routledge.

Sousa Santos, B. "Beyond Abyssal Thinking: From Global Lines to Ecologies of Knowledges." *Review* (Fernand Braudel Center), vol. 30, no. 1, 2007, pp. 45–89.

Spronken-Smith, Rachel A. and Tony Harland. "Learning to Teach with Problem-Based Learning." *Active Learning in Higher Education*, vol. 10, no. 2, 2009, pp. 138–153.

Standards of Good Practice. The Forum on Education Abroad. n.d. https://forumea.org/resources/standards-6th-edition/standards-6-1/ (accessed July 1, 2020).

Statecraft Simulations. n.d. https://www.statecraftsims.com/ (accessed July 22, 2020).

Stoddard, Jeremy D. "Film as a 'Thoughtful' Medium for Teaching History." *Learning, Media, and Technology*, vol. 37, no. 3, 2012, pp. 271–288.

Stommel, Jesse. "How to Ungrade." March 11, 2018, https://www.jessestommel.com/how-to-ungrade/ (accessed August 25, 2020).

Strange, Hannah and Heather Gibson. "An Investigation of Experiential and Transformative Learning in Study Abroad Programs." *Frontiers: The Interdisciplinary Journal of Study Abroad*, vol. 29, no. 1, 2017, pp. 85–100. DOI: 10.36366/frontiers.v29i1.387.

Strong, Robert A. *Decisions and Dilemmas: Case Studies in Presidential Foreign Policy Making since 1945*, 2nd ed. 2005. M.E. Sharpe.

Stump, Jacob L. "Exploring Politics and Government with Popular Culture: Justifications, Methods, Potentials, and Challenges in Introductory Political Science Courses." *Journal of Political Science Education*, vol. 9, no. 3, 2013, pp. 292–307.

Styles, Kendall W. *Case Histories in International Politics*, 7th ed. 2013. Pearson.

Summers, Sarah and Brett Craig. "A Cross-Cultural Collaboration Between U.S. and Kazakhstani Students." *Double Helix*, vol. 4, 2016, pp. 1–12.

Sunderland, Sherie, Jonathan C. Rothermel, and Adam Lusk. "Making Movies Active: Lessons from Simulations." *PS: Political Science and Politics*, vol. 42, no. 3, 2009, pp. 543–547.

Suskie, Linda. *Assessing Student Learning: A Common Sense Guide*, 2nd ed. 2009. Jossey Bass.

Sylvester, Christine. *War as Experience: Contributions from International Relations and Feminist Analysis*. 2013. Routledge.

Sylvester, "Experiencing War: An Introduction." In *Experiencing War*, ed. Christine Sylvester. 2011. Routledge, pp. 1–7.

Talbert, Robert. *Flipped Learning: A Guide for Higher Education Faculty.* 2017. Stylus.

Tan, Jason. "Revisiting the Chinese Learner: Changing Contexts, Changing Education." *Asia Pacific Journal of Education*, vol. 31, no. 2, 2011, pp. 227–238.

Tarrant, Michael Andrew. "A Conceptual Framework for Exploring the Role of Studies Abroad in Nurturing Global Citizenship." *Journal of Studies in International Education*, vol. 14, no. 52010, pp. 433–51. DOI: 10.1177/1028315309348737.

Tarrant, Michael and Kevin Lyons. "The Effect of Short-Term Educational Travel Programs on Environmental Citizenship." *Environmental Education Research*, vol. 18, no. 3, 2012, pp. 403–16. DOI: 10.1080/13504622.2011.625113.

Tedrow, Barbara. "Favorite Place Mapmaking and the Decolonization of Teaching." In *Engaging Difference: Teaching Humanities and Social Science in Multicultural Environments*, edited by Dovilė Budrytė and Scott A. Boykin, Rowman and Littlefield, 2017, pp. 75–82.

Tétreault, Mary Ann and Ronnie D. Lipschutz. *Global Politics as if People Mattered.* 2005. Rowman and Littlefield.

Tickner, Arlene. "Core, Periphery, and (Neo) Imperialist International Relations." *European Journal of International Relations*, vol. 19, no. 3, 2013, pp. 627–646.

Tickner, Arlene. "Hearing Latin American Voices in International Relations Studies." *International Studies Perspectives*, vol. 32, no. 2, 2003a, pp 325–350.

Tickner, Arlene. "Seeing IR Differently: Notes From The Third World." *Millennium*, vol. 32, no. 2, 2003b, pp. 295–324.

Tickner, Arlene B. and Karen Smith, ed. *International Relations from the Global South: Worlds of Difference*. 2020. Routledge.

Tickner, J. Ann. *Gender in International Relations: Feminist Perspectives on Achieving Global Security*, Columbia University Press, 1993.

Topping, Keith J. "Trends in Peer Learning." *Educational Psychology*, vol. 25, no. 6, 2005, pp. 631–645

Tufts University. "Formative and Summative Feedback." https://sites.tufts.edu/teaching/assessment/assessment-approaches/formative-and-summative-feedback/ (accessed August 15, 2020).

UNBC. *Indigenous Students Viewbook*. 2020. https://www.unbc.ca/sites/default/files/sections/future-students/unbcviewbookindigenous2020–21.pdf (accessed August 15, 2020).

U.S. Adults' Knowledge of the World. n.d. https://cdn.cfr.org/sites/default/files/report _pdf/NatGeo_CFR_US%20Knoweldge.pdf (accessed June 6, 2020).

US Department of Education. *Evaluation of Evidence-Based Practices in Online Learning: A Meta-analysis and Review of Online Learning Studies*. 2010. https://www2.ed.gov/rschstat/eval/tech/evidence-based-practices/finalreport.pdf (accessed April 20, 2021).

Usherwood, Simon. "Building Resources for Simulations: Challenges and Opportunities." *European Political Science*, vol. 14, no. 3, 2015, pp. 218–227.

Vachris, Michelle A. and Cecil E. Bohanon. "Using Illustrations from American Novels to Teach about Labor Markets." *Journal of Economic Education*, vol. 43, no. 1, 2012, pp. 72–82.

Valença, Marcelo. M. "O uso de simulações e cultura popular para o ensino de Relações Internacionais." *Estudos Internacionais*, vol. 8, no. 1, 2020, pp. 27–43.

Valença, Marcelo M. and Ana Paula Balthazar Tostes. "O storytelling Como Ferramenta De Aprendizado Ativo." *Carta Internacional*, vol. 14, no. 2, 2020, pp. 1–23.

Valeriano, Brandon. "Teaching Introduction to International Politics with Film." *Journal of Political Science Education*, vol. 9, no. 1, 2013, pp. 52–72.

Van Belle, Douglas A. *A Novel Approach to Politics: Introducing Political Science Through Books, Movies, And Popular Culture*, Fourth Edition. CQ Press, 2018.

Verloo, Mieke. "Multiple Inequalities, Intersectionality and the European Union." *European Journal of Women's Studies*, vol. 13, no. 3, 2006, pp. 211–28. https://doi .org/10.1177/1350506806065753 (accessed April 20, 2021).

Verwoord, Roselynn and Heather A. Smith. "The P.O.W.E.R. Framework: Power Dimensions Shaping Students as Partners Processes." In *The Power of Partnership: Students, Staff, and Faculty Revolutionizing Higher Education, Editors*, ed. Lucy Mercer-Mapstone and Sophia Abbott. 2020. Center for Engaged Learning, pp. 29–42. https://www.centerforengagedlearning.org/books/power-of-partnership/chapter-1/ (accessed July 15, 2020).

Via, Sandra. "Gender, Militarism, and Globalization: Soldiers for Hire and Hegemonic Masculinity." In *Gender, War, and Militarism: Feminist Perspectives*, ed. Laura Sjoberg and Sandra Via. 2010. Praeger, pp. 42–53.

Vlcek, William and Adam Bower. "Teaching IR at the University of St. Andrews (Scotland)." *International Studies Perspectives*, forthcoming.

Waldron-Moore, Pamela. "Seeking a Just and Humane World: Motivating Minority Students to Become Global Citizens." *Journal of Political Science Education*, vol. 7, 2011, pp. 224–239.

Walt, Stephen M. "One World, Many Theories". *Foreign Policy*, no. 110, Special Edition: "Frontiers of Knowledge", 1998, pp. 29–32, 34–46. http://Www.Jstor.Org/Stable/1149275 (accessed February 3, 2009).

Walvoord, Barbara E. Fassler and Virginia Johnson Anderson. *Effective Grading: A Tool for Learning and Assessment*, 2nd ed. 2010. Jossey-Bass.

Wang, Chun-Min. "Instructional Design for Cross-cultural Online Collaboration: Grouping Strategies and Assignment Design." *Australasian Journal of Educational Technology*, vol. 27, no. 2, 2011, pp. 243–258.

Ward, Jamie. *The Student's Guide to Cognitive Neuroscience*, 3rd ed. 2015. Psychology Press.

Warf, Barney. "Textbooks in Human Geography: An American perspective." *Royal Geographic Society*, 2017. https://doi.org/10.1111/area.12401 (accessed April 20, 2021).

Weber, Cynthia. "The Highs and Lows of Teaching IR Theory: Using Popular Films for Theoretical Critique." *International Studies Perspectives*, vol. 2, no. 3, 2001, pp. 281–287.

Weber, Cynthia. *International Relations Theory: A Critical Introduction*, 4th ed. 2014. Routledge.

Wehlburg, Catherine. *Promoting Integrated and Transformative Assessment: A Deeper Focus on Student Learning*. Jossey-Bass, 2008.

Weldes, Jutta. *To Seek Out New Worlds: Exploring Links between Science Fiction and World Politics*. 2003. Palgrave Macmillan.

Wemheuer-Vogelaar, Wiebke, Ingo Peters, Laura Kemmer, Alina Kleinn, Luisa Linke-Behrens and Sabine Mokry. *The Global IR Debate in the Classroom*. In International Relations from The Global South: Worlds of Difference, ed. Arlene B. Tickner, and Karen Smith. 2020. Routledge, pp. 17–37.

Werder, Carmen, et al. "Students as Co-Inquirers (Special Section Guest Editors' Introduction)". *Teaching and Learning Inquiry*, vol. 4, no. 2, Sept. 2016, pp. 5–7. DOI: 10.20343/teachlearninqu.4.2.2.

West, Charlotte. "Breaking Barriers to Study Abroad." *International Educator*, vol. 28, no. 4, 2019, pp. 30–35.

West, Lucy and Dan Halvorson. "Student Engagement and Deep Learning in the First-Year International Relations Classroom: Simulating a UN Security Council Debate on the Syrian Crisis." *Journal of Political Science Education*, 2019. DOI: 10.1080/15512169.2019.1616298.

Whitman Cobb, Wendy N. "Turning the Classroom Upside Down: Experimenting with the Flipped Classroom in American Government." *Journal of Political Science Education*, vol. 12, no. 1, 2016, pp. 1–14.

Whitworth, Sandra. "Feminism." In *The Oxford Handbook of International Relations*, ed. Christian Reus-Smit and Duncan Snidal. 2018. Oxford University Press, pp. 391–407.

Wiggins, Grant and Jay McTighe. *Understanding by Design*, 2nd ed. 2005. Association for Supervision and Curriculum Development.

Williams, Helen and Nicola Smith. "Feedback: Critiquing Practice, Moving Forward." *European Political Science*, vol. 16, no. 2, 2017, pp. 159–78.

Williams, Leonard and Mary Lahman. "Online Discussion, Student Engagement, and Critical Thinking." *Journal of Political Science Education*, vol. 7, no. 2, 2011, pp. 143–62.

Wilson, Bruce M., Philip H. Pollock and Kerstin Hamann. "Does Active Learning Enhance Learner Outcomes? Evidence from Discussion Participation in Online Classes." *Journal of Political Science Education*, vol. 3, no. 2, 2007, pp. 131–42.

Wilson, Edward O. *On Human Nature*. 2012. Harvard University Press.

Wilson, Matthew Charles. "Crowdsourcing and Self-Instruction: Turning the Production of Teaching Materials into a Learning Objective." *Journal of Political Science Education*, vol. 14, no. 3, 2018, pp. 400–408. DOI: 10.1080/15512169.2017.1415813.

Wolfe, Angela. "Implementing Collaborative Learning Methods in the Political Science Classroom." *Journal of Political Science Education*, vol. 8, no. 4, 2012, pp. 420–432. DOI: 10.1080/15512169.2012.729451.

Womble, Lynsee, et al. "A Model for Designing Faculty-Led Study Abroad Programs in the Business Curriculum." *Academy of Educational Leadership Journal*, vol. 18, no. 3, 2014, pp. 93–110.

Wong, Mary S. "Supporting Diversity and Internationalization through Transformative Learning Experiences." *Forum on Public Policy Online*, Winter 2007 edition. https://forumonpublicpolicy.com/archivespring07/wong.pdf (accessed April 20, 2021).

Worcester, Kent. 2013. "Graphic Novels in the Social Science Classroom." In *Teaching Politics Beyond the Book: Film, Texts, and New Media in the Classroom*, ed. Robert W. Glover and Daniel Tagliarina. 2013. Bloomsbury, pp. 87–102.

Worthen, Molly. "The Misguided Drive to Measure 'Learning Outcomes.'" *New York Times*, February 28, 2018. https://www.nytimes.com/2018/02/23/opinion/sunday/colleges-measure-learning-outcomes.html (accessed April 20, 2021).

Wunische, Adam. "Lecture Versus Simulation: Testing the Long-Term Effects." *Journal of Political Science Education*, vol. 15, no. 1, 2019, pp. 37–48.

Ya Ni, Anna. "Comparing the Effectiveness of Classroom and Online Learning: Teaching Research Methods." *Journal of Public Affairs Education*, vol. 19, no. 2, 2013, pp. 199–215.

Yates, William Butler. *Easter 1916. The Norton Anthology of Poetry*, 3rd ed. 1983, original 1916. W. W. Norton and Company.

Young, Candace C. "Program Evaluation and Assessment: Integrating Methods, Processes, and Culture." In *Assessment in Political Science*, ed. Michelle D. Deardorff, Kerstin Hamann and John Ishiyama. American Political Science Association, 2009, pp. 117–139.

Yuksel, Peri, and Frank Nascimento. "Breaking Barriers: Developing Faculty-Led International Trips for Underserved Students." *Scholarship of Teaching and Learning in Psychology*, vol. 4, no. 3, 2018, pp. 189–197. DOI: 10.1037/stl0000120.

Yuval-Davis, Nira. *Gender and Nation*. 1997. Sage.

Zajonc, Arthur. "Contemplative Pedagogy: A Quiet Revolution in Higher Education." *New Directions in Teaching and Learning*, no. 134, 2013, pp. 83–94.

Zalewski, M. (1996). "All These Theories Yet The Bodies Keep Piling Up: Theories, Theorists, and Theorising." *International Theory: Positivism And Beyond*, ed. Steve Smith, Ken Booth and Marysia Zalewski. 1996. Cambridge University Press, pp. 340–353.

Zimmerman, Barry. "Becoming a Self-Regulated Learner: An Overview." *Theory into Practice*, vol. 41, no. 2, 2002, pp. 64–70.

Zvobgo, Kelebogile and Meredith Loken. "Why Race Matters in International Relations." *Foreign Policy*, June 19, 2020. https://foreignpolicy.com/2020/06/19/why-race-matters-international-relations-ir/ (accessed April 20, 2021).

Index

300 133

accountability 152, 184, 201, 203, 205, 209, 212
Acharya, Amitav 31, 46
active learning 1, 3–6, 32, 45, 67–9, 77–8, 90, 117–18, 124, 130, 132, 145–6, 148, 179, 186, 189
   assessment in 201–12, 214–23
   renewing commitment to 35–7
   trends in 4–5
activism 54
Africa Today 181
African Union 24, 50
Akbaba, Yasemin 185
Allen, Michael A. 180
Allison, Graham T. 69
Alves, Cia 220
American Association of Higher Education 214
American Council on Education 29
American Political Science Association 5–6, 28, 36
Amnesty International 18
analytic eclecticism 132
Andersen, Espen 74
Anderson, Bret 77–8
application cards 207
Aristotle 27, 108, 111
Asal, Victor 91, 180
assessment in active learning 201–12, 214–23
Association of American Colleges & Universities 117, 121, 218
asylum seekers 2
Auchter, Jessica 55
Avalon 114

Ba, Alice 118–19
Bachner, Jennifer 185
backward design 13, 32–3, 119–22, 150

Baranowski, Michael K. 222
Barasuol, Fernanda 41, 46
Başkan, Filiz 185
Beck, Robert 186–7
Beckham, M. 158
Behera, Navnita Chadka 43
Belarus 55
Biswas, Bidisha 206
Black Lives Matter 64
Blaney, David L. 42
blogs 8, 180, 186, 195, 218
Bloom, Benjamin 27–9, 32–3, 178
Bloom's Taxonomy 32–3, 129–33, 138–9
Boehrer, John 64
Bolívar-Cruz, Alicia 206
Booth, Ken 61
brainstorming 78
Braskamp, Larry A. 163
Braveheart 133
Brazil 39, 45–8, 50
Brookfield, Stephen 195
Brown, Colin M. 206
Burch, Kurt 147, 151
Buzan, Barry 43

Capture the Flag 109
Carter, Ralph G. 70
cartooning 209, 211–12
Carvalho, Gustavo 93–4, 104
case studies 66–76, 108, 111
Chabal, Patrick 50
Challenge Game 220
China 2
Cho, Hoyun 211
citizenship 21, 25, 58, 60, 117, 121, 133
civil war 18, 29, 35, 66–7, 70, 162
Clausewitz, Carl Von 109
climate change 11, 162, 180
Cold War 47, 134
collaborative learning 189–99

colonialism 6, 21, 45, 49, 60, 62, 84, 197
comics 33
communication skills 2, 121, 127
concept mapping 130–31, 133, 209–12
conflict *see* war
constructivism 18, 22–3, 25, 58, 67,
    96–7, 119, 128, 133, 135, 145,
    177, 182
Coughlin, Richard W. 221
Council on Foreign Relations 14
COVID-19 pandemic 2, 19, 30–32, 35–6,
    46, 64, 70, 176, 184, 187
Cox, Eric 94
Cox, Robert 191
Craig, John 29–30
critical theory 40, 67
critical thinking 1–2, 15, 22–3, 33–4, 67,
    89, 121, 127, 130–31, 150, 170,
    203, 208, 222
cross-cultural diversity *see* diversity
crowdsourcing 197–8
curious feminism 58
Curran, Roisin 196–7
cybersecurity 3–4, 35

da Silva, André Reis 41, 46
Dalig and Vadan game 107–9, 116
Danielson, Robert W. 132
Darby, Flower 27, 196
Davidovitch, Nitza 120
Dawson, Bryan L. 60
de Swielande, Tanguy 70
de Wit, Hans 162
debriefing questions 207–8
Deciancio, Melisa 46–8
decision-forcing cases 69–70, 72
decolonization 6–8, 33, 46–50
democratization 30, 55, 157, 165
dependency theory 46–7
Devereaux, Charan 70
Dewey, A. Gordon 28
Dewey, John 27, 30, 34–5, 146
Dillenbourg, Pierre 189
Diplomacy 106, 108, 113–14, 116
disability 56, 61, 182
distance learning 35
    see also online learning
diversity 5–8, 11, 31–2, 35, 88, 160–74,
    181
Dominican Republic 85

drones 3
Duck of Minerva 180
dynamic tensions 33–4

Economist, The 181
Ecuador 85
empathic scaffolding 7
engagement *see* student engagement
Enloe, Cynthia 27, 58
environmental issues 2, 21–2, 29, 46–7,
    53, 63, 90, 98–9
    see also climate change
Epley, J. 93
ethics 19
ethnicity 6–7, 25, 52–4, 83, 86, 181
European Union 18, 24, 61, 90, 221
EuroSim 221
experiential learning 77–89, 117, 208,
    218

faculty-led study abroad programs 77–89
Fanon, Franz 49
feedback mechanisms 195–6, 198, 202,
    204, 206–7
Fees Must Fall 48
feminism 6, 18, 22–3, 25, 40, 52–64, 67,
    97, 135, 182, 190–93
fiction *see* film; literature
film 33, 35, 129–39, 179–80
Fisher, Kathryn 52
Fleming, Ian 134, 139
flipped classroom 30, 122–7, 186,
    217–18
food security 162
foreign policy 21–2, 40, 57, 77, 90, 99,
    212, 220
Forest, James J. F. 162
Forum for Education Abroad 87
fragmentation 3, 35
free markets 24
Freedom House 186
Freire, Paulo 27, 31, 33, 44, 192
Fung, Courtney J. 206

Gallup 14
game theory 156
games 45, 105–16
Gannon, Kevin 8, 181, 189, 192, 194

Index

gender 6–7, 19, 52–8, 60–61, 63–4, 83, 86, 110, 163, 181–2
genocide 42
Gibson, Heather 78
Giroux, Henry 191
Glazier, Rebecca A. 187
Global IR 23–4, 36, 39, 43–4, 51
Global North 5, 7, 23, 25, 38–9, 57, 171
Global South 3–4, 6–7, 23, 31, 38–51, 171
globalization 2–3, 5, 14, 18, 25, 30, 33, 35, 42, 84, 180, 185, 187
Golich, Vicki L. 68, 72, 74
González-Betancor, Sara M. 206
graphic novels 33
Great Debates 40, 46–7
Greenpeace 18
group work 84, 157, 183–4, 218–19
groupthink 99

Hakel, Milton D. 131–2
Halpern, Diane F. 131–2
Halvorson, Dan 221
Hamid, Mohsin 63–4
Hastedt, Glenn 70
Haufler, Virginia 206
Healey, M. 146
Healey, Mick 192
health 19, 35, 70, 87
    see also COVID-19 pandemic
Hegel, G. W. F. 49
Hendrickson, Petra 220
Henning, Jeremiah A. 219
Hensel, N. 158
High Impact Practices 218
Hobbes, Thomas 112
Hobbes Game 108, 111–13, 116
Hoffman, Matt 118–19
Hoffman, Stanley 40
hooks, bell 192
Houghton, David P. 70
Hovey, R. 42
Howard, Kimberley 79
human rights 2–3, 11, 21–2, 24, 29, 46, 66, 157, 180, 187
human security 2, 29, 46, 56, 64
humanism 50
hybrid learning 30, 32, 186

iClickers 183
idealism 133
identity and poetry exercises 106, 108
Imamoğlu, Ektrm 172–3
immigration 19, 42, 61, 63
indigenous knowledge 47
innovation 34–5
international cooperation 21–2, 35
International Criminal Court 50
international development 21–2
international law 18, 21–2, 186–7
International Monetary Fund 18
international organizations 18, 21–2, 90, 185
international political economy 18, 21–2, 33, 40, 47, 180
International Political Education Database 30
international relations, teaching
    active learning *see* active learning
    with case studies 66–76
    collaborative learning 189–99
    commitment and innovation in pedagogy 27–37
    critical time for 2–3
    engaging in inquiry 145–58
    engaging with diversity through technology 160–74
    essentials for introductory courses 11–25
    in the Global South 38–51
    intersectional pedagogy in 52–64
    with the IR theory toolkit 117–28
    with literature and film 129–39
    more effective online learning 176–88
    political violence with games and simulations 105–16
    through study abroad programs 77–89
    using Statecraft 90–104
International Studies Association 5–6, 11, 31, 36, 118–19
    workshops 19–23, 36, 78
internationalization 162–3
internships 218–19
intersectionality 7–8, 53–64
introductory courses to IR 11–25
IR theory toolkit 117–28
Iranian Plane simulation 220

Ishiyama, John 30
Ivens, Sven 205

James, Patrick 137
James, Sarah E. 206
James Bond franchise 130, 134–6, 139
Jenkins, A. 146
Jenkins, Leeroy 109
Johnston, Alastair Iain 97
Jones, Rebecca 221
journaling 84
   see also learning journals

Kaftan, Joanna 94, 113
Kahoot 183
Kant, Immanuel 49
Kaussler, Bernd 133
Kehl, Jenny 30
Keller, Brian 79
Keller, Jonathan W. 93
Kille, Kent J. 5, 185
Killick, David 163
Kiltz, Linda A. 70
knowledge plurality 41–3, 46, 48
knowledge retention 3–4, 15, 35, 105,
   131–2, 137, 146, 184–5, 208, 214,
   217–20
Knowlton, Dave S. 177
Koomen, Jonneke 6
Krain, Matthew 5, 130, 185, 205
Krishna, Sankaran 42
Kuzma, Lynn 64

Lang, James M. 27, 196
language barrier 168–70, 173
Lantis, Jeffrey S. 5, 64, 74, 185, 205
learning goals 13–15, 19–20, 32–3, 85,
   95, 120–21, 202–3, 218
   Bloom's Taxonomy 32–3, 129–33,
      138–9
learning outcomes 1, 9, 24, 68, 76–7, 82,
   94–5, 117, 120, 124, 145, 150–51,
   155, 158, 160, 164, 173, 178, 195,
   202, 214, 216, 218–19
learning journals 195–6
Learning Management System 180, 183,
   186
Leunig, Johanna 205
Levin-Banchik, Luba 220

LGBTQIA+ 4, 6, 58, 61, 86, 191, 219
liberalism 18, 21–3, 25, 58, 67, 96–7,
   117, 121, 131, 135, 182
lifelong learning 67, 222
Linantud, John 94, 113
Lipschutz, Ronnie D. 57
literature 33, 35, 63–4, 129–39
Liu, T. T. T. 42
living conditions 198
Lord of the Rings 130, 136–8
Lynn, Laurence E. 72, 74

Madden, Timothy M. 80
Mafia *see* Werewolf
Malewski, Erik 84
Marxism 18, 22–3, 40, 54, 67, 133, 135
Matrix trilogy 133
McCall, Leslie 55–6
McEachern, Susan 119
Me Too 64
Mechanical Turk 185
memoirs 33
memorization 34
mental health 86
mentoring 1, 33, 80, 148, 150, 156, 158
Michelsen, Niall 93, 95
militarism 60, 62
military 58, 66
Miller, William J. 217
Mingst, Karen A. 70
"minute" papers 207
Mislan, David B. 70
mixed-method approach 156–7, 205
Model Diplomacy 108, 113, 116
Model UN 90, 203, 219, 221
Monkey Cage, The 180
Mori, Katsuhiko 70
Morocco 85
Morreale, Joseph C. 78
motivation 13, 42, 67, 160, 170, 178,
   183–5, 187, 197, 217, 219–20
movies *see* film
multiculturalism 45
Munich 133

National Geographic 14
nationalism 60, 62, 133
nativism 2
neoliberalism 50

neuroscience 4
non-governmental organizations 11, 18, 61
novels *see* literature

Oberle, Monika 205
Oblinger, Diana 132
Oblinger, James 132
O'Byrne, Sarah 185
Ogg, Frederic 28
oil crisis 47
Olson, Christa L. 162–3
online learning 30–32, 125–7, 176–88, 208–9
open education resources 194–5
open-ended questions 75, 169, 204–5, 207–8
Orientalism 38
Osborne, Carolyn 211
outcomes *see* learning outcomes

pandemics 14, 86
    see also COVID-19 pandemic
passive learning 67–8, 118, 122–4, 127, 132, 139, 146, 214, 217
patriarchy 62
Peace Research Institute Oslo 186
pedagogy 7, 12, 21, 25, 38, 41–2, 44–5, 87, 210, 212, 214, 216
    see also individual teaching methods
    commitment and innovation in 27–37
    feminist interventions 52–64
    see also feminism
    history of pedagogical thinking 27–32
    of online learning 177–8
peer learning 161, 164, 169–71
Perusall 183
Peterson, V. Spike 54
Pew Charitable Trust Foundation 29
Phillion, Joann 84
Pipitone, Jennifer M. 84
Planet Money 180
pluriversal IR 39–40, 43–4, 47–8, 51
podcasts 180–81, 186, 195
political economy 18
political science 5, 12–14, 27–9, 33, 118, 149, 216

political violence 36, 105–16
polythink 99
populism 2, 161, 165, 172
positivism 29, 191, 210
post-colonialism 4, 23, 53–5, 58, 182
post-modernism 22–3
post-structuralism 40, 54–5, 58
Powel, Brieg 43
power relations 6, 21–2, 24, 53, 64, 66, 84, 162, 192
PowerPoint 180
predation theory 138
privacy 198
problem-based learning 32, 34–5, 145–8, 150–58, 218
professionalization 29
prostitution 58

quality of life 2
Qualtrics 185
Querejazu, Amaya 43

race 6–7, 19, 25, 42, 46, 52–3, 56–7, 83–4, 110, 162, 181–2
racism 6, 61, 162–3, 182
radicalism 131
Rafshoon, Ellen G. 63
Ramsey, James D. 70
Rasmussen, Amy Cabrera 56–7, 59
Raymond, Chad 93–4
realism 6, 18, 21–3, 25, 28, 67, 95–6, 106, 112, 114, 124, 131, 133, 135, 182
Red Card game 108, 115–16
refugees 2, 66, 70
regionalism 46–7
religion 56–7, 61, 86, 161, 165
Remains of the Day 133
research-focused learning 145–6, 148–58
Resistance 114
retention of knowledge 3–4, 15, 35, 105, 131–2, 137, 146, 184–5, 208, 214, 217–20
retrospective cases 69, 71
Rhodes, Carolyn 70
Rhodes Must Fall 48
Riegg, Natalya 59
Rock Paper Scissors 112
role-playing 27, 218, 221

Rose, Gideon 70
Rosen, Amanda 91, 180
Ruane, Abigail E. 137
rubrics 205
Runyan, Anne Sisson 54
Russia 2

Saiya, Nilay 93–4, 113
Sanders, Tobie 211
Schiano, Bill 74
scholarship of assessment 216
scholarship of teaching and learning 4–5, 8, 30, 32, 37, 117, 127, 216
Secret Hitler 114
secularism 165
self-assessment 154, 204, 206, 208, 220–21
self-regulated learning 123, 195
service learning 5, 78, 83, 89, 189, 218–19
Seven Days in May 133
sexual orientation *see* LGBTQIA+
sexual violence 4, 62, 163
Shellman, Stephen M. 220
Shor, Ira 192–3
Shostya, Anna 78
Simpson, Archie W. 133
simulations 45, 105–16, 180, 189, 218–22
  Statecraft 90–104, 108, 113, 116
Sinatra, Gale M. 132
Sjoberg, Laura 52, 54–5
Skype 164–72
Slavin, R. E. 164
smartphones 3, 129
Smith, Daryl 162–3
Smith, Hayden 93, 95
Smith, Heather A. 70, 190
Smith, Karen 43
Snow, Donald M. 70
social deception games 114–16
social media 3, 7, 25, 129, 179, 185
socioeconomic class 52–3
Socrates 27
Soroka, George 206
South Africa 24, 39, 45, 48–50, 59
sovereignty 3, 20, 24, 42, 59–60, 64, 135
Statecraft 90–104, 108, 113, 116
Steich, Philip 70
Stommel, Jessie 192, 196

Strange, Hannah 78
Strong, Robert A. 70
structural violence 53, 61–2
student engagement 1, 4–5, 27–37, 50, 52, 57, 66–7, 69, 94, 105, 116, 131, 145, 147, 152–5, 158, 168, 170, 181, 184–7, 193, 195, 197, 201, 204, 209, 214, 217–18
student-centered approaches 33, 120, 145, 177, 179, 214
study abroad programs 77–89
Styles, Kendall W. 70
Sunderland, Sherie 133
sustainable development 85, 90
Sweden 61
Sylvester, Christine 63

Tanzania 62
teacher training 29
teaching IR *see* international relations, teaching
teaching with purpose 32–7
technology 3, 160–74
Ted Talks 180
Tedrow, Barbara 59
terrorism 2, 18, 42, 55–6, 63, 86, 98, 133, 157
Tétreault, Mary Ann 57
textbooks 15–19, 21, 25, 39, 66, 135, 194–5
Thirteen Days 133
Tickner, Arlene B. 41, 43
Tickner, J. Ann 63
Tolkien, J. R. R. 136, 138
Topping, Keith J. 164
tourism 84
transformative learning 78, 86
transgender rights 4
  see also LGBTQIA+
transnationalism 18
Trump, Donald 171
Turan, Kürşad 220
Turkey 160–61, 163–5, 169–72, 185
Twitter 198

Ubuntu 49–50
United Kingdom 61
United Nations 18, 24

United States 2, 39–40, 42, 57, 61, 70, 88, 160–61, 163, 165, 171–3, 185, 216, 218, 221
United States Military Academy 162
U.S. State Department 29
Usherwood, Simon 94
utilitarianism 108, 111

Verano-Tacoronte, Domingo 206
video conferencing 164–6
    see also Skype
video games 33
virtue ethics 108, 111

war 11, 14, 18, 21–2, 24–5, 29, 33, 35, 47, 52, 55, 62, 66–8, 70, 105, 157, 162, 180, 187
war crimes 18, 66
Weapons of Mass Destruction 137–8
Weir, Kimberly A. 222
Werewolf 108, 115–16
West, Charlotte 80

West, Lucy 221
Wolfe, Angela 189
women *see* gender
Wong, Mary S. 162–3
workshops 19–23, 25, 36, 78
World Bank 186
World Development Indicators 186
World of Warcraft 109
World Today, The 181
World Trade Organization 135
writing skills 1–2, 20, 158, 215
Wunische, Adam 220

Yahlnaaw 197
Yates, William Butler 110
YouTube clips 179–80
Yuval-Davis, Nira 57

Zimbabwe 50
Zoom 183–5, 198
Zwingel, Susanne 54